THE STRUCTURE
AND DEVELOPMENT OF
RUSSIAN

THE STRUCTURE AND DEVELOPMENT OF RUSSIAN

BY

W. K. MATTHEWS

Professor of Russian in the University of London
and Head of the Department of Language and Literature at the
School of Slavonic and East European Studies, London

CAMBRIDGE
AT THE UNIVERSITY PRESS
1953

CAMBRIDGE UNIVERSITY PRESS
Cambridge, New York, Melbourne, Madrid, Cape Town,
Singapore, São Paulo, Delhi, Mexico City

Cambridge University Press
The Edinburgh Building, Cambridge CB2 8RU, UK

Published in the United States of America by Cambridge University Press, New York

www.cambridge.org
Information on this title: www.cambridge.org/9781107619395

First published 1953
First paperback edition 2013

A catalogue record for this publication is available from the British Library

ISBN 978-1-107-61939-5 Paperback

CONTENTS

PREFACE

I

I have tried here, in limited space, to present the facts of Russian consecutively from two different points of view, the descriptive (synchronic), which neglects the time factor, and the historical (diachronic), which sees language in relation to time. The facts in their totality are the same; it is the point of view that varies, making its own selection of facts and seeing them in a different set of relations. One point of view, however, supplements the other, and the twofold analysis of the language which they enable us to make gives an insight not only into its present system of symbols and meanings, but into the changes this has undergone in course of time.

A true historical perspective can exist only when we have historical records to draw on. Where they are wanting, as in still unwritten or till lately illiterate languages, or where they cover only a 'fraction' of time, as in Lithuanian and Albanian, it can be attained only by projecting linguistic record into the unrecorded past. Here we are obviously treading on uncertain ground, for however plausible the findings of the comparative-historical method of linguistic investigation may appear, we are ultimately obliged to admit that they can at best offer no more than an unverifiable approximation of the truth. Russian, fortunately for us, has records going back to the eleventh century, and we are therefore in a position to see a segment of it in historical flux. Though relatively brief, the vision permits us nevertheless to give the 'reality' of growth to what would otherwise be only a structure and a scheme.

2

The structure and development of Russian are dealt with in the first two parts of this book, and the third (Specimens) introduces passages of original Russian literature covering a space of nine centuries and arranged in chronological order. This illustrative matter, which I have put into English, will make it

possible for us to follow the evolution not only of Russian literature in its personalities and influences, but of the language in
its structural and stylistic changes. The passages with one ex-
ception (no. 14), are taken from Н. К. Гудзий, *Хрестоматия по
древней русской литературе XI–XVII веков*[4] (Москва, 1947).
No. 14 comes from Ф. Буслаев, *Русская хрестоматия*[4] (Москва,
1888). Gudzij prints all texts earlier than the sixteenth century
in their original spelling, which reproduces the errors and in-
consistencies of the MSS., and he uses the modern spelling for
the later ones, though he takes care to preserve their 'phonetic
and morphological peculiarities', as we do in reprinting six-
teenth- and seventeenth-century English. Buslajev, on the other
hand, 'normalises' his texts and naturally follows pre-Revolutionary practice in spelling. This has been modernised here to
make the text of no. 14 uniform with Gudzij's. Specimens later
than 1700 are also given in the modern spelling to preserve
uniformity and to lighten the reader's burden.

3

Three scripts are used in the text to represent Russian sounds,
viz. Cyrillic, which those who have studied Classical Greek will
find familiar up to a point; italics to transliterate the Cyrillic;
and boldface type, now often resorted to by the International
Phonetic Association, for our phonetic transcriptions. The I.P.A.
alphabet is fairly widely known, but I have not assumed that all
my readers will be acquainted with it. The Russian values of the
relevant symbols, interpreted approximately and for the most
part in terms of the sounds of the better-known European languages, are as follows:

(1) *Vowels*

i	as in Fr. 'm*i*ne'	ɐ	as in Port. 'di*a*'
ɪ	as in 's*i*t'	ɨ, ɨ	like the first vowel in the Cockney
e	as in Fr. '*é*t*é*'		pronunciation of 'm*oo*n'
ɛ	as in Fr. 's*e*pt'	u	as in Fr. 'f*ou*'
æ	as in 'm*a*n'	ʊ	as in 'p*u*t'
a	as in Fr. 'p*a*tte'	o	as in Fr. 'ch*o*se'
ü	as in Norw. 'h*u*s'	ɔ	as in Ger. 'K*o*st'
ə	as in '*a*go'	ʌ	as in 'c*u*p'
ö	as in Swed. 'd*u*m'	ɑ	as in Fr. 'p*a*s'

Normal Russian o is intermediate between o and ɔ. Along with all other Russian vowels except ɛ, it may form diphthongs (syllables of two vowels) with i, conventionally written j (as in '*y*et'), e.g. oj, ej, aj, ij, uj.

(2) *Consonants*

p as in Fr. '*p*omme'	s as in Fr. '*s*able'
b as in Fr. '*b*on'	z as in Fr. '*maison*'
m as in '*m*ay'	ʦ as in Ger. '*z*ehn'
t as in Fr. '*t*emps'	ʃ as in Fr. '*ch*ou'
d as in Fr. '*d*ame'	ʒ as in Fr. '*j*oli'
n as in Fr. '*n*appe'	ʧ as in '*ch*urn'
c as in Hung. '*ty*úk'[1]	j as in '*y*et'
ɟ as in Hung. '*nagy*'[1]	x as in Ger. '*noch*'
k as in Fr. '*c*orde'	ɣ as in North Ger. '*W*agen'
g as in Fr. '*g*rand'	l as in Am. Eng. '*l*ook'
f as in '*f*ace'	r as in Ital. '*c*aro'
v as in '*v*ery'	

All the foregoing consonants, except c, ɟ, j, and the 'sibilants' ʃ, ʒ, ʦ, ʧ, are frequently palatalised in Russian, i.e. pronounced with the middle of the tongue simultaneously raised. Palatalised consonants are indicated with a small 'hook', or comma, representing a miniature j (the symbol of palatalisation), attached to them (e.g. p̦, m̦, g̦, f̦). The sound ʦ is never, and ʃ and ʒ are rarely, palatalised, except in the older Moscow pronunciation, whereas ʧ always is, and c, ɟ, and j are palatal by nature.

4

I owe a debt of gratitude to my friend and former teacher, Professor N. B. Jopson, Fellow of St John's College, Cambridge, for reading my work in manuscript and for a great deal of constructive criticism and advice. I should also like to express here my grateful admiration of the Cambridge University Press for the care, patience, and efficiency expended on the production of this book.

W. K. MATTHEWS

UNIVERSITY OF LONDON, 1953

---

[1] See my article 'nouts on ðə hʌŋgɛəriən saund-sistim' (*Le Maître Phonétique*, no. 93; London, 1950).

PART I

THE STRUCTURE OF RUSSIAN

CHAPTER I

INTRODUCTION

I

Most European languages belong in grammar and vocabulary, or in what, by architectural analogy, may be called their structure, to a widespread language group, or complex, known as Indo-European, which at the present time comprises three major divisions in Europe—Germanic, Romance, and Slavonic. These

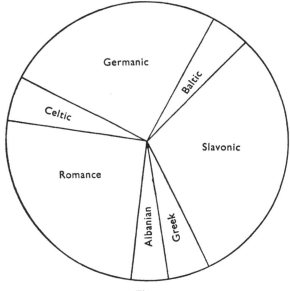

Fig. 1

divisions of Indo-European roughly coincide with the north-west, south-west, and east of the European territory respectively, and their margins are defined here and there by the presence of the still vigorous and no less characteristic Celtic, Albanian, Greek, and Baltic survivals, as will be seen from the accompanying

3

illustration (Fig. 1). Naturally the language map of Europe is not anything like so simple as this diagrammatic generalisation, whose only purpose is to suggest the relative geographical distribution of the various European types of Indo-European.

German may be taken as typical of the Germanic division, Italian of the Romance, and Russian of the Slavonic. Each division is made up of several members whose 'family likeness' requires no special linguistic aptitude to recognise. Besides Russian, the Slavonic division includes Ukrainian, Polish, Czech, Serbo-Croatian, and Bulgarian, as well as certain less-known languages used mainly outside the Soviet frontiers. It is customary, on the strength of certain phonetic criteria, to think of the Slavonic languages, which the intrusion of a continuous wedge of German, Hungarian, and Rumanian divides geographically into a northern and a southern sector, as a triad of western, southern, and eastern types.

West to East	West Slavonic	South Slavonic	East Slavonic
North	Cassubian	Slovene	Russian
	Polish		
to	Lusatian (Lower	Serbo-Croatian	White Russian
	and Upper)	Macedonian	Ukrainian
South	Czech	Bulgarian	—
	Slovak	—	—

From the numerical point of view by far the most important Slavonic language is Russian, which is spoken to-day by probably a hundred million native speakers living in both the European and the Asiatic part of the U.S.S.R. Geographically it is at once the northernmost and the easternmost Slavonic type, and its closest relatives, with which it shares a common literary origin and a recorded medieval development, are White Russian, the official language of the White Russian S.S.R. (capital Minsk), and Ukrainian, the official language of the Ukrainian S.S.R. (capital Kijev). These facts and the surviving affinities between the three East Slavonic languages inclined pre-Revolutionary Russian scholars to regard White Russian and Ukrainian as dialects of a common Russian language. Though erroneous, this view has not yet been completely discarded even in the U.S.S.R., where the term 'Great Russian', requiring the recognition, as complementary terms, not only of 'White Russian', but of 'Little Russian' (Ukrainian), is still used in dialect study.

2

Literary, or Standard, Russian is the official administrative language of the U.S.S.R. and of its capitals Moscow and Leningrad, and it is also the language of instruction, scholarship, literature, the stage, journalism, and public oratory. It is therefore a spoken as well as a written medium, but as a spoken language it has its basis and tradition in writing, which accounts for the choice of 'literary' as its Russian designation. Spoken Literary Russian is not now confined to a definable geographical area, though, history tells us, it had its origin in the administrative vehicle of sixteenth-century Muscovy and consequently belonged to the transitional zone between the two primary dialectal types of the language, viz. North and South Russian (see ch. v, pp. 89–91).

As the written form of Russian is of paramount importance for the study of the language, we may appropriately begin by familiarising ourselves with the characters it uses. The Russian alphabet, we shall see from the subjoined table, closely resembles the Greek capitals in its printed form, though it has several other characters, partly of non-Greek origin, which help to symbolise its more complicated phonetic material. For historical reasons (see Pt II) the alphabet is known as the Cyrillic and in its contemporary form as the 'civil' (*graždanka*), which goes back to Peter the Great and the first years of the eighteenth century. Similar alphabets are used to-day by all the other Slavs of the Orthodox communion—the Ukrainians, White Russians, Serbians, Macedonians, and Bulgarians.

Comparison of the Cyrillic with the corresponding Greek characters (see p. 6) shows a close resemblance in eighteen cases, and we also observe that, unlike the Greek and Latin alphabets, the Cyrillic does not distinguish the shapes of capital and small letters, except in two cases, viz. Б/б and E/e. The written forms of the Cyrillic characters disclose a number of divergences from

THE RUSSIAN ALPHABET

Printed form		Written form		International transliteration	Corresponding Greek uncial	Printed form		Written form		International transliteration	Corresponding Greek uncial
Capital	Small	Capital	Small			Capital	Small	Capital	Small		
А	а	_A_	_a_	a	A	Р	р	_P_	_p_	r	P
Б	б	_Б_	_δ_	b		С	с	_C_	_c_	s	C (Σ)
В	в	_B_	_в_	v	B	Т	т	_M_	_m_	t	T
Г	г	_Г_	_ι_	g	Γ	У	у	_У_	_у_	u	Y
Д	д	_D_	_∂, g_	d	Δ	Ф	ф	_Ф_	_φ_	f	Φ
Е	е	_Е_	_е_	e, je	E	Х	х	_X_	_x_	ch	X
Ё	ё	_Ё._	_ё_	jo		Ц	ц	_Ц_	_ц_	c	
Ж	ж	_Ж_	_ж_	ž		Ч	ч	_Ч_	_ч_	č	
З	з	_З_	_з_	z	Z (min. ʒ)	Ш	ш	_Ш_	_ш_	š	
И	и	_И_	_и_	i	H	Щ	щ	_Щ_	_щ_	šč	
	й		_й_	j			ъ		_ъ_	—	
К	к	_К_	_к_	k	K		ы		_ы_	y	
Л	л	_Л_	_л_	l	Λ		ь		_ь_		
М	м	_М_	_м_	m	M	Э	э	_Э_	_э_	e	
Н	н	_Н_	_н_	n	N	Ю	ю	_Ю_	_ю_	ju	
О	о	_О_	_о_	o	O	Я	я	_Я_	_я_	ja	
П	п	_П_	_п_	p	Π						

the printed norm. One of the most remarkable is the 'tripodic' _m_, which is associated with an earlier printed form III, so easily confused with the Semitic-looking 'trident' Ⅲ (cf. Heb. ש, Ar. س); another is the alternative and frequently used form for д (_g_), and still another the stylised alternative for small т (ј). A marked peculiarity of Cyrillic, which differentiates it from the Slavonic characters of the Latin alphabet, notably those of Czech and Croatian, is the relative absence of distinguishing marks diacritics). The only two Cyrillic characters provided with these are ё, invented by Karamzin at the end of the eighteenth century for the earlier digraph iô and till quite recently confined to elementary-school practice, and й, introduced by academic decree in 1735 for '*i*-consonant' (*j*). Russian Cyrillic, in common with the Ukrainian, White Russian, and Bulgarian varieties, differs from Serbian and Macedonian Cyrillic in having special vowel-letters to indicate the 'soft', or palatalised, quality of the preceding consonant (e.g. ё, ю, я), which Serbian, following an alphabetic rather than a syllabic principle of notation, does more consistently with Vuk Karadžić's Latin j (e.g. jo, jy, ja). The front-vowel letters e and и also perform the same function, and have 'hard', or non-palatalised, correlatives in э and ы. This gives two parallel series of 'hard' and 'soft' vowel-letters (*not*, of course, vowel sounds), viz.

Hard	ы	э	a	o	y
Soft	и	e	я	ё	ю

The two series are completed by the parallelism of two 'signs' (*znaki*), 'hard' ъ and 'soft' ь, variously called 'semivowels', *jery*, or 'surds' (*gluchije*), which formerly symbolised vowels and have now the value of merely diacritic marks, ъ representing for the most part the presence of j between the softened final consonant of a prefix and the following vowel (e.g. объём—aḅ¹jom 'size'; 'volume'), and ь the palatalised quality of the preceding consonant (e.g. соль—soḷ 'salt'). A further peculiarity of the Cyrillic alphabet as used in Russian is the existence of three small, or 'lower-case', letters which have no corresponding capitals, viz. ъ, ы, ь. The total number of characters in it has been thirty-three since 1917, when four others were abandoned as superfluous. These were i, ѣ, ѳ, and ѵ, now replaced by и, e, ф, and и respectively, and the first three of them often occur in pre-Revolutionary print. The vowel-letter i was used before other vowel-letters and to distinguish the identically pronounced words (homophones) мiръ 'world' and миръ 'peace', both now spelt мир (mị̧r); ѣ had the phonetic value of e in a large number of words which had to be learnt by heart in school (e.g. лѣсъ 'forest' and звѣзда́ 'star', now spelt лес—ḷes, звезда́—zvị̧¹zda); ѳ figured in loans from the Greek (e.g. ариѳме́тика 'arithmetic', now spelt арифме́тика—əṛif¹m̧eṭikə), and ѵ, a recognisable variant of Greek ypsilon, was found in мѵро 'myrrh' and in a few other rare forms. All these discarded characters, except the eccentric ѣ, were of manifestly Greek origin. Along with them, ъ was extensively used before the Revolution, as it followed every 'hard' vowel-letter. To-day its application has been severely restricted, and at one period, soon after the spelling reform, it was replaced even in its rare diacritical function by the apostrophe (e.g. объём was written об'ём in the 1920's and after).

3

Russian spelling, which makes use of the relatively simple alphabetic system we have just examined, was devised for a pronunciation very different from that of the modern literary language, particularly in the representation of vowel sounds. Indeed, it is a fairer picture of the vowel system of North Russian than of South Russian, which has influenced the dialect of the central area, where the literary language originates (see ch. v, p. 89). The vowel letters therefore often tend to be misleading, especially when they are not stressed (e.g. города 'towns' is pronounced gəra'da; переговóры 'discussions'—piṛiga'vori), and unless the position of the stress is known (and this can be acquired only with practice), it is quite impossible to pronounce the majority of Russian words, except monosyllables, correctly. A simple vowel-letter such as e, if it occurs under stress, may have as many as eight different phonetic values, viz. e, je, ɛ, jɛ, o, jo, ö, jö. In contrast to the vowel-letters, those representing consonants are generally 'true to type', except when unvoiced in final position (e.g. рожь 'rye' is pronounced roʃ) and before the symbols of voiceless sounds (e.g. лóдка 'boat' is pronounced 'lotkə).

The principles underlying Russian spelling, like those underlying English, French, and German spelling, are not uniform, but of several distinct categories, though one of these certainly tends to predominate. In Russian, as in German, the morphological, or 'etymological', principle, which is paramount, overlooks purely phonetic values in the interests of grammar: thus fem. nom. sing. рожь is not written рош, as it would be if the phonetic principle prevailed, but retains both ж and ь, because the rest of the paradigm of declension to which it belongs has ж and illustrates a 'soft-ending' type (see ch. III, p. 50), i.e. has a gen.-dat.-loc. form ржи—rȝi. The other, less prominent, principles of Russian spelling, intersecting with the morphological, are the phonetic and the traditional, or historical, which governs both English and French spelling. The phonetic principle is followed in the representation of stressed vowels, and, as we have seen, the 'hardness' and 'softness' of consonants are indicated by the shape of vowel letters. This has inevitably resulted in a profuse vowel symbolism. Traditional spelling, no doubt phonetic at first, has not kept pace with phonetic developments and now survives in a relatively small body of words of the жить (ȝit) 'to live' and шип (ʃip) 'thorn' type, in which the front vowel и (i) indicates the earlier palatalised hush-sibilants ʃ, ȝ, both of them grown 'hard' (ʃ, ȝ) in modern Russian. A further traditional complication derives from the presence of numerous Old Church Slavonic (Old Bulgarian) borrowings (see sect. 5, p. 14), which have retained their original spelling and accordingly differ in detail from their Russian counterparts (cf. житие—ȝiti'je 'life (of a saint)' and житьё—ȝi'tjo 'mode of living'; гражданин—grəȝda'ɲin 'citizen' and горожанин—gəra'ȝaɲin 'townsman'). Such doublets are easily distinguished from each other by orthographic differences (e.g. горящий—ga'rӕʃtʃij 'burning' and горячий—ga'rӕtʃij 'hot'), but where homophones occur and give rise to misunderstanding, diacritic marks, for instance the acute accent, are resorted to: thus что—ʃto 'that' (conjunction) is contrasted with the indirect interrogative чтó 'what'.

All the foregoing principles of spelling are rarely found singly. The spelling рожь, for instance, is not only morphological, but traditional, because the 'soft sign' not only fixes the declensional type of the word, but recalls the original 'softness' of ж.

The choice of capital letters in Russian is determined by considerations often identical with those that are operative in English: the first word of a sentence, whether it is preceded or not by a full stop, a proper name, personifications (e.g. Ро́дина—ˈroɟinə 'homeland'), and the beginning of a line of verse are all capitalised, though there may be exceptions to the last, as in the practice of other languages. But the Russian use of capitals shows differences in detail from the English and affinities with the French. Adjectives derived from proper names are often written with small letters (e.g. пу́шкинская эпо́ха—ˈpuʃkinskəjə iˈpoxə 'the age of Puškin'), and this usage applies equally to adjectives derived from the names of countries and peoples (e.g. англи́йский язы́к—anˈglijskij jiˈzik 'English', тата́рское и́го—taˈtarskəjə ˈigə 'the Tartar yoke'), as well as to common nouns of nationality (e.g. он ру́сский—on ˈruskij 'he is a Russian'). Titles and modes of address, except the polite 2nd person plural of the personal pronoun (Вы—vi 'you') and its case variants, are generally not emphasised orthographically (e.g. т. Ива́нов—taˈvariʃtʃ iˈvanəf 'Comrade Ivanov'), and the names of institutions which run into several words are mostly treated French fashion by writing with a capital letter the first member of the group only (e.g. Отделе́ние языка́ и литерату́ры—əɟɟiˈleɲijə jiziˈka i ɭiʈiraˈturi 'Department of Language and Literature', with which we may contrast Акаде́мия Нау́к—əkaɟˈemijə naˈuk 'Academy of Sciences').

Russian punctuation follows mainly German example and prefers 'grammatical' stopping to stopping by sense and breath groups, as in English. Subordinate clauses are always kept apart by commas, which accordingly precede relative and conjunctive pronouns like кто—kto 'who' and что 'that'. Commas are also used, as in English, to separate the homogeneous terms of a sequence, as when there are nouns in apposition, several attributes of a noun, a series of adverbs, or a succession of co-ordinate verbs, and they help to isolate vocatives, parenthetic particles, and interjections. The comma then has a great variety of uses. By contrast the semicolon and colon are less frequently used in Russian than in English, but French example has popularised the *points suspensifs* (*mnogotočije*), the dash, often used to indicate a change of speaker in reported dialogue and as a substitute for parentheses and the copula, and the exclamation mark, which is closely associated with the imperative. Quotation marks differ in place and aspect. When inverted commas are used, they always go in pairs and appear everted thus: „ ". Far more common, especially in recent years, are French-style angular brackets, viz. « », with the angles outwards.

4

Many of the technical details of written Russian—alphabet, spelling, punctuation—as well as its structure and style may now be illustrated by an exercise in translation from English into Russian.

A familiar passage in Rudyard Kipling's *Jungle Book* ('Mowgli's Brothers') reads: 'The Law of the Jungle, which never orders anything without a reason, forbids every beast to eat Man except when he is killing to show his children how to kill, and then he must hunt outside the hunting-grounds of his pack or tribe. The real reason for this is that man-killing means, sooner or later, the arrival of white men on elephants, with guns, and hundreds of brown men with gongs and rockets and torches. Then everybody in the jungle suffers. The reason the beasts give among themselves is that Man is the weakest and most defence-less of all living things, and it is unsportsmanlike to touch him. They say too—and it is true—that man-eaters become mangy, and lose their teeth.'[1]

This passage could not go into Russian as it stands, but would have to be construed in something after the following fashion: '*Law* (m.) jungles-of, never not prescribing-*he* nothing-of without cause-of, forbids *every-to beast-to* (m.) to-eat people-of, apart *that-of case-of* (m.), when he kills, teaching *own-of children-of* (m.) to-hunt. And also this (n.) allows-self only beyond limits-with land-of *own-of pack-of* (f.) or *own-of tribe-of* (n.). *True reason* (f.) this-of (n.) hides in that-in, that murder man-of draws after self-with, early or late, appearance *whites-of people-of* (m.) on elephants-on, with rifles-with, and hundreds-of *browns-of people-of* (m.) with gongs-with, rockets-with and torches-with. Then misery *all-to jungles-to* (m.). But beasts explain-they other other-

---

[1] See *The Jungle Book* (London, 1907), pp. 8–9.

to *this rule* (n.) thus: Man—*most weak, most helpless creature* (n.); along-this (n.) hunter-to unseemly to-touch he-of. They also speak-they—and this (n.) *very truth* (f.),—that maneaters sicken-they mange-with and lose-they teeth.'

As we read through this bewildering reconstruction, we begin to realise that there are notable differences between English and Russian. In contrast to English, Russian has no definite article, distinguishes both sex and animate gender in noun and adjective, and makes these two parts of speech, which are declined, agree with each other in gender, number, and case (as shown by our italics). It submits its cases to government by prepositions (e.g. on elephants-on) and verbs (e.g. sicken-they mange-with), harmonises subject and verb in person, number, and, we may add here, even in gender (in the singular of the past tense), does not use the verb 'to be' in the present tense, and resorts to commas to separate clauses, as well as parts of speech in apposition. The expression of gender in the verb is not illustrated by the foregoing passage, but there are many instances in it of the genitive-style accusative case (e.g. to-eat people-of), which is invested by an animate object in the masculine singular and the masculine-feminine (or epicene) plural and is perhaps the most striking way of distinguishing animate gender in Russian. Naturally the characteristics we have listed very far from exhaust the differences between the two languages in form and usage, but they suffice to show nevertheless the extent of the gulf that divides them as grammatical structures. This is widened still further by the written appearance of Russian. Our passage, translated into that language, represented by Cyrillic characters, and accented, would be:

Закóн джýнглей, никогдá не предпи́сывающий ничегó без причи́ны, запрещáет всякому звéрю есть людéй, крóме тогó слýчая, когдá он убивáет, учá свои́х детéй охóтиться. Да и э́то разрешáется тóлько за предéлами земли́ своéй стáи и́ли своегó плéмени. И́стинная причи́на э́того крóется в том, что уби́йство человéка влечёт за собóй, рáно и́ли пóздно, появлéние бéлых людéй на слонáх, с ружья́ми, и сóтен кори́чневых людéй с гóнгами, ракéтами и фáкелами. Тогдá гóре всем джýнглям. А звéри объясня́ют друг дрýгу э́то прáвило так: Человéк — сáмое слáбое, сáмое беспóмощное существó; поэ́тому охóтнику неприли́чно тро́гать его́. Они́ та́кже говоря́т — и э́то су́щая пра́вда, — что людое́ды заболева́ют чесо́ткой и теря́ют зу́бы.

If we now transcribe this passage into the Czech-style Latin characters of the International transliteration of Cyrillic[1] and indicate the stressed vowels of words of more than one syllable with an acute accent, we shall have the following:

Zakón džúnglej, nikogdá ne predpísyvajuščij ničegó bez pričíny, zapre-ščájet vsjákomu zvérju est' ljudéj, kromé togó slúčaja, kogdá on ubivájet, učá svojích detéj ochótit'sja. Da i éto razrešájetsja tól'ko za predélami zemlí svojéj stáji íli svojegó plémeni. Ístinnaja pričína étogo krójetsja v tom, čto ubíjstvo čelovéka vlečót za sobój, ráno íli pózdno, pojavlénije bélych ljudéj na slonách, s ruž'jámi i sóten koríčnevych ljudéj s góngami, rakétami i fákelami. Togdá góre vsem džúngljam. A zvéri objasnjájut drug drúgu éto právilo tak: Čelovék — sámoje sláboje, sámoje bespómoščnoje suščestvó; poétomu ochótniku neprilíčno trógat' jegó. Oní tákže govorját — i éto súščaja právda, — čto ljudojédy zabolevájut česótkoj i terjájut zúby.

Of course, unless we knew that *ch* and *j* have their German values, that *č* is pronounced like our ch, *š* like sh, and *ž* like s in 'treasure', we should not be able to pronounce all the sounds in this transliteration, but even if we knew the phonetic values of its characters, we should still be unable to read the passage to the satisfaction of a Russian. The reason for this is that Russian has a very different set of sounds from English, and the written form of the language is hardly a satisfactory guide to Russian pronunciation, though we shall probably concede on nearer acquaintance with it that it is more 'phonetic' than English spelling.

5

The structural differences between Russian and English turn in part on differences in the rate of development of the two languages. Here the recorded history of both comes to our aid. Comparison between eleventh-century and Modern Russian shows that the language has evolved relatively slowly, and the task of learning to read Old Russian with a preliminary knowledge of Modern Russian presents no real difficulty. On

---

[1] See my pamphlet-offprint, 'The Latinisation of Cyrillic Characters', *The Slavonic and East European Review*, xxx, 75; London, 1952.

the other hand Old English (Anglo-Saxon), as compared with Modern English, might be a different language: indeed it is easier to learn Old English with the help of Modern German than of Modern English. Leaving aside, however, the possible reasons for the different rate of development as between Russian and English, let us observe that in the latter part of the tenth century, when Old Russian began to be written, Old English, as a structure, was much less conservative than Old Russian, whose inflections (see ch. VI, pp. 117–23) present complexities unknown to the former.

English and Russian literary beginnings were also very different, because each was associated with the geographically nearest centre of Christian culture in Southern Europe. The Old English alphabet and literature show the effects of contact with Latin influence, both direct and through Irish, but that influence was not overwhelming, as was Greek influence on Wulfila's Gothic (fourth century) or on the Old Bulgarian (Old Church Slavonic) of St Cyril and St Methodius (ninth century). Old English literature, as the literary technique of *Beowulf* shows, must have had a long tradition of oral poetry. On the other hand the much later Old Russian was from the outset, if we ignore the supposedly twelfth-century *Lay of Prince Igor'*, a bald transcript of the closely related Old Bulgarian, which, though a giver in relation to Russian, was itself, like Gothic, a mainly servile imitation of Byzantine Greek in vocabulary and syntax. Its numerous abstract words were, for the most part, loan-translations, and its elaborate periodic style, braced by the use of particle and subordinate clause, was a translation of Byzantine models. This language then, in a necessarily Russian recension, is, as we shall learn more fully afterwards, at the source of Russian literature, and the subsequent history of both Russian language and Russian literature has been in a sense a long process of emancipation from the initial and paralysing influence of Byzantine culture working through the medium of Bulgarian. We shall not do more at this stage than anticipate part of a later detailed survey (see chs. VII–XI). Let us note cursorily that the process of emancipation, retarded with the renewal of 'reactionary'

South Slavonic contacts in the fifteenth century, was accelerated in the sixteenth and seventeenth centuries under the impact of West European, including Latin, example. Polish influence was operative throughout the long period of medieval rivalry between Poland and Muscovy; German influence, aided by Dutch, prevailed in the late seventeenth and early eighteenth centuries, and French influence dominated the next hundred years. German patterns of style helped in some measure to reinforce the Byzantine-Bulgarian stylistic trend of the Middle Ages, especially its addiction to involved usage, and French patterns helped to counteract the rigour of both Byzantine and German influence in unexpected, but effective alliance with spoken Russian. The last, as the language of the common people, was a potent creative factor and seems to have had a long history of use, if we may judge from the simple syntax of the medieval writs, law code, and unbookish parts of the solitary *Lay of Prince Igor'*. West European influence on Literary Russian, however, was actively combated in the name of the Byzantine-Bulgarian tradition in the late eighteenth and early nineteenth centuries, and the solution of the problem of a uniform literary style came only after the French Revolution. The style was worked out by leading Russian authors and publicists of the Romantic Age as a judicious mixture of native Russian, West European, and Byzantine-Bulgarian ingredients, and, perfected in the late nineteenth-century period of Realism, is valid in a modern adaptation to this day.

6

We are in serious danger of falling into error when we speak of a national Russian style, because style inevitably varies with social factors and literary fashions. It is better therefore to attempt a definition of the language, though not in national terms. We cannot go far wrong if we rely exclusively on linguistic characterisation, and this will be given in due course (chs. II–IV). Here we need only point out that Literary Russian is grammatically more like Latin and Ancient Greek than like French and English: it is, as it were, half-way between the old and the new, a language type still free from a too rigid word-order. In common with the older languages, Russian expresses the grammatical relationship of words in sentences by inflections, or changes in the forms of its nouns and verbs. In contrast to what obtains in Latin and Ancient Greek, its system of declension is more conservative and complex than its system of conjugation, which, even including aspect (see ch. III, pp. 61–3), is relatively straightforward. Russian syntax too, for all that it has experienced the cumulative influence of Byzantine Greek, Latin, and German, resembles on the whole to-day the simpler West European patterns, as our translation of the extract from Kipling (pp. 12–13, above) has shown.

Up to now we have dwelt on Russian as a receiver. But the language has given liberally to others both of its own and especially of what it has borrowed. This is best seen not so much in the relatively few loan-words, including remodelled political terms, which West European languages have taken over from Russian, as in the modern vocabularies of the heterogeneous languages of the U.S.S.R., which abound in Russian words and phrases. An examination of the pages of, say, a recent Votyak (Udmurt) dictionary[1] reveals in that Finnic language the presence of such Russian and russianised loan-words as *akt*, *blok*, *boj* (battle), *zona*, *kartina* (picture), *ledokol* (ice-breaker), *more* (sea), *nalog* (tax), *okrug* (district), *reč* (speech), *slon* (elephant), *truba* (chimney), *ukol* (injection), *česnok* (garlic), *špion* (spy), and *električestvo* (electricity). This is typical of most of the languages of the Union. But besides such lexical influence we find a deeper syntactic influence, though this varies considerably from one language to another. Votyak, which had a literature before the Revolution, retains its own characteristic usage, but Kamchadal (Itel'men), which belongs to the Palaeoasiatic (Palaeosiberian) group of incorporative, Amerindian-style languages, has simple sentences of Russian type.[2]

---

[1] В. М. Вахрушев и др., *Удмуртско-русский словарь* (Москва, 1948).

[2] See *Ntanselqzaankicen: Itelmenan anselnoan kniga* (*Let's Learn: A Text-book of Itel'men*; Leningrad, 1932).

The language of our study, whose characteristics, history, and influence we have just passed under preliminary review, must now claim our attention first as a structure and then in its development. The chapters on structure visualise Russian as it is now; those on its development visualise the concatenated stages of its growth, or that sequence of structures which, like the successive, infinitesimally different images of a film, provide the 'stills' of a moving pattern, extending, in this case, over nine centuries.

CHAPTER II

SOUNDS

I

Speech precedes writing, as writing is primarily a representation of speech with visual symbols, and speech, on analysis, resolves itself into a sequence of sound impressions made through the appropriate channels on the central nervous system and interpreted by the brain in terms of a particular system of language, which gives the sounds meaning. Sound and meaning go together, yet their relationship is not such that they cannot be considered separately. We shall therefore make our first approach to Russian through its sounds, but to do this we shall need to know something about the character and 'mechanism' of articulate sounds in general. The study of such sounds is the province of phonetics, if we study them merely as sounds apart from their meanings, and of phonology if we study them as the expression, or 'realisation', of a particular language-system. The difference between phonetics and phonology arises out of the difference between speech and language, the concrete act and the abstract system. The Swiss linguist Ferdinand de Saussure[1] was responsible for emphasising and popularising the contrast between speech and language, and Prince N. Trubetzkoy[2] for 'opposing' phonetics to phonology. Since the 1930's it has been usual to make this distinction with Trubetzkoy, and we shall observe it here for clarity of exposition.

Phonology is called 'phonemics' by Americans, and this designation of our science derives from the name of the minimum phonological unit, or phoneme,[3] which is contrasted with sounds, or 'phones', the units of phonetics. A clear instance of the dif-

[1] *Cours de linguistique générale* (Paris, 1916).

[2] *Grundzüge der Phonologie* (Prague, 1939). An expanded French version of this appeared as *Principes de phonologie* (Paris) in 1949.

[3] For a recent exposition from the English standpoint, see D. Jones, *The Phoneme: its Nature and Use* (Cambridge, 1950).

ference between the two may be seen in the two types of *l* in English (cf. the *l*-sounds in 'land' and 'well'), both of which, though distinct, constitute only one phoneme, as they are mutually exclusive and do not serve to differentiate meaning. By drawing a sharp distinction between phoneme and sound, the comprehensive and the particular, however, we expose ourselves to the possible error of ignoring the physical basis of the phoneme, which is 'realised' in a sound, as language itself is 'realised' in speech. In our subsequent investigation of the Russian phonemes we must be careful not to forget this: we shall try to view them, for practical purposes, not merely as abstractions, or the paper components of a language pattern, but as fundamental, or typical, sounds in that pattern.

In a book on the system of a language it is still customary to list its phonemes first and then to consider the words, or semantic groupings, of which they are a part. Attempts have been made in the U.S.S.R. recently to reverse this orthodox, or 'synthetic', procedure[1] by studying the sentence first and the phoneme last. This would obviously be the natural thing to do if we were concerned with a language to be recorded for the first time. But if the language in question has already been analysed phonetically and grammatically, as English and Russian have, the clearest presentation of it would give priority to the phoneme.

2

The Russian system of phonemes, like that of any other language, consists of characteristic elements known as vowels and consonants. These terms were first used by the Classical grammarians, but applied to letters rather than to sounds. We shall give them the values they have in modern phonetics and regard vowels as articulate sounds made by the breath in uninterrupted passage through the mouth (oral) cavity and consonants as articulate sounds made either by momentarily checking or by hindering its progress there.

---

[1] See the sketch of Votyak grammar appended to В. М. Вахрушев и др., *Удмуртско-русский словарь* (Москва, 1948).

Both vowels and consonants are classified according to the way they are made and the place they are made in and, whereas the advancement or retraction of the lips may be important for vowels, voice or its absence is an essential characteristic of consonants. Only the middle (phoneticians call it the 'front') and the back of the tongue help to form vowels by rising to various set

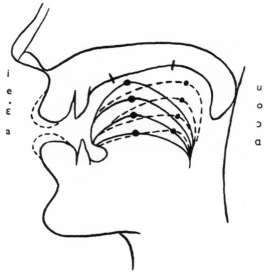

Fig. 2

positions opposite the hard and the soft palate, or palatal arch and velum, respectively, and occasionally 'central', or intermediate, types of vowels require the use of the surface of the tongue common to the front and back areas. The positions assumed by the tongue in relation to the palate are now commonly called 'close' (e.g. i and u) and 'open' (e.g. a and ɑ, as in French).[1] The four vowels i, a, ɑ, u are marginal types, i.e. they

[1] The terms 'close' and 'open' really refer to the relative approximation of the lower jaw to the upper. When the jaws are close together the tongue, which is embedded in the lower jaw, tends to be high, and when they are open the tongue is low. Henry Sweet used 'high' and 'low' for 'close' and 'open', and Russian phoneticians still adhere to his terminology.

represent the highest and lowest positions of the tongue in the formation of vowels, and they are connected vertically by intermediate types known as 'half-close' (e.g. e and o) and 'half-open' (e.g. ɛ and ɔ). The tongue and lip positions of all these vowels appear in Fig. 2. It will be observed that the back vowels (e.g. u, o, ɔ) are generally made with the lips pursed, or advanced, and the front vowels with the lips retracted (e.g. i, e, ɛ). This is the normal practice in English and Russian, but 'rounded' (lipped,

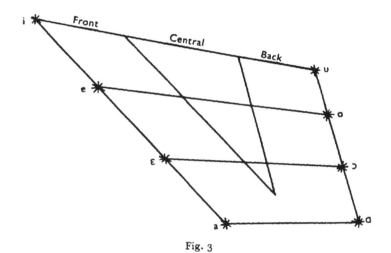

Fig. 3

or labialised) front vowels occur in both French and German (e.g. y in Fr. *lune* and Ger. *grün*), and an 'unrounded' back vowel (ɨ), to be described later, occurs in Russian. For purposes of classification and reference the tongue and lip positions of selected vowel-types have been 'fixed' by being recorded on gramophone records and photographed by X-ray lighting. These 'cardinal' vowels, as Daniel Jones calls them, constitute an ideal system and provide a suitable means of defining the vowels of any language. The diagram of the cardinal vowels is usually stylised as a quadrangle, and if we look at Fig. 3 we shall notice that it distinguishes what we may call 'areas of characterisation', in which the approximations of the cardinal types as they occur in a particular language are plotted.

In recent years the cathode-ray oscillograph has been successfully used to record the cardinal vowels as wave-forms on sound-recording film.[1] There are three main types of wave-forms, viz. the curvate i-type, the serrated a-type, and the embattled u-type (see Fig. 4). Close inspection of the wave-forms reveals that e resembles i, but is rather more angular; ɛ and a, whose waves resemble each other most closely of all, are pointed and refined

Oscillographic Wave-Forms of the Cardinal Vowels

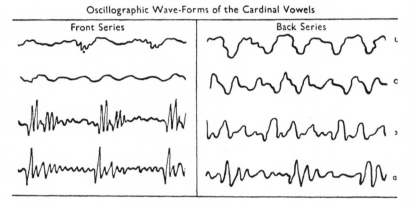

Fig. 4

variants of the a-wave; and ɔ resembles a, but is distinctly coarser and approaches the o and u types, being formally nearer to o than to u. Accordingly the cardinal vowels, in terms of oscillographic analysis, present three sets: i-e, ɛ-a-a, and ɔ-o-u.

Consonants are first classified broadly into two main groups— the occlusives, formed by occlusion (closure) of the oral cavity (e.g. Eng. p, t, m, n), and the constrictives, formed by constriction (stricture) of the oral cavity, so as to compress the exhaled breath into a narrow channel (as for f or s), or divide it (as for l), or interrupt its outflow by a series of rapid closures (as for Scotch r). Occlusives may be plosive (p, t) or nasal (m, n), and con-

[1] See *Proceedings of the Second International Congress of Phonetic Sciences* (Cambridge, 1936), p. 197.

strictives may be fricative (f, s), lateral (l), or vibrant (Scotch r). Affricates, which are treated as constrictives and transcribed with two letters, are plosives with a fricative release (e.g. Eng. ʧ in 'church'). The illustrations given here in parentheses symbolise consonants made at different 'places of articulation', viz. between both lips (bilabial p), between lips and teeth (labiodental f), between specific parts of the surface of the tongue and the surface of the palate (alveolar s, palatal j, velar k), and between the vocal chords, or lips of the larynx (glottal h). In all cases the consonant is articulated by the operation of an active part of the vocal organs—lips, tongue, vocal chords—but the places themselves, at least in English practice, are normally defined in terms of the part articulated against (cf. the subdivision of the entire area of the palate into alveolar, palatal, and velar places, or foci, of articulation).

3

The Russian vowel-phonemes show, in pattern, the typical triangular groupings of many European vowel-systems, with i, u, and a at the 'angles'. The following diagram contains six distinct vowel-types, viz.

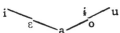

but these can be reduced to five phonemes, because i and ɨ are phonologically variants of the i-phoneme. Here, if anywhere, we begin to realise the need of viewing sounds from a phonetic as well as a phonological point of view. Phonology, primed by the science of meaning, or semantics, regards i and ɨ as phonematic ('phonemic') variants, because they are not used to differentiate meaning, which is the test of a phoneme, but to the ear the two sounds are obviously different, i being a front, and ɨ a back, vowel, and unless the difference is observed in speech, the native Russian may not understand at all. Acoustic tests confirm this, for L. V. Ščerba has measured the number of vibrations per second characteristic of the Russian vowels in isolation and has obtained the following results, viz. i—3044, ɛ—1816, ɨ—996, a—980, o—756, u—432.[1] These figures make it clear that i is a vowel which has more in common with the back than with the front series. The value of phonetic discrimination is thus obvious, and in the ensuing description of the Russian vowels we shall use it wherever it may seem necessary.

Two important considerations in the study of the Russian vowel-phonemes are that they depend (i) on the incidence of stress, which gives a clearer articulation, and (ii) on the quality

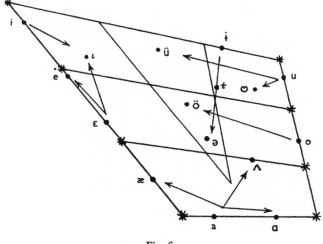

Fig. 6

of adjacent, especially sequent, consonants. The five-phoneme pattern we have discussed indicates only the stressed vowels. This is the bare minimum of the Russian vowel-system, and we see that it is adequately represented by the orthography. Indeed, the orthographic and the phonematic systems are obviously related, as Jones's 'broad transcription' of English shows, and modern phonology has learnt from traditional orthography what it has systematised for hitherto unwritten languages.

In addition to the stressed vowel-phonemes already given we have the following subsidiaries, which may be placed in relation

[1] *Русские гласные в качественном и количественном отношении* (СПБ, 1912).

to the principal, or typical, members by using the Jones quadrangle of cardinal vowels (Fig. 6). It will be seen from this diagram that each principal phoneme, except o, has at least one variant, which to phoneticians approaching Russian 'from the outside' would represent a distinct vowel-sound. In dealing with the Russian vowel-phonemes individually we shall enumerate the subsidiaries in each case.

We may begin our survey with the front vowels, viz. i, ɛ, and a. The first has the sound of English i: in 'seen', but is not long, even under stress. That is why a Russian, pronouncing English long vowels, tends to make them short. Russian i, when it is followed by a non-palatalised consonant (as in мимо—ˈm̦imə 'past, by'), is, like English i:, below cardinal level, but before a 'soft', or palatalised, consonant it is more like the cardinal sound. Here we have a phonetic context which is sometimes called 'interpalatal' position, because, as a front vowel, Russian i must invariably be preceded by a soft consonant (e.g. лить—ˈl̦iț 'to pour'). A lowered and retracted variety of i, represented by the undotted iota (ι), occurs in unstressed position (cf. the two types of i in или—ˈil̦ι 'or'), but, like the other unstressed vowels, will not be specially indicated in our transcriptions. It is rather closer than the short ι of 'city' (ˈsιtι), as its articulation gravitates towards i, whereas that of English ι gravitates towards e. Russian ι is also invariably shorter than Russian i, but difference of length (quantity) has no phonological value in the language, in contrast to what obtains in, say, English and German.

Russian ɛ is a typically open sound before hard consonants and occurs rather more frequently than its close variant e, which appears in interpalatal position (e.g. это—ˈɛtə 'this', эти—ˈeți 'these'). It recalls somewhat English ɛ in 'set' (sɛt), and sharply contrasts with the closeness of e, which is like that of French 'été'.

Russian stressed a is more front than back in normal usage, i.e. it resembles the first element of the English diphthongs aι (in 'night') and aω (in 'out') and not the vowel of 'far' (fɑ:), which is a markedly back vowel. Unstressed ʌ occurs only in the syllable immediately preceding the stress, or first pretonic syllable (e.g. ˈвода—vʌˈda 'water'), is rather more advanced than English

25

ʌ (in 'shut'), and may perhaps be adequately represented by ɐ, which fits into the bottom (open section) of the central wedge in the vowel quadrangle. Another variant of a is interpalatal æ, as in пять—р̜æ̜t̜ 'five', which is nearly the same sound as the English vowel in 'sat' (sæt), and still another, the ɑ preceding velarised 1 (e.g. спал—spɑl 'he slept'), is like the English back ɑ of 'far'.

As vowels of the front series, i, ɩ, e, ɛ, and æ require to be preceded by a soft consonant, and this, as we have seen in the account of Russian spelling (ch. i, p. 7), is indicated by the Cyrillic characters и, е, я respectively.

The back series of Russian vowel-phonemes comprises two rounded (labialised) types, u and o, both of which have subsidiaries, and the exceptional, unrounded ɨ, which is a member of the i-phoneme and has perceptible phonetic variants of its own in unstressed position, viz. ɪ and ə.

Russian u, as in ум—um 'mind', is related to cardinal u in the same way as Russian i is to cardinal i. Both Russian vowels, when stressed, are lower in tongue position, but quite as retracted as the cardinal sounds. The English vowel in 'moon' (muːn) is somewhat different from its Russian counterpart, being not only much longer, but rather more advanced. Unstressed ꭒ is, like unstressed ɩ, a lowered and more 'centralised' variety of u. As such it resembles English ꭒ in 'put' (pꭒt), but tends more towards u than towards o, to which the English sound gravitates. A central subsidiary member of the u-phoneme is found in interpalatal position (e.g. любить—ļüˈʹbit 'to love') and resembles the second vowel-element in the English dialectal pronunciation of 'moon' as mɨün.

Russian ɨ is a vowel about whose character phoneticians are still not entirely agreed. Some of them are inclined to hear it as a close back, others as a close central, vowel. Comparison with Polish ɨ, written y, or with the corresponding Ukrainian sound (и), which are both definitely 'central', suggests that Russian ɨ, as in бык—bɨk 'bull', falls within the close back area, though comparison with cardinal ɯ (the ideal unrounded u) makes it clear that ɨ is an advanced type of this vowel. There is no Standard English counterpart to ɨ, but its acoustic effect may be obtained by unrounding the uː of 'moon', as is done in, say, the Cockney diphthongisation of this word. The unstressed form of Russian ɨ tends to be both lower and more centralised (e.g. дáмы—ˈdamɨ 'ladies'), sometimes approaching the quality of the invariably unstressed ə (e.g. in the Moscow pronunciation of рýсский—'Russian' as ˈruskəj), which is the typical sound of the central vowel-area in Russian, as it is in English.

Russian o, the only exclusively stressed vowel in the language, is another sound about which there is not a consensus of opinion. Ščerba and Miss M. I. Matusevič[1] think that it resembles the distinctly open French ɔ in *note* and Italian ɔ of *notte*, whereas V. A. Bogorodickij and the Serbian R. Košutić, who reproduce Henry Sweet's threefold 'vertical' (formative) classification of vowels into high, mid, and low, consider it to be a medium vowel, and Jones places it between his half-close and half-open types, but nearer the latter. Comparison with the closely related Polish again shows Russian o to be a closer sound than Polish ɔ and accordingly closer than cardinal ɔ. Miss Matusevič is also right in pointing out that the Russian vowel is often diphthongised to uo, but errs, I think, in defining the second term of the diphthong as a half-open sound. Russian o to my ear is a medium sound with a tendency to closeness, which is proved by its admitted 'disintegration' into uo. In interpalatal position it becomes central ö, like the sound often heard in French *le* (e.g. тётя—ˈt̡öt̡ə 'aunt').

Russian ə is always found in unstressed syllables, including the relatively 'strong' first 'pretonic' (preaccentual), and it is invariably either final or followed by a hard consonant. It resembles English and German ə and varies in quality according to its position, being closer before the stress and more open after (cf. городá—gəraˈda 'towns' with гóрод—ˈgorət 'town').

Besides all these vowels, Russian has a body of diphthongs which, unlike the English ones, are all of one type. A diphthong is phonetically a single syllable beginning with one vowel and ending in another. To Jones it appears as a 'gesture', a movement

---

[1] *Введение в общую фонетику*[2] (Ленинград, 1948), which I have reviewed in *Archivum Linguisticum*, II, 2 (Glasgow, 1950).

performed by the tongue, and in this view a diphthong, unlike the stationary pure vowel, is primarily mobile, though the element of vowel resonance is naturally present in both. It may be conveniently identified by reference to its second component, or terminal vowel, and this may be used as a criterion of classification. In English there are three types of diphthongs, represented by such words as 'light', 'air', and 'south', i.e. -ι (front), -ə (central), and -o (back) types. In Russian none of these occurs, and some Russian phoneticians, among them Matusevič, prefer to deny the existence of diphthongs in their mother tongue altogether and to regard them merely as combinations of a vowel with j. In point of fact the j-position is not always reached in articulation, and so, where a vowel 'tails off' into another, the result is normally an i-diphthong. Any of the Russian vowels we have enumerated, except ε, may constitute a diphthong with j, which we shall retain in our transcription for convenience. The diphthong εj is impossible in Russian, because a palatal or palatalised consonant requires to be preceded by half-close e. The Russian series may be divided into stressed and unstressed diphthongs, the first comprising ij (in кий—ķij 'cue'), ej (in пей! —ɓej 'drink!'), æj (in чай—ʧæj 'tea'), aj (in рай—raj 'paradise'), ɨj (in выйти—vɨjti 'to go out'), uj (in дуй!—duj 'blow!'), üj (in плюй!—pḷüj 'spit!'), oj (in рой—roj 'swarm'), and öj (in семьёй —ʂimḷjöj 'by the family'), and the second series ιj (рýсский— ˈrusķιj), ɨj (in дóбрый—ˈdobrɨj 'kind'), oj (in рáтуй!—ˈratoj 'struggle!'), ʌj (in тайгá—tʌjˈga 'forest'), and əj in (дóброй— ˈdobrəj ' of/to the kind (one) '). These are all diphthongs phonetically. Phonologically, however, they do not exist in Russian, as they are not contrasted with simple vowels.

Study of these diphthongal series suggests that, making due allowance for the presence of variants, or subsidiaries, the Russian five-vowel phonological system is reduced to three by the elimination of e and o in unstressed syllables. The play of phonemes then is subject on occasion to prohibitions: certain types of sounds are not permitted in particular phonetic contexts. Of the three 'extreme' vowels—i, a, u—surviving in unstressed syllables, a (as ʌ) is confined to the first pretonic and becomes ə or ι elsewhere, according to whether it is spelt a or я. When и (i) is preceded by a hard consonant it is pronounced ɨ (e.g. жизнь—ʒɨʒn̩ 'life'). Between soft consonants o and u become centralised, and a is raised to æ. Knowledge of these and other similar rules makes it possible to reduce sound symbols to a minimum, and indeed such limitation is a matter of principle to the phonologist as well as a matter of convenience. He requires no more than six vowel-symbols, viz. i, e, a, o, u, ə, with an appropriate device, e.g. the postliteral hook, for discriminating between the palatalised and the non-palatalised sets of consonants. By means of these he is able to construct, among other things, schemes like the following, which shows the distribution of the vowel phonemes of Literary Russian in relation to stress.

Distribution of Russian Vowels

Pretonic syllables		Stressed syllable	Post-tonic syllables	
2	1		1	2
i/ɨ	i/ɨ	i/ɨ	i/ɨ	i/ɨ
i	i	e	i	ə
ə	a	a	ə	ə
ə	a	o	ə	ə
u	u	u	u	u

The general observation here is that the variety of vowels diminishes with distance from the stressed syllable. The two close vowel-phonemes i/ɨ and u survive in lowered, or relaxed, form, whatever the distance, e and o are always stressed, and a may occur in the first pretonic syllable. In weak position, i.e. in syllables other than the stressed and the first pretonic, e is replaced by i (more precisely ι), and a and o by ə.[1]

4

Manner of formation and place of articulation, or formative and local ('focal') criteria both enter, as we have seen, into the phonetic definition of consonants, and their concurrent application gives us the following table of the Russian system of con-

[1] Initially and even finally this ə tends to be pronounced ʌ, i.e. like the a of the first pretonic syllable. It appears as ə in our transcriptions. These also generally have a for ʌ and ɑ, i for ι, ɨ for ɨ, and u for ω.

sonantal phonemes, in which, incidentally, voice is indicated merely by the right-hand position of the symbol, whether it stands alone or is one of a pair of correlates. The symbol on the left will then represent a voiceless vowel.

		Bilabial	Labio-dental	Dental	Alveolar	Palatal	Velar
Occlusive	Plosive	p, b	—	t, d	—	—	k, g
	Nasal	m	—	n	—	—	—
Constrictive	Fricative	—	f, v	s, z	ʃ, ʒ	j	x
	Lateral	—	—	—	l	—	(l)
	Vibrant	—	—	—	r	—	—
	Affricate	—	—	ʦ	—	—	—

Of the foregoing 'hard' series of consonants, all but ʃ, ʒ, j, and ʦ can be 'softened', or palatalised, so that, corresponding to these, we have a nearly complete parallel set of 'soft' consonants. The alveolar fricatives ʃ and ʒ are normally hard, but ʃ occurs soft before ʧ in the consonant group represented in Cyrillic by щ, сч, зч (e.g. щи—ʃʧi 'cabbage soup'), and when long, as they may still be heard in the Moscow pronunciation, both are invariably soft. Moreover long ʒʒ, as in вóжжи—ˈvoʒʒi 'reins', has a complex variant in ʒʤ (ˈvoʒʤi). The palatal j can naturally not be palatalised. The affricate ʦ is always hard, as the affricate ʧ (i.e. tʃ) is always soft, and neither has a voiced correlate, except positionally, i.e. before a voiced consonant. The incomplete soft series of consonants may be arranged as follows:

p̡, b̡	—	t̡, d̡	—	k̡, g̡
m̡	—	n̡	—	—
—	f̡, v̡	s̡, z̡	—	x̡
—	—	—	l̡	—
—	—	—	r̡	—
—	—	—	ʧ	—

The effect of palatalisation on the ear is a function of the manner in which the soft consonants are formed. Their peculiar articulation requires the assistance of the 'front' (actually the middle) of the tongue. By simultaneously raising this towards the palatal arch an i- or j- colouring is obtained, which assures a substantial difference in quality between the hard and soft pairs. This difference is more noticeable in some cases than in others: thus it is not so obvious in the labials as in the dentals, alveolars, and velars. An English ear may seize the difference by comparing the hard French ʃ of *chou* with the relatively soft English ʃ of 'shoe'.

We may begin our survey of the Russian consonantal phonemes with the plosives, whose manner of formation consists in closure of the oral cavity at one of three different points, viz. the lips, the upper teeth, against which the tip of the tongue is pressed, and the soft palate, where occlusion is effected with the back of the tongue. The bilabial pair p/b are like their English counterparts, except that p is not noticeably 'aspirated' when stressed. There is considerable acoustic difference on the other hand between Russian and English t/d: the Russian pair is dental, as in French, the English alveolar. In both cases articulation is apical, i.e. with the tip of the tongue, but the area of contact for the Russian sounds is restricted to the upper teeth. As for k/g, the Russian and the English pairs show the same difference as the two sets of bilabials: in both cases only the English voiceless plosives are aspirated, and this applies to English t as well.

Normally the various pairs of plosives (oral occlusives) have corresponding unpaired, or single, nasals. The English plosives p/b have m, t/d—n, and k/g—ŋ (as in 'song'). The Russian plosives, on the contrary, have an incomplete set of nasals, k/g being without a nasal counterpart. Russian n too differs from English n, being dental, i.e. of homogeneous formation with t/d, whereas the English sound is characteristically alveolar, though the strong nasal resonance in both cases tends to obscure the difference, which is so marked in the plosives.

All the Russian occlusives, whether oral or nasal, present themselves in two parallel series, hard and soft, the latter, as we already know, accompanied by an i-articulation, which generally makes them 'bifocal' (to use Ščerba's term).[1] The co-existence of two articulation-points is best seen where the tongue makes contact with only one, as in the formation of the palatalised bilabials p, b, m.

The constrictive series of consonantal phonemes in Russian, though more numerous than the occlusive, as in most other

[1] See my article 'baifoukl a:tikjuleiʃn' (*Le Maître Phonétique*, no. 98; London, 1952).

languages, exhibits notable gaps. There are no bilabial fricatives of the type of English **w**, no dentals, i.e. the two sounds represented by the English spelling *th* (e.g. 'this thing'), and no glottals like English **h**, and there are only a solitary voiced palatal **j**, which tends, as in English, to become semivocalic, and an almost equally solitary voiceless velar **x**, of the type represented by Scotch and German *ch*, which has a sporadic correlate in the voiced ɣ of бóга—ˈboɣə 'God's'.[1] The most numerous fricatives are the sibilants s/z and ʃ/ʒ, both sets being quite distinct from their English counterparts. The Russian hiss-sibilants (*svistjaščije*), as in соль—soḷ 'salt' and зоб—zop 'gizzard', differ from the English type in having a 'dorsal' articulation as opposed to the English 'apical' articulation, i.e. they are made with the tip pressed against the lower teeth, whereas English s/z (as in 'same' and 'rise') require the tip to be raised to the level of the upper. In both cases a narrow channel of varying depth is formed down the middle line of the tongue and a tenuous stream of breath projected against the upper teeth and gums. The Russian hush-sibilants (*šipjaščije*) ʃ/ʒ are both of them primarily hard, whereas the corresponding English fricatives strike the Russian ear as soft, being slightly, but perceptibly palatalised (cf. Russian шут—ʃut 'jester', жук—ʒuk 'beetle' with English 'shoot'—ʃuːt, 'pleasure'—ˈpleʒə). The difference in acoustic effect is here due to the difference between the English 'dorsal' and the Russian 'coronal' articulation: the tip and edges of the blade are raised and the body of the tongue laterally contracted for the Russian sounds, and though the front of the tongue does not participate, as it does for the English, the back is slightly raised, making Russian ʃ/ʒ 'bifocal', or with two places (foci) of articulation, in contrast to its 'unifocal' hisses (s/z). The laterals and vibrants belong with ʃ/ʒ to the alveolar group by their principal articulation-point. Russian l, as in лук—luk 'onion', is 'bifocal', like the English sound in 'well' or 'cold', but the 'dark' quality (lower resonance) is more marked

---

[1] Voiced ɣ also occurs positionally (e.g. грех дýмать—grɛɣ ˈdumət 'a sin to think'). Positional correlates of other unpaired consonants (m, n, l, r) are comparatively rare.

and recalls the General American l. In contrast to this, English prevocalic l, as in 'land', has a clear articulation nearly like the normal l-sound in French and German. Russian r, as in рот— rot 'mouth', is a lingual vibrant (trill), whereas the English sound, especially in its more pronounced varieties, is a retroflex fricative, made by keeping the tongue stationary and its tip slightly bent back from the teeth-ridge. A sound of the Russian type is the Scotch vibrant, which, like the Spanish rr of *perro* 'dog', is much more pronounced because of its more numerous vibrations. Russian soft ļ, like Italian *gl* (in *paglia* 'straw'), and ŗ, which has an Irish equivalent, are very different in acoustic effect, from their hard correlates.

In addition to all these relatively simple consonants Russian has an affricate ʦ, for instance in цеп—ʦɛp 'flail', which is a retracted t released without puff, or plosion, into the allied (homorganic) fricative s. The sound is invariably hard and has no voiced counterpart, except as a positional variant before voiced sounds (e.g. отéц был здесь—aˈʦɛʣ bil ˈzdeş 'father was here'). The English letter-group ts, as in 'wits', lacks the cohesion of the Russian sound and does not constitute a consonantal unit, i.e. is not an affricate. On the other hand both Russian and English ʧ (cf. час—ʧas 'hour' with English 'church') are affricates and nearly equally soft, but while English ʧ has a voiced correlate in ʤ, as in 'joy', Russian ʤ, like ʣ, is a mere subsidiary of the corresponding voiceless phoneme (e.g. ночь—noʧ is pronounced noʤ in the sentence ночь былá тёмная—ˈnoʤ bila ˈtomnəjə 'the night was dark').

Of the two 'registers'—the 'hard' and the 'soft', as S. I. Karcevski(j)[1] calls them, the first is regarded, where vowel is opposed to consonant, as the normal. Accordingly the soft series of consonants must be felt as secondary, the later outcome of palatalisation, although from the phonetic and sometimes from the phonological point of view, hard and soft consonants are distinct sounds. The incomplete correlation of the two series, with the hard just predominating, and the relative mobility of

[1] 'Remarques sur la phonologie russe' (*Cahiers Ferdinand de Saussure*, III; Geneva, 1943).

the hard consonants, which are less restricted in their distribution than the soft, suggest the limitations and the 'inferiority' of the latter. Another antithesis, this time uniting both series, is that between voiced and voiceless consonants, whose interplay shows the exclusive presence of the voiceless in final position as in German (e.g. груб—grup 'coarse'; cf. Ger. *grob—grɔp*).[1] The anomalies of the Russian consonantal system as a phonological whole may be seen in the gaps of the following tabulation, adapted from Karcevski(j):

Articulation points	Consonants	Sonants
Bilabial	p, b	m
Labio-dental	f, v	—
Dental	$\left\{\begin{matrix} t, d \\ s, z \\ t \end{matrix}\right.$	n
Alveolar	$\left\{\begin{matrix} ʃ, ʒ \\ tʃ \end{matrix}\right.$	$\left\{\begin{matrix} l \\ r \end{matrix}\right.$
Palatal	j	—
Velar	$\left\{\begin{matrix} k, g \\ x \end{matrix}\right.$	—

5

Up to now we have considered Russian only as a system of isolated sounds. But these normally occur in sequences, and the sequences tend to group themselves into syllables defined by relative sonority (loudness) and stress. Sonority ranges sounds as a scale of acoustic prominences, with the vowels and sonants (i.e. nasals and 'liquids') at one end and the voiceless consonants at the other. The vowels in Russian constitute the nucleus of the syllable, but sonants may do this in other languages, including some of the Slavonic ones (e.g. Czech *vlk*, 'wolf', Croatian *vrlo* 'very'). Stress provides emphasis, and its pulsations, which run into several degrees, help to number the syllables. A string of syllables may be uttered without very pronounced stress, as in French, but more usually, as in Russian, one or more syllables in a word is characterised by the presence of a greater volume of

[1] The voicelessness of final consonants is a feature of the phonological systems of a number of languages (e.g. Polish, Bulgarian, Geg Albanian).

energy, which is generally associated with increased quantity (length) and a higher pitch. Where the muscular energy of utterance is very noticeable, we have dynamic, or 'expiratory', stress, as in both Russian and English. The significance of dynamic stress in Russian has already been dwelt on in the tabulation of the complex, stress-governed patterns of vowel-incidence. Here we may note its distribution. Compared with stress in Polish, Czech, and French, Russian stress, like English, is unfixed and irregular, but, unlike English stress, it is mobile in the same paradigm (cf. село—ṣiˈlo 'village' with сёла—ˈṣolə 'villages'). In this respect it has parallels outside Slavonic in Greek and Lithuanian. There are several degrees of stress, as we have already stated, the strongest being the primary stress of the 'stressed' (tonic) syllable, which in Russian usually exhibits a slightly lengthened vowel. A distinctly weaker position is the first pretonic syllable, and the weakest of the 'unstressed' syllables are probably the second pretonic and the first post-tonic, which may lose their vowels in rapid speech (e.g. городовой—gər(ə)daˈvoj 'policeman'; gen. sing. нового—ˈnov(ə)və 'of the new'). In English we recognise secondary stress in the longer words (e.g. 'combination'—ˌkɔmbiˈneiʃn). To Russian ears a secondary stress is not evident, but the first pretonic syllable is defined by a recognisably 'pure' (non-central) vowel in contrast to the 'reduced', or more 'obscure', vowels of the weaker syllables.

It has been observed that the vowels of the Russian stressed syllables are rather longer than those of the unstressed, but this difference has no phonological bearing. Such length is an integral part of stress, and the native speaker is unaware of it, except in obvious cases of emphasis. Compared with English vowel-length, which is both marked and phonological, it has not even the value of intermediate length between long and short, as we can observe for ourselves by listening to a Russian's treatment of English long vowels. On the other hand Russian has long as well as short consonants, and this difference in quantity may be a phonological, as well as a phonetic, feature (cf. сжечь—ʒʒetʃ 'to burn up' with жечь—ʒetʃ 'to burn').

The heightened pitch of the Russian stressed syllable is not equivalent either to the syllabic tone of certain European languages (e.g. Serbian, Lithuanian, and Swedish), which does not necessarily differentiate meaning, or to the significant syllabic tone of Chinese and of certain Papuan and African languages. On the other hand, like English and French, Russian has characteristic types of sentence intonation which carry notable differences of meaning. 'Intonation', according to V. Vsevolodskij-Gerngross, 'is the coefficient that converts the written word into the living one.'[1] Russian intonation patterns have a number of things in common with the more familiar and so far better-studied English 'tunes', and may be indicated, for practical purposes, by either curves or a notation of dots for unstressed syllables and larger dots, or strokes, for stressed. The second course, introduced by H. Klinghardt,[2] is now generally adopted, though it is occasionally varied by substituting small strokes for the dots, and the Morse-style sequence of 'dots and dashes' is sometimes enclosed in frames for ease of reference. If we assume, as an empirical condition, the existence of three levels of voice—middle (normal), high, and low—we shall be able to indicate the relative pitch of successive syllables on or between the three lines representing these levels, for it is the relative pitch that is important, and not the absolute, which belongs to the province of music. The syllable with the strongest stress will show the essential character of the intonation. In Russian there are four types of this in dispassionate speech, viz. falling ($\searrow$), high rising ($\nearrow$), rising ($\nearrow$), and rising-falling ($\searrow$):

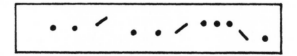

1. Я прочёл замечáтельную кнúгу.

(ja pra^ɪtʃol zəmɪ^ɪ tʃæţɪlnuju ^ɪknɪgu)

I have read a remarkable book.

[1] See Classified Bibliography, I.

[2] *Französische Intonationsübungen* (Cöthen, 1908), and *Übungen im englischen Tonfall* (Cöthen, 1920). The author uses large and small dots.

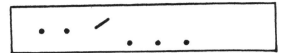

2. Вы давно́ уже́ здесь?
   (vɨ daˈvno uʒɛ z̦deș?)
   Have you been here long?

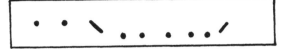

3. Она́ ско́ро прие́дет сюда́?
   (ana ˈskorə pr̦ijed̦it șuˈda?)
   She will be arriving here soon? (surprise).

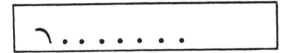

4. Сде́лайте э́то, пожа́луйста.
   (ˈzd̦eləjți etə paʒalstə)
   Please, do this.

The falling intonation, like its English counterpart, accompanies a feeling of certainty; the rising, on the contrary, is coloured with doubt and perplexity. Statements, commands, and exclamations have each a falling intonation, but the peremptory command may invest the high rising one (e.g. не шуми́!—n̦i ʃumi! 'silence!': ··╱). Questions can have either a rising or a falling intonation, the former, at a high level, being used if there is no specific interrogative word, the latter where this is present (cf. кто́ там?—ˈkto tam? 'who is there?': ╲· with э́то о́н?—etə ˈon? 'is it he?': ··╱). Where emotion intrudes into even a simple statement it can change the stressing and concomitantly the entire character of the intonation (e.g. он сла́вный челове́к— on ˈslavnɨj t͡ʃilaˈv̦ɛk 'he is a fine fellow', is pronounced with the following emphatic intonation: ·╲.... instead of the more usual: ·╱╰·╲). The example in the foregoing sentence illustrates an intonation of emphatic contrast, but emphasis may involve a mere intensification of utterance, and in this case the only difference between the intensified and the normal type of sentence is not in the character of the intonation, but in the interval between the beginning and the end of the characteristic tone (e.g. оста́вьте же меня́!—asˡtaf̧ți зə m̦iṇa! 'leave me alone!': ·╲. . . .).

In involute constructions such as may occur in read narrative, the intonation pattern varies not only according to the meaning of each sentence, but also according to its grammatical structure. The invariable falling tone at the end of a complex sentence is contrasted with rising tones at the end of preceding constituents, whether they are grammatically phrases or clauses (e.g. если бы он зна́л, что она́ не придёт, то он не оста́лся бы до́ма—jeş̧li bɨ on ˡznal ʃtə ana ṇi pr̦iˡd̦ot, to on ṇi aˡstalsə bɨ ˡdomə 'if he had known that she was not coming he would not have stayed at home': · · · ·╲. . . . .╱╿. . . .╱·╲.), but the rising tone is not there merely to express contrast, as in simple sentences with several stressed syllables: it is the nucleus of, as it were, a 'suspended' intonation, expressing the 'uncertainty' of incompletion and expecting the final, conclusive fall to round off the sentence. There is a general parallel to this in English, but in contrast to English, Russian rarely uses a level tone and usually substitutes either a rising or a falling one according to the tonal nature of the final stress. If this is accompanied by a rising tone, all the preceding stressed syllables will have falling ones and vice versa.

Stress, quantity, and intonation are all of them attributes, or accessories, of sounds or syllables, the 'prosodies' of Trubetzkoy, or the 'suprasegmental phonemes' which American phonologists contrast with 'linear' phonemes, i.e. with the successive sounds in word and sentence. Being detachable from the sounds with which they are associated, they have been subjected to separate scrutiny as 'supplementary'. In point of fact they are an essential part of the utterances from which they have been isolated, for, as we have already seen, the priority is always with utterance, and phonemes and their attributes are no more than products of analysis.

Phonetic analysis of phonemes in contact discovers the phenomena of assimilation, which arise from the overlappings of articulation, the anticipation of a succeeding sound while one is already being formed. Assimilation may be complete or partial, progressive or regressive. Complete assimilation ultimately creates length, the outcome of identification, which doubles, or 'geminates', the assimilating sound (e.g. отделять—ǝd̦ḍiˈļæț 'to divide'). On the other hand partial assimilation may lead to the identification of adjacent sounds in one particular, for instance in voice (thus молотьба 'threshing' is pronounced mǝlaḍˈba, where voiceless ț is assimilated to voiced b). Progressive influence involves that of the first of two adjacent sounds on the second (e.g. English 'observe'—ǝbˈzɜːv), and the more common regressive influence shows the second of two sounds assimilating the first, as in Russian (e.g. трубка—ˈtrupka 'pipe'). The paramountly regressive type of assimilation in Russian may be seen in the Russian speaker's natural tendency to introduce it into his English speech (e.g. 'what do you want?' becomes uˈod du ju uˈont? instead ofˈ(h)wɒt du juˈwɒnt?). Assimilation may lead not only to the identification of successive sounds, but to the lapse (syncope) of one of them when it is part of a phonetically difficult complex (cf. известный—izˈv̦ɛsn̦ij 'noted' with English 'whistle'—ˈ(h)wisl). In some cases it is a question of simplification rather than of assimilation (e.g. здравствуйте!—ˈzdraṣți! 'how do you do!').

Assimilation also gives rise to apophony, or gradation (Ger. *Ablaut*), which affects both vowels and consonants and may be either synchronic (contemporary) or diachronic (historical). The synchronic apophonies are never noted in a mainly morphological spelling, yet they take place in speech. They may assume the guise of an alternation of phonemes, for instance ǝ/a/o (водород—vǝdaˈrot 'hydrogen', вода—vaˈda 'water', воды—ˈvod̦i 'waters'), or merely of phonological variants like ɛ/e in сел—ṣɛl 'he sat down' and сели—ˈṣel̦i 'they sat down'. Diachronic apophonies have already found reflection in the accepted spelling and entail the variation of stem-forms, as in плакать—ˈplakǝț 'to weep', плачу—ˈplatʃu 'I weep' (плак-/плач-); nominative singular лоб—lop 'forehead', genitive лба—lba (лоб-/лб-). Such apophonies must obviously have been synchronic at one time and were determined by standards of pronunciation which are now obsolete. The classic instance of a diachronic apophony is in the Germanic languages, where it has been exploited to vary meaning (e.g. English 'sing—sang—sung').

CHAPTER III

WORDS AND FORMS

I

Words are more easy to recognise than to define, and awareness of them as units of speech, which depends on the existence of phonological norms (e.g. final voiceless consonants in Russian), precedes their recognition as spatially isolated written forms. Writing helps to define their limits and grammar to fix their categories according to form and usage. But a full study of words in their grammatical diversity is possible only with the aid of semantics. Form detached from meaning is not enough.

The impact of semantics is first felt in the analysis of the complete sentence, which discovers the antithesis of subject and predicate. These two elements may be considered to be tacitly present even in elliptical constructions of a 'logical' order, which eliminate one or other of them. Further analysis of the sentence resolves the major divisions into smaller ones known as 'syntagmas', or word-groupings. These subdivisions of subject and predicate are the parts of speech, which were originally extracted from a study of Ancient Greek by native philosophers and grammarians and later transferred from Ancient Greek to Latin. Modern European languages have inherited the parts of speech from the Classics, and although some modern languages, among them English and Russian, cannot be satisfactorily fitted into the special framework of Classical grammar, they nevertheless readily lend themselves to grammatical analysis into parts of speech. These then are a semantic reality, although their formal expression differs in detail from one language to another.

The reality of the word, denied out of context by A. A. Potebnja,[1] was accepted by most of his pupils and is admitted by the present generation of Soviet grammarians. To one of these—the

[1] See Classified Bibliography, III.

late L. V. Ščerba[1]—it is the minimum linguistic unit, which cannot be further analysed grammatically, but to his pupil V. V. Vinogradov[2] this formulation seems insufficiently elastic. We are invited to see in the structure of the word a function of the language-system of which it is a fragment. It can therefore vary from one language to another according to phonological norms, which are anything but uniform for all languages. The complexity of the word as a linguistic concept is due to the co-existence of two modes of approaching it—the formal and the semantic. The importance of the first is more apparent in Russian than in English. 'In a language like Russian', says Vinogradov, 'there are no lexical meanings which are not grammatically formalised and classified', or, to put it differently, the word in Russian is a system of forms and meanings which serves as a field of inter-action for the grammatical categories. The emphasis on form in this definition of words must not obscure their semantic (lexical) aspect or neglect them as bearers of meaning. Indeed, the only satisfactory definition of words is one which refuses to eliminate either.

Approaching Russian words from the combined formal (structural) and semantic points of view, we recognise the existence of two major types, viz. words of full meaning, which comprise the major parts of speech, and subsidiary words, which comprise the prepositions, conjunctions, and other particles. Russian grammarians have long been aware of this distinction and have attempted to define it: the two types of words were known to the formalist F. F. Fortunatov[3] as 'full' and 'partial' and to Potebnja as 'lexical' and 'formal' respectively. If we restrict the traditional application of the term 'parts of speech' to noun, adjective, numeral, pronoun, verb, and to the adverb as a 'lexical' unit, we shall be able to refer to prepositions, conjunctions, and the adverbial particles as 'particles of speech'.

---

[1] *О частях речи в русском языке* (Русская Речь. Новая серия ɪɪ, Ленинград, 1928).

[2] *Русский язык. Грамматическое учение о слове* (Москва-Ленинград, 1947).

[3] *Сравнительное языковедение. Лекции* (Москва, 1900).

This will leave us with interjections, which belong to the sphere of affective, or emotional, symbols. Vinogradov's 'modal words', representing the intrusion of the speaker's mood into the 'logic' of the sentence (e.g. едвá ли вам удáстся кóнчить к срóку 'you will hardly finish your work on time'), are manifestly connected with adverbial usage.

We are now in a position to classify and arrange the parts and the particles of speech as they exist in Russian. The nominal class, which is made up of the substantive, adjective, and numeral, and its associate, the pronominal, are opposed both formally and semantically to the verbal, which, as the nucleus of the predicate, attracts to itself a variety of 'complements'—not only adverbial 'extensions', but members of the nominal class functioning as objects. The verb itself may be absent from the predicate, as it generally is in Russian when it takes the form of the copula in present time (e.g. он здесь 'he is here', lit. 'he here'), and this state of things reveals, like the presence of non-verbal elements in the predicate, that noun and subject on the one hand and verb and predicate on the other are not co-extensive terms.

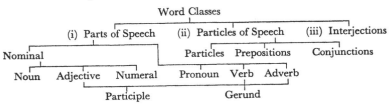

Moreover, the existence of hybrid parts of speech like the participles and gerunds breaks down the nominal and verbal classes as mutually exclusive groupings. Participles are the link between verb and adjective, gerunds the link between verb and adverb, and the adverb is, formally, a great reservoir, in which all the three members of the nominal class meet on nearly equal terms. All the parts of speech in the restricted sense of the expression have characteristic formal indices, constituting more or less complex systems and reflecting the presence of various notional, or semantic, categories (e.g. nouns have gender and case, verbs person, tense, and aspect, and adverbs share the

43

degrees of comparison with the adjective). In contrast to the parts of speech, the particles are formally invariable and blend function with meaning. Adverbial particles and prepositions may appear in the same sentence, and conjunctions bind sentences either on equal terms or by subordinating one to another. The table on p. 43 epitomises the word classes.

2

Classical grammar distinguished between variable and invariable words, and this distinction was taken up by Russian grammarians, whose mother tongue, like Ancient Greek and Latin, had preserved, as we have learnt, a considerable number of formal characteristics, or 'inflections'. To Russian grammarians like Fortunatov and Trubetzkoy it seemed expedient to contrast flexion (the formal expression of word relationships in the sentence) with derivation, or word-formation, a purely lexical category of relationships. Thus the genitive-case ending or the ending of the 3rd person singular of the present tense are both inflections, whereas the association of го́рдый 'proud' with го́рдость 'pride' is derivational and belongs therefore not to grammar, but to the vocabulary. The Russian system of flexion finds the nominal and verbal classes on opposite sides. The former presents the following correlations: (i) singular/plural (number), (ii) masculine/feminine/neuter and animate/inanimate (gender), (iii) attributive/predicative (syntactic usage), and (iv) nominative/oblique (case). These correlations are expressed formally by means of characteristic endings (terminal morphemes), and their systematic presentation gives rise to the paradigms of declension. Such paradigms are a feature of all three nominal parts of speech and extend to the participles. Declension then may be conceived as the systematised formal criteria of the nominal class.

In contrast to the relative complexity of nominal declension, we have in Russian the relative simplicity of verbal conjugation. Within the limits of the verb itself the invariable infinitive form is contrasted with the inflections of the finite verb in its principal moods, the indicative and the imperative. The primarily nominal category of gender, which permeates noun and adjective, intrudes not only into the hybrid participle, lending it an adjectival appearance and declension, but also into the past tense of the verb, which differs formally from the present in not expressing the verbal category of person, but in distinguishing nominal gender. The reason for this is historical: the modern Russian past-tense form is an indeclinable participle, which was originally associated with the verb быть 'to be', and participles, as we have seen, express gender, like adjectives. Apart from this anomaly, the Russian finite verb represents the intersection of the categories of number, person, tense, mood, voice, and aspect, and, as such, resembles its French and English counterparts, even in the last particular, though, as a formal device, aspect is a characteristic feature of the Slavonic verb. Formally the Russian system of conjugation is not quite so simple as the broad practical division into two types according to the 3rd person endings, singular and plural, of the present tense, viz. into a -je-/-ju- type (1st conjugation) and an -i-/-ja- type (2nd conjugation), may suggest (cf. читáет—читáют 'reads—read' with хóдит—хóдят 'walks—walk'). There are various degrees of miscegenation (e.g. хóчет—хотя́т 'wants—want'), and much scope is offered to the interplay of various apophonies (e.g. ч/т in the foregoing pair; also ж/д in брожу́/брóдишь 'I roam/he roams').

The flexional processes are operated by the affixation of one or more morphemes to the basic morpheme ('root') of a word. Morphemes, as Trubetzkoy conceives them, are unanalysable morphological, or formal, elements, which comprise prefix, root (base), suffix, ending, composition, and the word-morpheme. This represents analysis carried to its logical limits: if the variable complex of morphemes is to be contrasted as a unit with an 'amorphematic' word-unit, then that unit, which corresponds either to the root or to the whole of the complex word, must in the nature of things also be a morpheme. For practical purposes we may exclude invariable words, which in any case lie outside paradigms, and consider the traditional root and affix, the latter including prefix, suffix, and ending, as the formal elements of flexion. The root, however, may be subject to apophony, both vocalic and consonantal (e.g. a/e in ся́ду 'I sit down', сесть 'to sit down'; ш/с in ношу́ 'I carry', но́сишь 'thou carriest'), and this adds substantially to the complexity of plain morphematic interchange in declension and conjugation (e.g. nom. sing. ла́мпа 'lamp', gen. ла́мпы, dat. ла́мпе, acc. ла́мпу, or 1st–3rd pers. sing. pres. tense игра́ю-игра́ешь-игра́ет 'I–you–he play(s)').

The grammatical system of flexion is, as we have seen, contrasted with the lexical system of derivation. Here again the broad line of division into nominal and verbal parts of speech becomes apparent. The nominal base gives rise by affixation, or accretion, to diminutive, abstract, agentive, feminine, singulative, adverbial, and comparative forms; the verbal base to perfective and imperfective forms with the aid of prefixes and suffixes respectively, as well as to semelfactives (e.g. пры́гнуть 'to jump'), iteratives (e.g. подпры́гивать 'to keep jumping up'), and the determinate-indeterminate, or particular-general, antithesis (e.g. лете́ть 'to fly', лета́ть 'to be capable of flying'). Unlike flexion, which relies exclusively on suffixation for its formal discriminations, derivation makes considerable use of the prefix.

3

The nucleus of the nominal class is the noun (substantive), which is essentially appellative and names, or 'stands for', either concrete objects or 'objectified' ideas (e.g. челове́к 'human being', кни́га 'book', сла́ва 'glory'). In Russian it presents these in association with the grammatical categories of gender, number, and case, all of which may, indeed, occur in the forms of its antithesis, the verb, and yet, apart from number, are not essentially verbal categories. Several criteria may be applied to the classification of nouns, and in each case we discover an opposition of two complementary types. Thus common nouns (appellatives) are contrasted with proper names, concrete nouns with abstract, singulative with collective, 'normal' with diminutive, hypocoristic (meliorative) with pejorative, positive with negative. In all these and other similar pairs, formal indices may suffice to designate the noun type, but generally its meaning and form require to be considered together in deciding on its class.

The formal element of the noun is very much in evidence in Russian and assumes the appearance of the complicated system of significant morphematic relations known as declension, in which case is closely associated with the expression of gender and number. One form, for instance the accusative singular человéка, may blend all these categories in a single affix, viz. the ending -a. It is customary to consider gender first, then number and case.

Gender, described by I. P. Lyskov[1] as 'the most typical morphological index' of Russian nouns, is an 'obligatory' nominal category, even where a noun is devoid of the other two (e.g. пальтó 'overcoat'). The three genders—masculine, feminine, and neuter—are variously related in form and express not only differences of sex, but the category of animation, conceived as an antithesis of animate and inanimate. The various correlations observable in the Russian generic system are expressed by appropriate oppositions of the three genders. Sex is expressed by the semantic correlation masculine/feminine, which does not fully coincide with the existing formal criteria: thus the typically feminine ending -a/-я may be found in nouns which are masculine in meaning (e.g. воевóда 'voyvode'; дядя 'uncle'). Animate gender is a predominantly masculine category and emerges clearest in the gen.-acc. sing. form (e.g. слонá 'elephant('s)', коня 'horse('s)'), which is unknown either to the feminine singular or to the neuter in both numbers. Historical records and the testimony of other Slavonic languages, for instance Polish, suggest that the semantic basis of animate gender was the expression of person in a patriarchal, i.e. a predominantly masculine, society. It is significant that when adjectives become animate nouns they assume masculine form (e.g. рабóчий 'workman'; лóвчий 'huntsman').

The expression of sex-gender, though not of animate gender, is formally confined to the singular of nouns. The plural has a special animate accusative of genitive form, like the masculine

---

[1] *О частях речи* (Москва, 1920).

singular, and this does duty for animate nouns of both genders. Accordingly masculine and feminine constitute one formal category in the plural as opposed to the neuter, though this antithesis appears only in the nominative and accusative cases. As an antithesis it is characteristic of the Russian treatment of the neuter gender, which, in the written language at least, is effectively isolated from the other two. The neuter is, as it were, the abstract expression of the world of objects. It contains little trace of personality, which may be seen *inter alia* in the formal identity of the neuter and masculine paradigms outside the nominative and accusative, as well as in the 'neutralisation' of substantivised parts of speech (e.g. гро́мкое ура́ 'a loud hurrah'). The neuter also comprises invariable loan-words (e.g. бюро́ 'office', клише́ 'cliché', пари́ 'bet'). In the opinion of S. P. Obnorskij[1] it is the least vigorous of the genders, and in South Russian it is being absorbed by the feminine. The extension of the process to the literary language may lead to the creation of a two-gender (bigeneric) system as in Romance, Celtic, the modern Baltic languages, and Hindi.

Number as a category in Russian is one of the links between noun and verb. Its use with nouns shows a conflict of conceptions. Multitude in terms of individual units is expressed by identical masculine and feminine endings in the nom. plur., viz. -ы/-и (masc. plur. столы́/враги́ 'tables/enemies'; fem. plur. ры́бы/кни́ги 'fishes/books'), whereas the collective notion is formulated in the mainly stressed ending -а/-я/ья (e.g. города́ 'towns'; учителя́ 'teachers'; ли́стья 'leaves'). This contrast suggests morphematic variety in the expression of the plural, and indeed there are so many plural endings in Russian that the semantic parallelism of singular and plural is formally somewhat obscured, for besides the typical -ы/-и and -а/-я endings of the masculine-feminine and the neuter respectively, we have masculines in -а/-я (e.g. леса́ 'forests') and neuters in -и (e.g. я́блоки 'apples'; у́ши 'ears'), masculines in -е (e.g. гра́ждане 'citizens') and neuters in -ена (e.g. имена́ 'names'), *singularia tantum* (e.g. нефть 'oil': ко́фе 'coffee') and *pluralia tantum* (e.g.

са́ни 'sledge'; ша́шки 'draughts'). The masculine and neuter nom. plur. ending -ья (e.g. князья́ 'princes') is only an expression of collectivity. There is often no need to go to the plural for this: зверь 'game' and зо́лото 'gold', морко́вь 'carrots', and ба́бьё 'womankind' are all singular in form. Some of these nouns (e.g. зо́лото) are used only in the singular. But the same idea of undifferentiated mass may emerge from a plural form (e.g. the intensive моро́зы 'frost'; пески́ 'sands'). Abstract nouns appear clearest in the singular (e.g. доброта́ 'kindness'). Paired objects (e.g. но́жницы 'scissors') are inevitably plural now, though they used to be dual (e.g. берега́ 'river banks'; пле́чи 'shoulders').

Case, the third formal category of the noun, is, as its Ancient Greek and Latin names (πτῶσις, *casus*) suggest, a metaphor derived from dicing: the differences in the fall (πτῶσις) of the dice were transferred by a natural semantic mutation to the differences in the 'cadence' of the noun and its cognates. We may conceive case then as a system of interchanges or substitutions. It is not merely a form of inflection, but the focus of a great variety of semantic categories, viz. space, time, causation, possession, and so on. The net result of this is that even the extant diversity of case-endings in Russian cannot do formal justice to the diversity of meanings imposed on them. There is a glaring contrast between poverty of form and richness of meaning. The functional limits of nominative, accusative, and dative are fairly clear. Genitive and locative ('prepositional') combine two cases each, the first—the genitive and ablative, the second—the locative and prepositional (Bogorodickij's 'explicative').[1] The meaning of the latter depends rather on the prepositions with which it is invariably used than on its inflections. The other cases too, except the 'neutral' nominative, are associated with prepositions as part of their usage. The 'peripheral' meanings of the cases (e.g. the instrumentals of comparison, time, and manner) are on the borderline of noun and verb.

Examination of the case-endings reveals a considerable number of homophones, whose semantic differentiation is made

[1] See Classified Bibliography, III.

possible by their distribution among the six (3 × 2) units of gender and number. As there are six cases in Russian, this gives a theoretical total of thirty-six, to which we may add the formal distinctions made in certain nouns between the masculine genitive and partitive (e.g. чáя/чáю 'of tea/some tea') and the separation of the locative and prepositional cases in others (e.g. в лесý 'in the woods'; о лéсе 'about the woods'). The three genders emerge most obviously in the nominative singular, where we encounter the following types of endings:

Gender ...	Masculine			Feminine				Neuter			
Type	1	2	3	1	2	3	4	1	2	3	4
Nom. sing. ending	—	-ь	-й	-а	-я	-ия	-ь	-о	-е	-ие	-мя

Here we observe that the consonantal ending, including -й (-*j*), is typical of the masculine noun. But there is also a feminine soft-consonant type, and this makes it difficult for the beginner to decide to which gender a noun ending in a soft consonant belongs (cf. masc. зверь 'beast', день 'day' with fem. дверь 'door', тень 'shadow'). Forms like дя́дя 'uncle', дéдушка 'grandpa' offer no difficulty, for though masculine in meaning and qualifiable by formally masculine attributes, they are grammatically feminine and fit easily into the scheme of the feminine paradigms (e.g. nom. sing. мой дéдушка 'my grandpa', gen. моегó дéдушки). As between feminine and neuter the only apparent homophones are the nouns in -я (e.g. ня́ня 'nurse') and -мя (e.g. плéмя 'tribe'), but the presence of -м- in the neuter ending is decisive, and historical linguistics comes to our aid in keeping the two apart. In the nominative plural there is complete identity between the typical masculine and feminine forms, viz. ы/и, and for the most part these are clearly contrasted with the neuter -а/-я. The oblique cases of the singular, except the accusative, are generally identical for both masculine and neuter. The neuter -ие and -мя types, however, have their idiosyncrasies. In the oblique cases of the plural there is an intergeneric uniformity of endings, except in the genitive and accusative, which help to differentiate the three genders and, as we have seen, point the contrast of animate and inanimate in the masculine and feminine. The differentiation of homophones, which is an essential part of the Russian system of noun declension, may be seen in the choice of the same case-ending -ы/-и for the feminine gen. singular and the masculine as well as the feminine nom. plural. The difference in this instance as between feminine singular and feminine plural is established not only by context, but by stress (thus страны́ 'country' is the gen. singular of страна́, стра́ны its nom.-acc. plural).

4

The adjective is closely associated, in both form and meaning, with the noun to which it refers and on which it depends. It is not autonomous, like the noun, but posits the existence of the noun. Its material basis is quality, and the adjective of quality is perhaps the most characteristic type, though there are other varieties, some of which bring the adjective in touch with the numeral and the pronoun. Morphologically the Russian adjective is remarkable for its compact and transparent paradigms of declension, exhibiting a maximum of case-differentiation and few anomalies. The three genders are kept separate in the singular only, and they have a common form in the plural. Like the noun, the adjective distinguishes animate gender in the masculine singular and in the epicene plural form. There are three types of declension, and they are based on the now familiar apophony of hard and soft stems (e.g. m.-f.-n. nom. sing. но́вый-но́вая-но́вое 'new'; си́ний/си́няя/си́нее 'blue'), whose parallelism is disturbed by the existence of formally mixed types (e.g. высо́кий, высо́кая, высо́кое 'high'; хоро́ший, хоро́шая, хоро́шее 'good'). It may be noted that the mixed types are exclusively 'soft' and therefore regular in the plural (e.g. высо́кие, хоро́шие), and that, as between written and spoken Russian, there is a curious anomaly, which permits adjectives with a stressed stem in ж and ш (e.g. све́жий 'fresh'; вы́сший 'higher; highest') to be soft in appearance (spelling) and hard in acoustic effect (e.g. све́жий, вы́сший are pronounced ˈsʋɛʒɨj, ˈvɨʃʃɨj).

The adjective differs from the noun in distinguishing morphologically between predicative and attributive usage in the nominative and accusative of both numbers (cf. the predicative forms, sing. сух, сухá, сýхо, plur. сýхи 'dry' with the corresponding attributives сухóй, сухáя, сухóе, plur. сухи́е). Comparison between these two sets of forms shows that the attributive is the longer by a syllable, and this is due to historical causes. The long adjective was derived from the short by suffixing the forms of the personal pronoun, with its obsolete monosyllabic nominative and accusative (sing. и, я, е 'he, she, it', plur. и, ѣ, я 'they'), and the oblique case forms, which are peculiar to the long, represent to-day the fusion of a nominal and a pronominal declension. The antithesis of long and short is incomplete: there are some adjectives which have no long form (e.g. masc. nom. sing. рад 'glad'), others which have no short form (e.g. masc. nom. sing. большóй 'big'). On the whole the long adjective predominates, having invaded the arena of predicative usage (e.g. он си́льный 'he is strong' is synonymous with он силён) and restored something of its adjectival quality to the short adjective, which has been in serious danger of interpretation as part of the verbal system (Šachmatov's 'conjugable adjective') or as a member of the recently constituted 'category of state' (*kategorija sostojanija*), which we shall consider under the heading of the adverb.

In contrast to the relative simplicity of its flexion, the adjective, like the noun, has a well-articulated system of derivation, which includes a multitude of hypocoristic and qualitative suffixes. The former may be illustrated by such a form, say, as малю́сенький 'tiny, weeny', which represents an agglomeration of morphemes expressing diminutiveness, all of them attached to the root мал- 'small' and serving merely to intensify its meaning. As for the variety of qualitative suffixes, it will appear from the following by no means complete set of masculine examples: кост-ля́вый 'bony', бод-ли́вый 'butting', зуб-áстый 'toothy', дар-ови́тый 'gifted', замеч-áтельный 'remarkable', вон-ю́чий 'stinking', рв-áный 'tattered', бéг-лый 'fugitive', лóм-кий 'brittle', крит-и́чный 'critical', and маги́ческий 'magical'.

A type of flexion unknown to the noun and distinguishing the adjective from all other parts of speech, except the adverb, is comparison, which in Russian, as in English, may be either flexional or periphrastic ('analytical'): thus masc. nom. sing. краси́вый 'beautiful' has synonymous comparative forms in краси́вее and бо́лее краси́вый 'more beautiful'. Of the three degrees, the comparative is focal, for the superlative is often merely a development of the comparative, and the semantic existence of the positive as such is determined 'retrospectively' by that of the comparative form. The comparative is peculiar in using mostly the invariable flexional form predicatively and the declinable periphrastic form attributively. It is also rich in unproductive irregular forms (e.g. высо́кий/вы́ше 'high/higher'; у́зкий/у́же 'narrow/narrower'; гро́мкий/гро́мче 'loud/louder'). These, as will be seen, are pure comparatives, disclosing formal complexities beyond the parallelism of apophony (e.g. высо́кий/вы́ше has the consonantal alternation с/ш, but -ок- in the first is a formative suffix) and the curtailment of the normal ending -ee to -ей in rapid and colloquial utterance. 'Suppletive', or complementary, pairs occur as in English (e.g. хоро́ший/лу́чше 'good/better'). Other irregularities are such inflected attributive types as вы́сший 'greater', лу́чший 'better', and ста́рший 'older', which have a complete paradigm of declension. These comparatives may sometimes have simultaneous superlative force (e.g. лу́чший сорт 'the best kind'), and it is this type in -ший which has given us the largely bookish forms велича́йший 'greatest', нове́йший 'newest, latest', and others. Among superlatives in -а́йший/-е́йший superlative force is occasionally lacking, but the forms have an affective colouring (e.g. э́то миле́йший челове́к 'he is a very lovable man'). Indeed, affective colouring is a prominent characteristic of these suffixes. Unmistakably superlative meaning, free from the ambiguities of the foregoing forms, may be obtained by using periphrastic devices (e.g. са́мый большо́й 'the very biggest') or, on occasion, prefixes (e.g. the bookish наи- as in наилу́чший 'best'). The latter are normally devices of affective expression (e.g. предобре́йший 'most kind').

The mechanism of comparison involves the use of either particles (e.g. чем 'than') or the genitive case of the second term (e.g. он вы́ше меня́ ро́стом 'he is taller than I'), which, in usage, is ablative. The genitive case appears only in connection with the invariable form of the comparative. The periphrastic, with its qualified positive nucleus, requires the use of the conjunction (e.g. бо́лее (ме́нее) уда́чный чем 'more (less) successful/effective than').

5

The third nominal category, the numeral, has its own distinctive features, but at the same time it is formally allied to both noun and adjective. It is semantically the abstract expression of number, divested, as the result of generations of mathematical thinking, of every vestige of concreteness. Unlike noun and adjective, the Russian numeral, except in its lowest (1–2) and highest units (from 1000 on), does not express the category of gender. The unique series оди́н/одна́/одно́ 'one' certainly illustrates all three genders in the singular, each with a full paradigm of declension, but has a common plural form (одни́), and два/две 'two' differentiate gender in the nominative and accusative, with the masculine два doing duty for the neuter as well, but again the mainly plural-type oblique cases (e.g. gen.-loc. двух, dat. двум) are generically invariable, and moreover number is not distinguished. In contrast to два/две, the forms о́ба/о́бе 'both' maintain the difference of gender in the oblique cases (e.g. gen. masc. обо́их, fem. обе́их). Masculine полтора́ 'one and a half' and feminine полторы́ are the only other numerals with gender, but, as in два/две, this is confined to the nominative, the invariable oblique полу́тора being common to both. Три 'three' and четы́ре 'four' are declined like два/две, and all three numerals 'govern' the genitive singular, i.e. they were once adjectival and qualified dual nouns (e.g. два, три, четы́ре челове́ка 'two, three, four persons'). Пять 'five' is a noun in form and government, and is accordingly followed by its noun in the genitive plural (e.g. пять челове́к 'five persons'). The higher units and all the other cardinals govern the same case. Unless they are substantivised, the cardinals, except those from миллио́н upwards, which are nouns, are incapable of being qualified by an attribute: one cannot, for instance, say кру́глый (or кру́глая) пять 'a round five', but кру́глая пятёрка 'a round pentad' is possible. All the cardinals, apart from со́рок 'forty', девяно́сто 'ninety', and сто 'hundred', which have only two cases each, viz. a nominative and an oblique, present a paradigm of six cases, though there are a great many homophones (e.g. пять has only two oblique case-forms, пяти́ and пятью́, which are spread over the six cases, the latter representing the instrumental, and the former all the rest). The cardinals from пятьдеся́т 'fifty' to во́семьдесят 'eighty' and those compounded with сто (e.g. две́сти 'two hundred', три́ста 'three hundred', пятьсо́т 'five hundred') inflect both members of the complex (e.g. gen. двухсо́т, трёхсо́т, пятисо́т). Compared with noun and adjective, the numeral then has a deformed system of declension, which displays a curious duality syntactically: the nominative-accusative case-forms function as nouns and govern; the oblique case-forms qualify and agree like adjectives (cf. три неде́ли 'three weeks' with о́коло трёх неде́ль 'about three weeks'). The latter peculiarity leads to such complexities as тремя́ ста́ми шага́ми да́льше 'three hundred paces further on', which are felt as a burden in arithmetical calculations.

The system of ordinals is more regular and rigid, and comports itself to the cardinals as the adjective does to the noun. It is the point of contact, formal and semantic, between adjective and numeral, and its paradigm of declension has the clarity of the adjectival paradigm. The ordinal units present diverse types from the standpoint of word-formation (e.g. пе́рвый 'first', второ́й 'second', тре́тий 'third', etc.). From девя́тый 'ninth' on, the radical consonant -т- prevails, except in the unique, once 'extranumeral' сороково́й 'fortieth', in ты́сячный 'thousandth', and in миллио́нный 'millionth'.

The collectives are essentially substantivised forms (e.g. дво́е 'couple', тро́е 'trio', че́тверо 'quartet'), govern their nouns (e.g. дво́е су́ток 'forty-eight hours'), and decline like plural adjectives (e.g. gen. двои́х, четверы́х). The designations of indefinite quantity and number (e.g. мно́го 'much', не́сколько 'a few', сто́лько 'so much') take us into the sphere of the pronoun and adjective. Their nominative forms, unless they are adjectival (e.g. мно́гие 'many'), function as nouns, as may be seen in their government of the genitive case (e.g. мно́го наро́ду 'a lot of people', ма́ло вре́мени 'little time'), but their oblique forms are adjectival (e.g. по́сле не́скольких лет 'a few years later'). Nouns of the type у́йма, тьма, бе́здна, про́пасть, and ма́сса, which denote an innumerable multitude, may also be considered here as allied in meaning. We are accordingly led to conclude that the boundaries of the parts of speech are not hard and fast, and that linguistic material is, as it were, in a state of movement, constantly passing out of one word class into another. This movement will become even more obvious when we study the adverb.and its associations.

6

Thinking in terms of a common type of sentence, one finds the noun in its appellative function paramount as the subject and governing the verb. But noun and subject are not co-extensive and synonymous, and the normal sentence can dispense with the noun and substitute the pronoun. This part of speech, however, is not a mere substitute for the noun, as its name (Ancient Greek ἀντωνυμία, Latin *pronomen*) erroneously implies, but, at least in its personal form, a reflection of reality in individual terms. It is connected with both noun and verb and participates in the categories and inflections of both. Primarily it is the abstract expression of the category of person, which is extranominal, but an essential element of the verb and the basis of the system of conjugation. It links up with noun and verb through number. As a nominal type, the pronoun expresses gender, but only in the third person, which is of demonstrative origin (e.g. э́тот, э́та, э́то; э́ти 'this; these'), and its conception of number in the 1st and 2nd persons is peculiar, for the plurals мы 'we' and вы 'you' are not strictly multiples of я 'I' and ты 'thou' respectively, but mean 'I and another' and 'thou and another'. In the 3rd person the idea of plurality is less trammelled by that of person, for the personal polarity is я/ты ('I/thou'), and accordingly the 3rd person plural они 'they' can mean either several or a great many units made up of он, она́, оно́ 'he, she, it'. Of the first two persons, the inclusive plural мы can appear with the second singular or plural defined comitatively, i.e. in terms of the instrumental case (e.g. мы с тобо́й/ва́ми 'we two/we') and constitutes an opposition to the unqualified exclusive мы. The polite capitalised Вы resembles the latter in its exclusiveness.

Personal Pronouns

Singular

	1st	2nd	3rd	
			он (m.)/оно́ (n.)	она́ (f.)
Nom.	я	ты		
Gen.	меня́	тебя́	(н)его́	(н)её
Dat.	мне	тебе́	(н)ему́	(н)ей
Acc.	меня́	тебя́	(н)его́	(н)её
Instr.	мно́ю (мной)	тобо́ю (тобо́й)	(н)им	(н)ей
Loc.	мне	тебе́	(н)ём	(н)ей

Plural

	1st	2nd	3rd
Nom.	мы	вы	они́
Gen.	нас	вас	(н)их
Dat.	нам	вам	(н)им
Acc.	нас	вас	(н)их
Instr.	на́ми	ва́ми	(н)и́ми
Loc.	нас	вас	(н)их

The system of pronominal declension differs in several particulars from that of the noun, but resembles that of the adjective, which it has historically determined. The fundamental types of declension then are nominal and pronominal. The adjective once shared in both these, but in modern Russian it adheres exclusively to the latter. Within the paradigm of the personal pronoun there is a contrast in flexion, as in number, between the first two persons, which have marked formal idiosyncrasies, and the third, which represents the true pronominal type. The oblique cases of the 3rd person pronouns, in all genders and in the plural, exhibit two synonymous forms, one with prothetic -н- after prepositions, and the other, absolute, form without. The essentially personal pronouns of the first two persons have identical forms in the genitive-accusative and the dative-locative singular and in the genitive-accusative-locative plural. In both persons, singular and plural, the instrumental case, as a unique form, is distinguished from the rest and calls to mind that the only masculine *i*-stem noun путь 'way' remains masculine because of its instrumental путём (cf. the fem. кóстью < кость 'bone'). The absence of gender, as characteristic a feature of the personal pronoun proper as it is of the reflexive, which, incidentally, has no nominative case and no plural (e.g. gen.-acc. себя́ 'self'), is also a feature of the interrogative кто? 'who?' and the negative никтó 'none', both of them epicene. Accordingly there is a contrast in gender only as between кто? and что? 'what?' and this turns on the expression of the animate-inanimate antithesis. Here we have the only expression of animate, as distinct from sex, gender in the pronominal class outside its adjectival uses, for we have seen (p. 57) that there is complete formal identity as between the genitive and accusative forms of all the personal pronouns. Where the pronoun lends itself to adjectival function (e.g. the masc. possessive мой 'my' or the masc. demonstrative тот 'that') animate gender emerges in the co-existence of two accusative forms, one identical with the nominative, the other with the genitive (e.g. nom.-acc. наш, gen.-acc. нáшего 'our'). Such pronouns, and they include the indefinites (e.g. masc. sing. весь 'all'), are declined like adjectives.

Unlike nouns, pronouns cannot generally be qualified by adjectives, unless they are substantivised (e.g. своё я 'one's own ego'). The epithet in some instances (as with indefinites) tends to follow the word qualified (e.g. ктó-то такóй 'some such person'). Forms like кóе-ктó 'someone', ктó-либо 'anyone' and the emphatic óн-то 'he' illustrate the susceptibility of the pronoun to combinations with hyphenated particles. The force of these modifying elements varies: it may be emphatic, vaguely selective, (ктó-нибудь), rather more definite (ктó-то), or adversative (онá же). The contrast between definite and indefinite appears in the prefixated forms никтó 'none' and нéкто 'someone'. Particles are also found in association with nouns (e.g. отéц же 'but father') and verbs (e.g. сядьте-ка 'do sit down').

7

The polarity of subject and predicate in the sentence translates itself to the plane of the parts of speech as the polarity of noun/ pronoun and verb, which was known to Ancient Greek grammar and philosophy and is a principle of modern logic. The verb defines action or state chiefly in relation to the subject, and all its equipment of categories and conjugations serves to express that relation. The most abstract expression of the verbal idea takes the form of the infinitive 'mood', and this, in its invariability, indicated by the endings -ть, -чь, -ти (e.g. спать 'to sleep', мочь 'to be able', вести 'to lead'), with or without the reflexive particle -ся/-сь (e.g. мыться 'to wash', нестись 'to speed'), is contrasted with finite verbs and participles, which are conjugable and declinable respectively. The link with the subject is established not only with the aid of number and person, but, on a more abstract plane outside the 'reality' of the sentence, through the hybrid class of the participle, which is adjectival in form and function.

The emphasis on the priority of the verb in the system of the parts of speech ascends, in the history of Russian grammar, to Potebnja, to whom linguistic development was an uninterrupted process of 'verbalisation'. His theory was taken over by D. N. Ovsjaniko-Kulikovskij and A. M. Peškovskij, but challenged by A. A. Šachmatov, who was the first to protest against the 'dithyramb to the verb'.[1] The importance of the verb, however, is undeniable, though its absence is not fatal to the organisation of the sentence, at least at elementary levels, as Russian constructions without the copula in the present tense will show (e.g. это так 'that is so'; кто он? 'who is he?'). In contrast to the noun, the verb is characterised, as a part of speech, by its greater elasticity and the pre-eminence of its structural aspect. The elasticity derives from its more abstract character and the agglutinative quality of its morphemes. This may be seen especially in the system of derivation, which draws largely on nouns and verbalises them by recourse to a variety of suffixes

[1] See Classified Bibliography, III.

(e.g. обéд-ать 'to dine', горе-вáть 'to grieve', пот-éть 'to sweat'). Some of these verbal suffixes have ceased to be productive, and the unproductive types of verbs generally show a formal difference between infinitive and present-tense stems (e.g. лечь 'to lie down'; лягу 'I shall lie down'). The total number of unproductive verbal groups is fairly considerable (cf. the English or German 'strong', or apophonic, verbs), but it is a mere fraction compared to the totality of verb-forms.

Of the verbal categories, person occurs, as we have seen, in the pronoun, but the concept of person is different in each case, for all that its source is the same. Pronominal person is a variety of that substance in the world of phenomena which the noun symbolises; verbal person, on the other hand, conceives substance as the agent or the object of action and presents it as a marked variant of the category of person. It is verbal person which plays the leading part in the organisation of the predicate. In Literary Russian the association of the pronoun with the verb is the rule, but the pure conjugable verb is used in colloquial speech, though necessarily without those affective overtones which its use would disclose in writing. Of the three persons, the third is the least personal and lends itself readily to impersonal constructions (e.g. моросúт 'it is drizzling'; мне не везёт 'I am out of luck'). But both the first and the second person may be used in a wider impersonal sense (e.g. поживём увúдим 'live and learn'; куй желéзо покá горячó 'strike the iron while it is hot'). Nevertheless the antithesis of the first and the second person to the third is plain even in the domain of 'impersonality', for the personal element cannot be completely excluded from them. Within the sphere of the first two persons the first is the more stable and definite, the second the more general and elastic. The relation of person to the verbal notion is expressed by prepositive pronouns as well as by pronominal suffixes. The significance of the former may be seen in the existence of such anomalies as знай я 'if I had known' and а мы и скажú емý 'and we went and told him', where the personal form of the verb, viz. the 2nd person singular, is at variance with the pronominal subject, viz. the 1st singular and the 1st plural respectively.

Number is intimately connected with person, whose presence, as we have learnt, modifies its customary nominal interpretation as a simple plurality. It is less 'material' in the verb than in the noun, but none the less an essential part of both. Gender, on the other hand, though alien as a grammatical category to the Indo-European verb, maintains a tenuous contact with the Russian, whose system it has invaded as the result of historical evolution through the 'verbalised' past participle active. Loss of the auxiliary 'to be', with which this indeclinable participle was originally associated, has made it a full verb in meaning without depriving it of participial gender or concurrently endowing it with the indices of person and making it conjugable (e.g. я, ты, он стоя́л 'I stood, thou stoodest, he stood', она́ стоя́ла 'she stood', мы, вы, они́ стоя́ли 'we, you, they stood').

The formal categories of the verb, apart from the general ones of person, number, and gender, are exclusively verbal, viz. aspect, tense, mood, and voice, none of which is expressed in Russian by any other part of speech, even by the chequered 'category of state' (see pp. 69–70). The triple division of time, familiar from English and French, exists in Russian, but is bound up with the less familiar notion of aspect. Mood appears in the finite verb, and voice in the participles, which fall into active and passive as well as into past and present types.

The dominant category of aspect, which reflects ways of conceiving the verbal process, is characteristically Slavonic and Russian, and the two antithetic aspects, as now understood, were first observed in Czech by V. J. Rosa as early as the seventeenth century. Rosa in his *Grammatica linguae bohemicae* (Prague, 1672) defined the imperfective as the expression of action *in fieri tantum* and the perfective as the formulation of accomplished fact. Russian scholarship has naturally expended much thought on the elucidation of this category, and its study already has a fairly long history. One of the earliest grammarians to systematise aspect seems to have been A. V. Boldyrjov, who in the second decade of the nineteenth century attacked Lomonosov's widely accepted 'European' theory of tense and confronted it with a Russian theory of aspect. The number of aspects has

varied since then from two to four. At one period (1839) a
diversion was introduced by G. Pavskij,[1] who constructed his
three 'degrees' of verbal action—semelfactive, imperfective, and
iterative—on the model of the degrees of comparison. At the
present time a broad twofold division is generally accepted, but
subdivisions are admitted in each case. The imperfective aspect
has three variants—durative (e.g. говори́ть 'to speak'), iterative
(e.g. пры́гать 'to keep jumping'), and frequentative (e.g.
ви́дывать 'to see often'). The first of these may be illustrated by a
continuous straight line, the last two by a broken one. In contrast
to the imperfective, the perfective limits action. It too can express three varieties of this, viz. completed action (e.g. написа́ть
'to finish writing'), the starting point of an action (e.g. запе́ть
'to start singing'), and momentary action (e.g. пры́гнуть 'to
jump'). These are known respectively as resultative (finitive),
inchoative (ingressive), and semelfactive (punctual), and may
be represented by the figures ⊣, ⊢, and I . Certain verbs
of motion may have two kinds of imperfective aspect, one
determinate, actual, or concrete (e.g. плыть 'to swim'), the
other indeterminate, potential, or abstract (e.g. пла́вать 'to be
able to swim').

The intersection of the two aspects occurs not only on the
semantic, but on the formal plane. Verbs of one aspect may be
derived, by using prefix or suffix, from the other. There is no
exclusive affix in either case, but the prefix по- and the suffix -ну-
are frequent as perfective indices (e.g. стро́ить/постро́ить 'to
build'; толка́ть/толкну́ть 'to push'), whereas the suffix -ыв-/
-ив- (as in чит-ыв-ать < чита́ть 'to read') is frequentative. Verbs
of the чи́тывать- type may be derived even from prefixated verbs,
and in this case the radical vowel is changed to intensify the
difference (cf. разбра́сывать with разброса́ть 'to throw about').
Any prefix attached to a verb of imperfective form makes it
perfective and simultaneously colours it with its own meaning,
though a great many prefixes have become almost devoid of
their original meaning in certain contexts (e.g. позва́ть < звать
'to call', сде́лать < де́лать 'to make', написа́ть < писа́ть 'to

[1] *Филологическия наблюдения*, I–II (СПБ, 1842–50).

write'). The use of all these formal elements may be seen in the 'agglutinative' formations adduced by S. Karcevski(j):[1]

Primary verb	толка́ть	(imp.)/толкну́ть (semelf. perf.)
	↓	
1st degree	вы́толкать	(perf.)
	↓	
2nd degree	выта́лкивать	(imp.)
	↓	
3rd degree	повыта́лкивать	(perf.)

But the parallelism of the two aspects, brought out by this 'genealogy', is broken by the existence of verbal forms which are neutral to aspect (e.g. such simple verbs as ра́нить 'to wound', очну́ться 'to wake').

The tripartition of time in grammar is an inheritance from antiquity, and in modern Russian it is found blended with the category of aspect into a complex pattern. The scarcity of tenses in the language is made up for by an abundance of aspective forms, which have considerably increased the subtlety and scope of the temporal category. The past tense (preterite) has the clearest outlines: there are four forms of it—two perfective (i.e. perfective and semelfactive) and two imperfective (i.e. imperfective and frequentative). But all these cannot be constructed from any verb. Such parallel 'suppletive' forms as сиде́ть and сесть and their derivatives offer suitable illustrations (e.g. past tense сиде́л 'was sitting', посиде́л 'sat for a while', сел 'sat down', си́живал 'used to sit'). One invariable imperative-like form of the past tense, found in some verbs (e.g. а он и сиди́ себе́ там 'and he kept on sitting there'), which Šachmatov traces back to the lost Old Russian aorist, is strongly affective and also subject to differences of aspect. The imperfective past tense is durative and descriptive, and gives no jolt or fresh turn to the movement of a narrative, this being the function of the perfective, the aspect which generally emphasises either initiated or completed action.

The contrast of present and future outside the copula, which has a defective present tense (with only есть 'is', and суть 'are'), but a complete set of future forms (e.g. бу́ду 'I shall be', бу́дут

---

[1] See Classified Bibliography, III.

'they will be'), is effected in Russian mainly by aspective oppositions: the imperfective present tense has present, the corresponding perfective has future, meaning (cf. де́лаю 'I do', сде́лаю
'I shall do'). A periphrastic future of the imperfective verb also
exists (e.g. бу́ду де́лать 'I shall do'), but here the emphasis is on
the imperfective process (cf. сейча́с бу́ду одева́ться 'I shall start
dressing at once' with сейча́с оде́нусь 'I shall get dressed at
once'). The present tense, like the obsolete aorist, is 'extratemporal', and so can be used in statements of abstract truths,
in proverbial expressions, in whatever is not a function of time
(e.g. ти́ше е́дешь, да́льше бу́дешь 'the slower you go, the further
you'll get'). A perfective present may occasionally be used in the
same fashion, if the expressed result is habitual (e.g. как ау́кнется,
так и откли́нется 'as you shout, so it will echo').

The relation of the tenses to one another in Russian may be
represented in a very simplified fashion by an adaptation of
G. Guillaume's[1] diagram, using the verbs пить 'to drink' and
вы́пить 'to drink up'. The linear process is indicated by я пил
in the imperfective past tense and вы́пью 'I shall drink' in the
perfective future, the boundary between them being represented

by the perfective past я вы́пил 'I have drunk up', which begins
at the point пью 'I drink'. The notion of бу́ду пить 'I am going
to drink' contrasts with that of пью and implies continuity in the
future. Я пил бы 'I should drink' also lies to the right of the
boundary, being conditional and potential and implying dura-
tion. The parallelism of я бу́ду пить/я вы́пью and the lack of
parallelism between я пил/я вы́пил suggest graphically the
extent to which the category of aspect interferes with that of
time, which, as a consecutive trinity of past, present, and future,
would admit of purely linear representation.

[1] *Temps et verbe* (Paris, 1929).

Mood, as this word suggests, involves the impingement of the speaker's attitude on the verbal idea. In Russian the names of moods (e.g. изъяви́тельное 'indicative', жела́тельное 'optative') are older than the name for 'mood' (наклоне́ние), which translates the Greek ἔγκλισις (Lat. *inclinatio*). Kant's discrimination between the antinomies of modality, viz. possibility/impossibility, existence/non-existence, and inevitability/chance, influenced the recognition of a threefold system of moods in Russian grammar—indicative, imperative, and subjunctive.[1] Potebnja added a conditional-optative, and Šachmatov the unreal, potential, and hypothetical. From the point of view of volition, or willing, there are only two moods—imperative and non-imperative. The latter is intellectual and distinguishes real (indicative) from unreal (hypothetical, conditional, subjunctive). Formally all this manifests itself in the divergent conjugation of imperative and indicative and in the choice of the 'unreal' past tense and the aoristic particle бы for the so-called conditional mood (e.g. на ва́шем ме́сте я э́того не сде́лал бы 'I should not do this if I were you'). The imperative is outside time, emphasises person, and has an agglutinative structure (e.g. пойдём-те-ка 'do let us go'). A detail in the opposition of imperative to indicative is the sharper distinction between the concepts of inclusiveness and exclusiveness in the former (e.g. incl. ся́дем, ся́демте 'let's sit down'; excl. ся́дьте! 'sit down!'). The imperative form can be transposed to conditional (e.g. уйди́ он, я не знал бы что де́лать 'if he went away, I should not know what to do') or to emphatic indicative use (e.g. вы гуля́ете, а я рабо́тай 'you are taking it easy, while I'm working').

Voice (diathesis) is the pre-eminent verbal category as well as the basis of the others. It indicates the trend of the action or process expressed by the verb, and it may define the relation of verb to object. The first gives the antithesis of active and passive, the second that of transitive and intransitive. The coexistence of these antitheses in the sphere of voice has led to conflicting views on its interpretation, and the difficulty of this has been

[1] И. И. Давыдов, *Опыт общесравнительной грамматики русского языка* (СПБ, 1852).

increased by the presence of the reflexive ending -ся/-сь (cf. the gen.-acc. of the reflexive pronoun себя), which communicates to the verb an entire scale of values varying from the purely reflexive (e.g. мы́ться 'to wash') and reciprocal (e.g. целова́ться 'to kiss') to extrareflexive ones modified by shades of 'middle' and 'passive' meaning (e.g. учи́ться 'to learn', возвраща́ться 'to return', роди́ться 'to be born').

Outside the system of the finite verb we have the formally recognisable infinitive, which presents the verbal idea as a noun and yet retains the transitive force of a verb (e.g. писа́ть письмо́ 'to write a letter'), and the participles, whose variety is multiplied by tense and voice. The participles may be illustrated by the following tabulation.

	Masculine			
	Active		Passive	
Infinitive	Present	Past	Present	Past
дела́ть (imp.)	де́лающий	де́лавший	де́лаем(ый)	де́лан(ный)
сде́лать (perf.)	—	сде́лавший	—	сде́лан(ный)

It will be noticed that the imperfective verb has a full set of participial forms and that the perfective has none in the present tense. The 'shorter', or predicative, participles are confined to the passive voice and, unlike the 'long', or attributive, forms, cannot be declined, but they share distinctions of gender with these in the singular (e.g. masc.-fem.-neut. sing. де́лаем/де́лаема/ де́лаемо 'being done'). Complete indeclinability as well as an invariable form distinguish the gerunds, present (e.g. де́лая 'doing') and past (e.g. де́лавши 'having done'), both of which are active and display the verb in transition to the adverb (cf. говоря́ 'speaking' with со́бственно говоря́ 'strictly speaking'). The declinability of the attributive participles puts them in this respect into the category of the adjective, but just as the infinitive differs from the pure noun of action (cf. стро́ить 'to construct' with строе́ние 'construction') in its ability to take an object, so the participle differs from the adjective, and the gerund from the adverb, in this particular (e.g. pres. part. act. де́лающий э́то 'one doing this'; ger. де́лая э́то 'doing this').

Apart from the system of derivation, which reveals the verb in its agglutinative complexity, there is the system of conjugation, which offers a relatively simple scheme. The infinitive stem is contrasted here with the indicative (e.g. брать 'to take', беру́ 'I take'), and classifiers of the verb have laid emphasis either on the one or on the other while using both as criteria. The infinitive group comprises, besides the infinitive mood, the past tense, past participle, and past gerund; the present-tense group—the exclusively finite forms: present tense, imperative, present participle, and present gerund. Another basis of classification is productivity. According to this there are five classes of productive morphemes, illustrated by the infinitive forms игра́ть 'to play', сине́ть 'to show up blue', рисова́ть 'to draw', храни́ть 'to keep', and толкну́ть 'to push'. The unproductive, or vestigial, series is still rather numerous, consisting of about 400 verbs: thus the соса́ть 'to suck' type comprises about 160 of these, the га́снуть 'to go out' (as a light)—60, and isolated types, including athematic (stemless) дать 'to give'—50 odd. A final element in the classification of the verb is stress, whose irregular incidence and mobility are well illustrated by this category. Stress may fall on the stem (e.g. пла́вать 'to swim') or on the stem suffix (e.g. игра́ть 'to play'). Its 'vertical' incidence through the paradigm of conjugation makes it possible to distinguish and contrast a fixed accent (e.g. чита́ть 'to read', чита́ем 'we read') and a mobile one (e.g. ходи́ть 'to walk', хо́дим 'we walk'), which pertains to some 200 verbs. Shift of stress may accompany affixation (e.g. вы́йти 'to go out'; итти́ 'to go'; чи́тывать 'to read at intervals'; чита́ть 'to read'). A similar 'horizontal' mobility is seen in the three ways of stressing the generic past-tense forms, viz. (i) нёс/несла́/несло́/несли́ 'carried', (ii) взял/взяла́/взя́ло/взя́ли 'took', (iii) знал/знала́/зна́ло/зна́ли 'knew'. These show that the exceptionally stressed form, where such exists, is the feminine.

8

The transition from the verb to the adverb is effected in Russian through the gerund, the hybrid word class partaking of both verbal and adverbial elements. The 'extratemporal' character of the gerund in the present tense readily lends itself to adverbial function, but its strongest link remains with the verb (e.g. it can epitomise an adverbial clause), and it cannot be ranged with the adverbs unless it loses this link (e.g. лёжа 'in a recumbent posture'; мо́лча 'in silence'). Russian adverbs are exceptionally numerous and of motley origin and form. Derivation shows a group of them to be particularly close to the adjective, with which these adverbs share the 'short' neuter form (e.g. бли́зко 'near') and the mechanism of comparison (cf. adj. глубо́кий 'deep', глу́бже 'deeper'; adv. глубоко́/глу́бже). Another feature which this adverbial type has in common with the adjective is the facility with which it forms hypocoristic diminutives (e.g. давне́нько 'a rather long time ago').

Contacts between adverb and pronoun may be seen in the threefold types of pronominal adverbs, viz. those of place, time, and manner, which we may arrange as follows:

	Pronominal Adverbs		
	Place	Time	Manner
Interrogative	где? 'where?'	когда́? 'when?'	как? 'how?'
Demonstrative	там 'there'	тогда́ 'then'	так 'so'
Negative	нигде́ 'nowhere'	никогда́ 'never'	ника́к 'in no way'
Indefinite	где́-то 'somewhere'	когда́-то 'once'	ко́е-ка́к 'somehow'

Thus we have the formal parallelism of к-то? 'who?' and ко-гда́, тот 'that' and то-гда́, ни-к-то́ 'no one' and ни-ко-гда́, к-то́-то 'someone' and ко-гда́-то, to name only one set of examples. The connection of the adverb with noun and numeral is often effected through case forms (e.g. instr. ря́дом 'side by side'; loc. вдвоём 'together'), which, when 'petrified' through isolation, drop out of their paradigm and become lexicalised. This process of inflected forms becoming invariable 'words' is all the plainer if the case form is governed by a preposition with which it constitutes a compact grouping, or syntagmatic unit (e.g. вглубь 'into the depths', сзади 'from behind'). In such fusions the links between adverb and preposition become apparent. The remaining part of speech—the conjunction—draws on the adverb for its more abstract uses, notably as an expression of time (когда́), place (где), and manner (как). These uses may be combined under the rubric of 'circumstance', and the adverbs illustrating it, together with the already noticed qualitative and quantitative types (e.g. ма́ло 'little'), make up the main divisions of the adverbial class.

The nearness of adverb to adjective has been remarked, for instance, in the domain of comparison, which is an essential part of orthodox grammar. Another domain, unknown to this, is that of 'state'. This new word class lies between noun and verb and recruits its membership from a wealth of sources, among which the most important are the adverb and the predicative adjective. Here then these 'allied' parts of speech meet again, but this time in synthesis. The 'category of state' (*kategorija sostojanija*) was first named by Ščerba to get over a difficulty of parsing. Others, like Šachmatov, have preferred to consider it as the 'predicative function of the adverb'; others still, like Peškovskij, to analyse it into its chief components, viz. adjective and adverb. The difficulty, which Ščerba solved by creating a new category, resides in the flexional invariability, predicative function, temporal colouring, and varied origins of the nominal predicate with or without the copula. Sentences like она́ здоро́ва 'she is well', он не прочь игра́ть 'he doesn't mind playing', мне хо́лодно 'I'm cold', уже́ пора́ 'it's high time', здесь шу́мно 'it's noisy here', and э́то нельзя́ 'that's not done', indicate in Russian a considerable variety of type, and yet the majority of the constructions are adverbial, and where nominal (e.g. уже́ пора́), can easily be recognised and interpreted as such. In all these cases, except the formalised нельзя́ 'not allowed', which cannot be used outside the limits of the present tense, the copula is posited, or 'understood', and its use becomes obligatory in the past and future tenses (e.g. я был рад 'I was glad', он ско́ро бу́дет здоро́в 'he will soon get well'). The introduction of the copula, which is not really, as Vinogradov thinks, a purely temporal form, but morphologically a finite verb in its own right, solves the difficulty of classification and enables us to detach adverb from adjective and noun. But if unity is sought, the application of the adverbial criterion как? 'how?', which often functions in Russian for our 'what?', will place the predicative nucleus of most of the sentences we have given into the elastic framework of the adverb.

The adverb modifies not merely other adverbs and adjectives, but both nuclei of the subject-predicate antithesis. Modification of the verb by the adverb is a common grammatical feature of languages and is usually regarded as the typically adverbial function (e.g. он усéрдно рабóтает 'he works assiduously'). Nevertheless, such instances as боксёр в тяжёлом вéсе 'a heavy-weight boxer' (lit. 'in heavy weight') show the adverb to be no less closely connected with the noun.

9

The relationship of adverb and particles (preposition and conjunction) has already claimed attention, and movements between the two word classes are aided by the absence of sharp lines of division. Semantically the particles are bereft of material meaning. They are 'formalised' words and serve grammatical and affective purposes, and their incidence in speech and writing is, according to statistical data, of considerably greater frequency than that of words of independent meaning. In Russian the most frequently used particles are the prepositions в 'in', на 'on', c 'with' and the conjunctions и 'and', a 'but'.

For purposes of grammatical analysis we may distinguish between the particles proper and the orthodox categories of the preposition and the conjunction. Particles are often, though not necessarily monosyllabic (cf. и, a, вот Fr. *voici*, да 'yes', and нет 'no' with тáкже 'also', причём 'moreover', and отнюдь не 'not at all'), and they may be orthographically isolated or hyphenated as enclitic morphemes (e.g. -же, -либо, -то). These adverbial functions and connections emerge from such syntactic groupings as почти вдвое больше 'nearly twice as much/many', where the first word can be construed either as an adverb or as an adverbial particle. The main uses of the particles appear to be emphatic (e.g. и вам не совестно! 'you ought to be ashamed of yourself!'), connective (e.g. даже его нет 'even he is absent'), definitive (e.g. именно она это сказала 'it was she who said so'), demonstrative (e.g. вот он 'here he is'), negative (e.g. ни я, ни вы 'neither I nor you'), comprehensive (e.g. кто-либо 'anyone'), and verbal (e.g. сядемте-ка 'do let us sit down'). Such particles as -ли (interrogative), что за! (exclamatory), and де ('reportative') illustrate other, more limited, groupings. Nearly all the groupings contain particles which readily lend themselves to affective speech.

10

In contrast to the frequently affective colouring and grammatical mobility of the particles proper, the preposition presents a 'logical' and stable category of largely monosyllabic and dis-syllabic words which are intimately associated with the case forms of nouns. One of the cases—the locative—is indeed completely dominated by the preposition and known to Russian grammar as the 'prepositional'. The maximum number of cases which a single preposition can govern is three (e.g. с 'with' governs the genitive, accusative, and instrumental), the minimum—one (e.g. к 'to' governs only the dative). This offers a formal criterion of classification. Another criterion is semantic, and according to this we may distinguish, among other types, local (e.g. в 'in'), temporal (e.g. в), causal (e.g. от 'from'), final (e.g. для 'for'), possessive (e.g. у Fr. *chez*), and comitative prepositions (e.g. с with the instr.). The local and temporal types have several common forms (e.g. в, от, на 'on', до 'up to'), as is inevitable in view of the 'relativity' of the notions of space and time and the natural tendency to interpret invisible time through visible space. The use of the possessive у 'near, at' is the Russian way of expressing the idea contained in our verb 'to have' (cf. у меня книга 'I have the book', lit. 'near me book'). And the plethora of case endings, found, for instance, in the Uralian and some North Caucasian languages,[1] is met in Russian by the varied functions of the prepositions in combination with case endings (e.g. comparative наподо́бие челове́ка 'in the likeness of a man'; allative к окну́ 'towards the window'; transgressive за го́ры 'beyond the hills', and distributive по кни́жке 'a book each').

Formally the prepositions fall into simple and complex types, the latter being often analysable into simpler components (e.g. во-кру́г 'around'). The simple prepositions are usually the more abstractly grammatical, and some of them tend to be little more than agglutinative morphemes (e.g. в, на, о 'about'). The spread of the tendency towards abstraction was aided at the end of the eighteenth and in the early nineteenth century by the example of French, which led to the use of prepositional constructions after verbs (e.g. отставáть от 'to fall behind') and to the extension of some of their existing uses (e.g. с усе́рдием 'assiduously'). Contrasted with the simple prepositions, the complex have rather more concrete meanings, especially where they constitute still transparent syntagmas, which have, in some instances, been orthographically unified (e.g. благодаря́ 'thanks to', насчёт 'concerning', вро́де 'like').

The existence of parallel, or variant, forms of some prepositions is due to phonetic rather than to grammatical considerations. Such 'full-vowelled' types as во 'in', со 'with', and обо 'about', for normal в, с, о(б) respectively, occur before words beginning with a consonantal complex (e.g. во всём 'in everything', обо мне́ 'about me'). Similar forms are found in prefix-compounds, in which the historic final ъ of the preposition functioning as a prefix has become о (e.g. войти́ 'to enter' < во + ити́).

The formal identity of most prepositions and prefixes should not mislead us into thinking that the two are synonymous. A number of prenominal and preverbal prefixes (e.g. вы- 'ex-', пере- 'over-', раз/рас Ger. zer-) cannot function as prepositions. Some are mere Church Slavonic doublets of these (cf. Russ. перед- with C.S. пред- 'in front of'); others, for instance воз-/вос- Ger. auf, have parallels in related languages (e.g. Latv. uz 'on').

---

[1] See my book *Languages of the U.S.S.R.* (Cambridge, 1951).

II

The connection between particles and adverbs is probably clearest in the conjunction, which borrows from the latter such words as it can use as connectives. The conjunction exists and functions within the limits of the sentence and is perhaps the word class with the minimum of semantic value. Its formalised character derives from its primary use as a link between words or clauses; its differences of meaning—from the varying relationship of the clauses to one another. The two main functions of this particle from the syntactic point of view are to express co-ordinate and subordinate relationships, and it is as an expression of the latter that the conjunction is most formalised and least independent. Within these major relationships we may discriminate between purely copulative usage (e.g. и 'and'), which is sometimes correlative (e.g. и...и 'both...and'), and various connective refinements such as opposition, disjunction, comparison, condition, concession, cause, purpose, time, and place. These give rise to adversative (e.g. а 'but'), disjunctive (e.g. или 'or'), comparative (e.g. чем 'than'), conditional (e.g. если 'if'), concessive (e.g. хотя 'though'), causal (e.g. так как 'as'), final (e.g. чтобы 'so that'), temporal (e.g. когда 'when'), and local (e.g. где 'where') varieties respectively. The ubiquitous subordinative conjunction что 'that', which is pronominal in form and origin, can be used in colloquial Russian as a relative pronoun. The close relationship between conjunction and relative pronoun is obvious, and some Russian grammarians seem inclined to classify even words like кто 'who' and masculine singular который 'which' as conjunctions.

Like the prepositions, the conjunctions are not uniform morphologically and in the main present two types, simple and complex, which cut across the syntactic subdivisions. The simple are often monosyllables (e.g. и 'and', а 'but'), the complex are either orthographic compounds (e.g. или 'or', всё-таки 'nevertheless') or syntagmas with some of their constituents orthographically isolated (e.g. после того как 'after'). The sources of the conjunctions reveal themselves especially from a study of the complex varieties. The presence of the copulative и and the relative что in these (e.g. итáк 'accordingly', чтóбы 'so that') will show that the monosyllabic conjunctions are capable of fusion with other elements.

The study and organisation of the conjunction, as of the preposition, in Russian is due to French influence, as is also the stylistic exploitation of asyndeton, or unconjunctive linking. The medieval language, imitating Bulgarian and Greek practice, used an abundance of conjunctions and particles. But it was a language divorced from everyday speech. This, then as now, preferred brevity and encouraged the use of elliptical constructions, to which asyndeton belongs.

12

According to Vinogradov there are numbers of hybrid words in Russian which do not present clear features to semantic analysis. Such words as итáк 'accordingly', бýдто 'as if', прáвда 'true' seem to hesitate between the classes of the conjunction and the 'modal word'. The latter is a relatively recent concept of Russian grammar, which since Fortunatov has shown a marked anxiety to bring order into the chaos of the particles. Earlier grammarians, like Vostokov and Greč,[1] as well as later ones, like Bogorodickij, have been content to leave the particles in the domain of the adverb. Potebnja noted their parenthetic as well as their affective character and called them 'interpolations' (*vvodnyje slova*). This term seems adequate, as many such expressions derive from complete parenthetic sentences. The term 'modal', as used in modern Russian grammar, emphasises their affective usage. Whether they require to be accommodated in a special category may be legitimately doubted. They comprise a heterogeneous assortment of words, and all of them represent the introduction of the speaker's mood into the sentence, which they seem to qualify in subjective terms (e.g. мол 'he said', кстáти 'by the way', знáешь 'you know', шут егó знáет 'who knows'). The

---

[1] А. Х. Востоков, *Сокращённая русская грамматика* (СПБ, 1831); Н. И. Греч, *Практическая русская грамматика*[2] (СПБ, 1834).

last example is an interjection as well as a complete sentence and ushers us into the 'extragrammatical' sphere and atmosphere of emotion.

13

The interjection may include 'nonce-sounds', which are emitted *ad hoc* and may be variable and unrepresented in the written language. The interjections proper are formalised and vary in kind from mere cries (e.g. ax! 'ah!', ox! 'oh!') and imitations of sounds (e.g. бац 'bump') to elliptical or complete sentences (e.g. у́жас! 'horror!', вон! 'get out!', вот тебе́ на! 'well I never!'). Such expressions are generally regarded as lying outside the bounds of grammar, yet they belong to language, at least in its 'living' spoken form, and as they draw for the most part on the other word classes, they cannot be entirely ignored. The relationship of the interjection to the verb, for instance, is plainly seen in the use of verbal interjections like стук 'knock', хлоп 'clap', бух 'bang' as substitutes for the verb to describe sudden and violent action (e.g. она́ хлоп на дива́н 'she flopped down on to the settee'). Here the difference between the 'non-grammatical' interjection and the 'grammatical' verb is contained in the observation that the former is incapable of assuming the characteristic formal indices of the latter. All the verbal interjections we have mentioned as well as several others (e.g. ax! ox!) can be easily converted into semelfactive verbs by means of the suffix -ну- (e.g. сту́кнуть 'to knock', а́хнуть 'to exclaim'). Moreover, like the genuine parts of speech, the interjection is productive and constantly enlarges its domain at the expense of the others.

CHAPTER IV

SENTENCES

I

We have already found that the fashion among grammarians to-day, especially in the U.S.S.R., sets in the direction of giving precedence to the sentence as the historically older formation and as the unit of meaning with which we are first confronted in learning to know a hitherto unwritten language. There is no need for us to accept the very dubious thesis of 'stadiality', first enunciated by N. J. Marr and elaborated by his pupil I. I. Meščaninov,[1] according to whom sentence-structures can be classified as earlier and later, in order to realise the capital importance of the sentence and syntax to language.

In the Russian system, as in others of the Indo-European pattern, the sentence in the speaker's utterance, when analysed by the speaker and re-created by the listener, divides into two interconnected segments, subject and predicate, and the first, when nominal, is defined by the nominative case. This type of sentence-structure is accordingly qualified as 'nominative', in contrast to ergative, possessive, and other types found in a variety of languages (e.g. Caucasian, Uralian, and Palaeoasiatic), with which, however, we are not directly concerned here. Any part of speech may serve as the nucleus of the subject, even those which, like adverbs and particles, remain invariable in form, but normally the subject is either a noun or a pronoun. The nucleus of the predicate may appear, in the same way, as one of several parts of speech, including the noun, pronoun, adverb, and even interjection (e.g. Татьяна—ах! 'Tat'jana exclaimed'),

---

[1] See my papers 'The Japhetic Theory' (*The Slavonic and East European Review*, xxvii, 68; London, 1948), and 'The Soviet Contribution to Linguistic Thought' (*Archivum Linguisticum*, ii, 1–2; Glasgow, 1950). Soviet linguistics now rejects stadiality.

but the normal nucleus is a verb. A common type of sentence is illustrated by со́лнце гре́ет 'the sun warms', дождь идёт 'the rain is falling', and соба́ка ла́ет 'the dog barks', in which subject and predicate are reduced to bare essentials. Both sides of the sentence may be expanded, the first by attributes (epithets), of which the simplest and commonest are adjectival (e.g. ле́тнее со́лнце 'the summer sun'), the second by an object, which is nominal or pronominal (e.g. со́лнце гре́ет зе́млю/её 'the sun warms the earth/it'), or by adverbial modifications (e.g. со́лнце си́льно гре́ет 'the sun warms greatly'). Starting from these simple extensions of the nuclei of the sentence we ultimately reach the expanded complex sentence, in which the attribute appears as an entire adjectival clause and the predicate as a concrete of verb-nucleus, object-clause, and adverbial clauses. Such involute sentence-types are not infrequent phenomena in Russian prose, whether intellectual or imaginative, which in this respect differs sharply from the much simpler structures of every-day Russian speech, especially where these are not subject to literary norms. Among the simpler structures we find not only plain two-part sentences like она́ вчера́ прие́хала 'she arrived yesterday' or ле́то бы́ло замеча́тельное 'the summer was re-markable', but such minimum one-part sentences as пожа́р! 'fire!' or хо́лодно 'it is cold', described by Russian scholars as 'appellative' (*nazyvnyje*). These may be analysed, referring to the subject-predicate antithesis, as elliptical, with the 'missing' part 'understood', though sometimes it is difficult to know what exactly the omission is. It seems better not to attempt to bring them under a wider structure, but to accept them as laconic 'nominative' labels alongside the logically acceptable syntactic antitheses. Such labels very often result from that affective frame of mind which creates interjections, the articulate forms of emotional emphasis. Just as interjections, like vocatives, inter-polations (Fr. *incises*), and particles like да 'yes' and нет 'no' do not form an integral part of the 'logic' of sentences, so the appellative type of sentence, which incidentally occurs in writing as well as in speech (e.g. По́езд сейча́с тро́нется. Después Після́дние рукопожа́тия. Поцелу́и. Приве́тствия. 'The train is just going

77

to start. The last handshakes. Kisses. Farewells', where the asyndetic, 'pointed' succession of detached words has an emotionally heightening effect), lies strictly outside the scope of grammatical analysis.

We shall confine ourselves from now on in this chapter to a study of the prevailing sentence-patterns in Russian.[1] These may be investigated and classified in terms of either form or meaning, i.e. they may be approached from the outside or the inside. Approach from the outside does not imply the absence of the semantic criterion, for a knowledge of the meaning of a sentence must inevitably precede its formal analysis. This distinguishes sentences of both simple and complex type, the latter sorted into varying degrees of intricacy. Here we come also on the fundamental dichotomy of co-ordination (parataxis) and subordination (hypotaxis). The latter is involved in the more intricate sentences, but co-ordination, whether it multiplies the subject or is extended to secondary elements like complements or adverbials, is very likely to be present. The unmistakably complex sentence requires a great deal of deliberate thinking out, and the formal device of punctuation is always at hand to assist in its analysis and to mark the significant pauses. These pauses are taken up, where such a sentence becomes speech, by intonation, which uses pitch movements at various levels to bind, contrast, and separate.

Applying the semantic criterion rather than the formal one to the study of the sentence, we may distinguish relatively dispassionate declarative sentences (statements) from such as express volition and various shades of emotion—surprise, annoyance, perplexity—and we may discriminate between the logical pairs affirmative/negative, affirmative/interrogative, and actual/hypothetical in the first category. This gives us indicative, imperative, and exclamatory sentence-types, the last of which is a 'logical' development of the interjection. We shall consider the indicative and its numerous variants on the one hand and the imperative on the other. The first presents the content of thought in all its subtlety, the second—the will in its direct simplicity.

[1] For illustrations of these see Pt III (Specimens) *passim*.

Thought has created for its expression the involved system of the finite verb, with its emphasis on aspect, tense, mood, and voice, as well as the auxiliary, participial, and gerundial constructions, which serve to extend and define. Further complexity is introduced by the various classes of conjunctions, and the conditional particle бы, and the devices of interrogation and negation complete the ramifications of verbal usage on the intellectual plane. On the volitional plane we find the compact system of the imperative, in which formal devices actively bring out the second person, while the first and third remain undifferentiated unless they are linked to the second (e.g. пойдёмте 'let us go').

The close association of formal and semantic elements will have become obvious from the foregoing, and we are now able to use both simultaneously as criteria to investigate the two terms of the sentence equation—subject and predicate. The subject, whether simple or expanded, takes logical, though not necessarily syntactic, precedence of the predicate, for it may on occasion be inverted and follow the latter. This occurs in narrative (e.g. настáло ýтро 'day broke'). Normal order, however, gives priority to the subject in the sentence. Within the expanded subject, or subject-complex, which is dominated by the noun, we find concord of noun and adjectival or participial attribute, involving agreement in both gender and number (e.g. тёплый сóлнечный день ' a warm, sunny day ', снéжная вершúна 'a snowy summit'). Participial concord (e.g. бýря, свирéпствовавшая всю недéлю 'the storm that raged all the week') implies a formal ellipse, for the participle, agreeing with its antecedent, summarises a subordinate clause and does away with the relative pronoun. Where the participle functions as an attributive adjective it assumes the adjectival position before the qualified noun (e.g. горящее здáние 'a burning building'). Attributive pronouns (pronominal adjectives) do the same, and this applies equally to the genitive case of possessives (e.g. егó 'his', её 'her', их 'their') and to the formally adjectival types (e.g. masc. мой 'my', ваш 'your', свой Lat. *suus*). But the genitive case of a qualifying noun always follows the nominative of the qualified. The scheme of the subject-complex may appear as follows:

Prepositive attribute	Noun	Postpositive attribute
си́льный ('strong')	ве́тер ('wind')	—
его́ ('his')	сестра́ ('sister')	—
кру́пные ('large')	ка́пли ('drops')	дождя́ ('of rain')
—	да́ча ('a villa')	находя́щаяся по сосе́дству ('situated in the vicinity')

The predicate, which is the principal segment of the sentence, may be either nominal or verbal. The nominal predicate is associated with the copula, and this appears mostly outside the present tense, which is neutral to time (cf. э́то был челове́к высо́кого ро́ста 'he was a tall man' with э́то челове́к высо́кого ро́ста 'he is a tall man'). Here we perceive the reason for the decay of the present-tense conjugation of быть 'to be' and the use of есть 'is' with plural subjects (e.g. у меня́ де́ньги есть 'I have money'). Another development is the extension of verbal ellipse in the nominal predicate (e.g. я к вам с про́сьбой 'I have come to ask you a favour', lit. 'I to you with a request'). The nominal predicate is particularly common in proverbs, i.e. in set expressions (e.g. бе́дность не поро́к 'poverty is not vice'). In contrast to the nominal predicate, whether full or elliptical, the verbal is more flexible and more frequently used. It groups verbs by either co-ordination or subordination. The first grouping may be unconjunctive, or asyndetic, even if there are several verbs in the co-ordinate chain, especially when they are concomitant or sequent in meaning (e.g. он сиди́т, перели́стывает кни́гу, зева́ет 'he is sitting, turning over the pages of a book, yawning'; лес ру́бят—ще́пки летя́т 'timber is being cut, splinters are flying'). Linking by conjunctions, however, is the rule in subordinative (hypotactic) constructions (e.g. она́ заяви́ла, что не придёт 'she declared that she was not coming').

Before examining the formal categories of the verb as they figure in the predicate, let us first consider its dependence on the subject, which normally announces and governs the verb, and endows it with its transferable qualities. This will involve study of the concord of subject and verb, which we have in English and which, in view of the more conservative structure of Russian, is even more salient in that language. All the nominal categories, except case, and the pronominal category of person find expression in the verb and generally agree on either side of the bipartite sentence. Thus a multiple subject will require a plural verb, the gender of the subject will be reflected in the past tense forms (e.g. она провела у нас лето 'she spent the summer with us'), and the person of the subject will reappear in the present tense forms (e.g. как вы поживаете? 'how are you?'). Number, however, is not always shared, for when there are several subjects following a verb, this may agree only with the first (e.g. вокруг был лес, поле, луга 'round about there was a wood, a field, and meadows'), and the dichotomy of multitude and mass may give rise to such hesitations as в дом вошло (or вошли) шесть солдат 'six soldiers entered the house', where the verb may agree either with the numeral, conceived as singular, or with the governed plural noun.

The association of verb and subject in the sentence involves also the consideration of the personal-impersonal antithesis. Sentences like я думаю 'I think' and the very much rarer мне думается 'it seems to me' (lit. 'methinks') present a contrast of emphasis. The first shows the subject dominant and in control of the verb, to which it has given its personal characteristics; the second shows the verbal notion dominant, with the 'logical' subject reduced to case dependence (here in the dative). This antithesis, however, is imperfect in Russian, where we also find an 'intermediate', semipersonal (logically impersonal) type of sentence. In this the verb appears as formally personal, but the accompanying 'personalising' pronoun is significantly absent (e.g. говорят, что они в отъезде 'they are said to be away', where говорят corresponds to the formally personal French construction *on dit* and the German *man sagt*).

The formal categories of the verb remain an inalienable part of its structure and, unlike those of the subject, are not transferred to the opposite segment (here the subject) in the act of sentence-building. Concord or formal harmony between subject and verb proceeds, as we have seen, from the subject and consists in the transfer of nominal categories to the verb. This then becomes charged with meanings, partly its own and partly those of the subject, and by virtue of such semantic complexity has emerged in Russian, and in Indo-European generally, as the premier and nuclear syntactic unit.[1]

Of the Russian verbal categories, aspect and tense are complementary and not in conflict, for they represent distinct planes of meaning, viz. a view of action, process, or state on the one hand and the triple grammatical division of time on the other. Aspect, we already know, has provided the language with an inflected future tense and to some extent restored the lost contrast of imperfect and aorist (see ch. VI, p. 122). The tenses as a rule express the interrelationship of the three areas of time in such a fashion that past, present, and future tense coincide with past, present, and future time, and yet usage permits the choice of any of the tense forms to express the temporal notion generally attached to the others. Thus the past tense can indicate present (e.g. пошёл! 'off with you!') and future time (e.g. вот сёли мы в самолёт, вот поднялйсь 'we shall take our seats in the plane and rise into the air'), the present tense future (e.g. зáвтра я éду домóй 'I am leaving for home to-morrow') and past time (in vivid narrative), and the future tense past (e.g. в прóшлое лéто, бывáло, встáну рáно, одéнусь, побегý нá реку купáться 'last summer I would get up early, dress, and run down to the river to bathe') and present time (e.g. до посёлка верстú две бýдет 'it is about two versts to the hamlet'). It will be seen, however, that auxiliary words of time appear in some cases (e.g. зáвтра 'to-morrow', бывáло 'usually'). In vivid narrative the time-factor is established unambiguously by preliminary sentences. As for temporal sequence in narrative or in the single complex sentence, it remains entirely free from the mechanical concords ('sequence of tenses') characteristic of French and English.

Similar transpositions (metatheses) to those found in the use of tenses occur in the use of moods, of which Russian formally

---

[1] See И. И. Мещанинов, *Глагол* (Москва-Ленинград, 1949) and my review of this book in *Archivum Linguisticum*, IV, 1 (Glasgow, 1952).

recognises three, viz. indicative, imperative, and conditional (subjunctive), if we overlook the infinitive, which is not strictly a mood. Of the three, the conditional is expressed by combining the past tense of the indicative as the 'unreal' counterpart of the present, with the particle бы, which is historically a form of the verb быть 'to be' and appears in the protasis (*if*-clause) as well as in the apodosis (result clause), for instance éсли бы это нé было так, то я бы вам это сказáл 'if it were not so, I should tell you'. The indicative and imperative have already been shown in formal antithesis: each has a distinct conjugation, which in the case of the indicative is modified by tense, whereas time is not a function of the imperative. Aspect is expressed in both conjugations, and the imperative offers a curious contrast between an affirmative perfective aspect and a negative imperfective (e.g. дáйте мне, не давáйте емý 'give it to me, don't give it to him') which, however, is by no means absolute.

As case is probably the fundamental category of the noun in its syntactic distribution, so voice is probably the fundamental category of the verb, and both these categories have this in common that they determine grammatical relationships. The function of voice has already been stated, and we may now study it in its syntactic bearings. The three types of subject-predicate relationship in terms of voice may be illustrated by the following parallel diagrams:

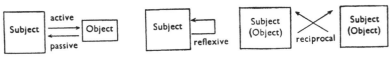

Fig. 7

In the active voice the action proceeds from the subject as agent in the nominative case and may directly affect an object, which in Russian assumes the form of the accusative (e.g. мáльчик нажáл кнóпку 'the boy pressed the button'). In the corresponding passive construction, the object, now nominative, suffers the action proceeding from the subject, which is conceived as the instrument of action and characteristically invests the instrumental case (e.g. кнóпка былá нажáта мáльчиком 'the button was pressed by the boy'). The idea of the passive, like that of the middle, voice also assumes the form of the reflexive verb, and this form may occasionally have reciprocal meaning. The subject of the reflexive verb is its own object (e.g. я одевáюсь 'I dress myself'), that of the reciprocal verb, which is always plural in form,—its opposed subjects. These are each simultaneously subject and object, the subject in each case being the object of the other and vice versa (e.g. онú чáсто встречáлись 'they often met').

As the nucleus of the predicative complex, the verb appears surrounded by two sets of complements, nominal and adverbial. The former include the two objects, indirect and direct. And both types of complement, except the indirect object, may appear either as single words or as entire sentences.

So far we have analysed the affirmative statement in its components, viz. verb, indirect object, direct object, and adverbial complements (e.g. он передáл мне письмó сегóдня ýтром за столóм 'he handed me the letter at table this morning'). The negative statement introduces an odd complication by requiring the direct object to appear in the genitive instead of the accusative case, as in the affirmative (e.g. я там не вúдел картúны 'I did not see a/the picture there'). This difference in case serves to emphasise the negation of the idea contained in the verb. Another peculiarity of Russian is that negatives are cumulative and do not cancel out or neutralise one another as in English. A sentence like онá никогдá никогó не вúдит 'she never sees anyone', lit. 'she never no one does not see' shows the reinforcement of the negative verb with a negative direct object and a negative adverbial complement.

The other antithesis of the affirmative statement is the interrogative, which may also be modified by the negative particle. Here the antithesis emerges clearest in the spoken form of the language, which opposes a rising to a falling intonation (cf. э́то прáвда/˙˙\. 'it is true' with э́то прáвда?/..∕. 'is it true?'). But there may be formal differences too, involving inversion (e.g. бы́ли вы там? or вы там бы́ли? 'were you there?') or the use of an enclitic particle (ли), especially with the negative verb (e.g. не éздили-ли они́ туда́ 'have they not been there?'). This particle was more widely used than it is now, functioning, as it did, in the nineteenth century in all interrogative sentences, except such as already had an interrogative or began with the surprise of ра́зве or неуже́ли 'really'. It is always enclitic and attaches itself to the word emphasised in the interrogation.

The final pattern of sentence syntax is that offered by the order of words. In the subject segment the attribute, or determinant, if adjectival in form or function, is prepositive, unless it constitutes an adjectival clause, in which case the subject-noun is its antecedent. In the predicate segment the verb may precede its objects or follow them, and is equally mobile in relation to its satellite adverbs. Of the two objects, the indirect has priority of place over the direct, and of the adverbs, the temporal precede the spatial, as in German. Here Russian is unlike English, which gives precedence to the more concrete (spatial) extensions of the verbal idea. A common 'logical' order of the constituents of the Russian simple sentence is the familiar sequence of subject-verb-object (e.g. он дал мне э́то 'he gave me this') or the less familiar one of subject-object-verb (e.g. он мне э́то дал), but this may be considerably modified by the needs of emphasis, which gives rise to inversions of it. Subtle relationships of rhythm, characteristic of the more involved types of sentence, introduce further changes into the customary order. Nevertheless, it often appears as one or the other of its two variants in constituent clauses.

CHAPTER V

DIALECTS[1]

I

The literary standard of Russian speech, whose structure we have just reviewed, is the development of a regional dialect that has received the sanction of history. Its historical development will be considered later. At this point we are concerned with its regional associations, which represent a horizontal cleavage of language in general contrast to the vertical cleavage into social dialects. Such a contrast of cleavages, however, does not strictly hold good of Russian to-day, because the regional dialects are primarily those of the collectivised peasantry. The contrast appears to be rather between these regional types of Russian on the one hand and the literary language on the other, and it involves a conflict between 'conservative' and 'progressive' linguistic trends in the remote villages as well as in the dialectally heterogeneous towns. In the latter the literary language tends to predominate because of the influence of school education, but in spite of this it lacks uniformity, for there is always the presence of 'centrifugal' regional elements, and these are complicated by a vertical division into professional dialects and slang, which are most in evidence in the great cities.

Although Literary Russian, like Standard English, has assumed features which do not tie it down to a particular area, its regional basis is unmistakable. It belongs to a narrow central zone, whose contemporary municipal nuclei are Kalinin (Tver'), Moscow, and Penza. North and east of this zone lies the vast and still mainly forested area of North Russian; south and west of it, to the White Russian and Ukrainian borders and to the lower Volga and the foothills of the Caucasus, the much smaller, mainly steppe area of South Russian. The approximate boundaries are indicated on the Durnovo-Sokolov-Ušakov 'tentative'

[1] For a fuller account of these see my paper 'Modern Russian Dialects' (*Transactions of the Philological Society*, 1950; London, 1951).

dialect-map (1915), which was revised and reproduced in miniature by N. N. Durnovo in 1927[1] and, again, by R. I. Avanesov in 1948[2] and P. S. Kusnecov in 1951[2] (see Map, which follows and

RUSSIAN DIALECT AREAS

simplifies Durnovo's). The dialect map indicates the distribution of the three East Slavonic languages in Europe in a form which will be modified only after the publication of the Russian linguistic atlas and the already planned Ukrainian and White Russian atlases. If the example of existing linguistic atlases like the French

[1] *Введение в историю русского языка*, I.
[2] See Classified Bibliography, IV.

and the German can serve as a guide here, it seems unlikely that the revised boundaries of the East Slavonic languages and their subdivisions will show any marked divergence from those which are already known, and we may therefore accept the Durnovo-Sokolov-Ušakov map as a fair cartographic statement of the Russian spoken in Europe. On the other hand the Russian language-area in Siberia and its dialectal pattern have not yet been adequately plotted, and although a great deal of material already exists on the Siberian dialects, a complete 'visual' account of them must await the appearance of the atlas of Russian in Siberia, whose compilation has been seriously mooted. In both European and Asiatic Russia, as we are aware, languages alien to Russian and of diverse typology are in common use.[1] The areas they occupy are also approximately known, and linguistic atlases of some of them are in active preparation. These languages are naturally not indicated on the Durnovo-Sokolov-Ušakov map, though their habitat is suggested in a number of cases by blank or faintly stippled patches. We have to bear their existence in mind to correct the false impression which the dialect map must inevitably leave.

Study of the 'tentative' dialect-map shows that the west and south of the European part of the U.S.S.R. are occupied respectively by White Russian, which has its main centres at Minsk (south-western dialect) and Smolensk (north-eastern dialect), and by Ukrainian, whose territory extends from Cholm and Transcarpathian Užgorod (Užhorod) in the west to Novočerkassk and Stavropol' in the east and includes the towns of L'vov, Kijev, Char'kov, Odessa, Dnepropetrovsk (Jekaterinoslav), and Rostov-on-Don, all of which, except Kijev, speak the South Ukrainian dialect. If we draw a straight line from Pskov in the north-west to Dzaudžikau (Vladikavkaz) in the south-east we shall have an approximate frontier dividing the territory occupied by these two types of East Slavonic from that of Russian, which comprises in general terms the entire north and east of European

---

[1] See my paper 'The Language Pattern of the U.S.S.R.' (*The Slavonic and East European Review*, xxv, 65; London, 1947), and the fuller account in *Languages of the U.S.S.R.* (Cambridge, 1951).

Russia and most of the Slavonic-speaking tracts of Siberia. We have already learnt that European Russia is divided into three unequal areas corresponding to the geographical extension of three dialect-groups, viz. North, Central, and South Russian. The main contrast is between North and South Russian. The territory of the former is made up of the basins of the Arctic rivers (Northern Dvina, Onega, Mezen'), the Volkhov-Neva river-system, and much of the course of the Volga and its northern and eastern affluents; that of South Russian occupies most of the Don Basin and the upper basin of the Oka. This gives Archangel, the environs of Leningrad (but not Leningrad itself), Novgorod, Vologda, Jaroslavl', Kostroma, Vladimir, Gor'kij (Nižnij Novgorod), Kirov (Vjatka), Ul'janovsk (Simbirsk), Ufa, Saratov, Ural'sk, and Čkalov (Orenburg) to North Russian, and Kaluga, Tula, Rjazan', Orjol, Kursk, Tambov, Voronež, Stalingrad (Caricyn), and Dzaudžikau to South Russian. There is, however, a considerable island, or enclave, of pure Southern speech in North Russian territory, east of Kujbyšev (Samara), and the lower course of the Volga from Stalingrad to Astrachan' belongs to both the major varieties of Russian. We are left with a narrow, arc-like zone extending from the valley of the Lovat' in the north-west to that of the Sura and beyond in the south-east. This is the home of the hybrid Central Russian, whose recognition as a distinct dialectal group was determined by the administrative and literary importance of Moscow Russian. In effect Central Russian, spoken also in an enclave north-east of Kostroma, is a transitional dialect between North and South Russian. Other transitional dialects are those between North Russian and the north-eastern variety of White Russian (Pskov-type)[1] and between South Russian and the north-eastern variety of White Russian (Brjansk-type).[2] Curiously enough there is no characteristic transitional dialect between Russian and Ukrainian, although there is one between the northern (Polessian) dialect of Ukrainian and the south-western dialect of White Russian (Černigov-type).

North Russian has by far the largest area and once predominated in Siberia, which was colonised till the mid-

[1] Dotted area on Map.　　　　[2] Hatched area on Map.

eighteenth century by immigrants mainly from North Russian territory. The Russian colonisation of Siberia began at the end of the sixteenth century and had reached the Pacific coast by the middle of the seventeenth. The eastern affluents of the Volga were the starting point, and the riverine area between latitudes 55–60° N. was the principal zone colonised. From the middle of the eighteenth century onwards the southern part of this zone (the so-called 'Moscow tract') was followed by settlers from other parts of Russia, including the Central Russian area, and the building of the Trans-Siberian railway towards the end of the nineteenth century added an impetus to their movement. Since 1917 there has been considerable and heterogeneous immigration into Siberia, and the old dialect 'boundaries' have been largely obliterated. In certain parts, for instance the Central Urals, the Kuznetsk basin, and the Maritime Province, there is much dialectal intermixture, and, according to A. P. Georgijevskij,[1] some dialects are spreading at the expense of others. In the towns Literary Russian, with school aid, is exerting a unifying influence and overlaying the local dialect, which inevitably becomes its 'substratum'. On the whole we may distinguish earlier from later dialects, but, as we have seen, classifications in terms of space and time do not coincide, and we have also to take into account the geographical distribution of the Uralian, Altaic, and Palaeoasiatic language-groups, which patchily cover the entire area of Soviet Asia. The geography of the Russian dialects in Siberia must therefore present a kaleidoscopic disorder, which historical dialectology organises into vaguely outlined areas reproducing the north-south dialectal cleavage of European Russia, but which descriptive dialectology sees only as areas of varying miscegenation.

The North Russian dialect, like its Central and Southern cognates, is by no means uniform. It is normally subdivided into five groups, viz. (i) the Northern, or Maritime, centred in Archangel and spoken in the lower valleys of the Onega, Northern Dvina, and Mezen', (ii) the Olonecian between Lake Onega and the river Onega, (iii) the Western, centred in

[1] *Русские на Дальнем Востоке* (Владивосток, 1926–30).

Novgorod and extending from Estonia to about longitude 35° E., (iv) the Eastern, with its principal foci at Vologda and Kirov, and (v) the Vladimir-Volga group, which is spoken along the upper and middle Volga and from Jaroslavl' and Kostroma in the north-west to Ural'sk and Čkalov in the south-east. Central Russian, even if we do not recognise it as a distinct dialect, but as a mixture of North and South Russian, exhibits a dialectal duality emanating from the nature of its northern 'substratum', viz. a western type, spoken in Kalinin and Moscow, and an eastern, centred in Penza. The eastern sector is by far the larger, beginning as it does close to Moscow and extending in a semicircle southwards to the latitude of Saratov.

South Russian, as opposed to North Russian, has an enclave outside its own territory, which we have already located, and falls into only three distinct types according to the character of the phonetic phenomenon known to Russian scholarship as *jakan'je* (яканье), or *ja*-vowelling. This may be preliminarily defined as the pronunciation of written е/я either as *a* or as *i/e* in the syllable immediately preceding the stress, or the first pretonic, and is broadly classified according to the diverse distribution of these vowels as: (i) dissimilative, (ii) moderate, and (iii) strong. In the first two types of *jakan'je* the influence of the stressed vowels introduces subtleties; in the strong type *a* prevails throughout. Dissimilative *jakan'je* is found in the western subdialect of South Russian, spoken at Kaluga, which has overlaid a Vladimir-Volga type of North Russian to create the western subdialect of Central Russian. Moderate *jakan'je* characterises the southern subdialect of South Russian, spoken in two sectors, viz. (i) at Orjol and Kursk, and (ii) along the lower Don and in the Northern Caucasus. This form of South Russian is also found, mixed with White Russian elements, in the Russian-White Russian transitional zone from Brjansk northwards. The eastern subdialect of South Russian occupies a considerable area, which extends from Rjazan' in the north to Stalingrad in the south, is heard at Tambov and Voronež, claims the enclave in the Vladimir-Volga subdialectal area of North Russian, and shares the lower Volga tract with the same type of North Russian south of Stalingrad.

2

Our account of the three major dialects of Russian must be prefaced by some general observations on the larger phonetic system, of which that of Literary Russian is only a part. It becomes obvious from this that the level of abstraction must be secondary rather than primary, i.e. we shall be dealing here not so much with actual sounds as with phonemes, or semantically generalised sounds, and not with the phonemes of one dialect, but with the parallel phonemes of several (cf. D. Jones's 'diaphones').[1] Avanesov distinguishes five major systems of stressed vowels in Russian, and these are not distributed according to the dialectal subdivisions whose territories have just been delimited. The systems present the usual triangular pattern with an *a*-base, and vary from five to seven phonemes. The 'extreme' vowels— *i, a, u*—occur in all of them. Differences arise in the distribution of the middle terms *ę/e* and *ǫ/o*, i.e. the close and open varieties of *e* and *o*.[2] The seven-phoneme system

is found, for instance, in the Ryazan' province. In this vowel-system close *ę* as in лѣто 'summer' and мѣра 'measure' is contrasted with the more open *e* of крест 'cross', and the close *o* of кот 'tom-cat' with the more open *o* of сон 'sleep; dream'. Here we are not concerned with the influence of adjacent palatalised consonants, which convert *e*, as in день 'day', into a close sound, but with a 'free' differentiation of the middle series of vowels into closer and more open varieties. In opposition to the seven-vowel system we have the five-vowel system

---

[1] *Outline of English Phonetics*[4] (Cambridge-Leipzig, 1934).

[2] The italicised symbols are phonematic, the boldface-type symbols phonetic. Thus *ę* and *e* correspond to e and ɛ, *ǫ* and *o* to o and ɔ.

of the literary language and of other dialects in all the three major dialect areas. Here the close and open varieties of *e* (cf. мел—m̧εl 'chalk' with мель—m̧el 'shallow') constitute one phoneme and are therefore merely positional variants. Intermediate vowel-systems of six phonemes, i.e. with two independent types of *e* and one type of *o*, are widespread in North Russian, in which we also find a five-vowel system, with an *e* tending towards *i* (e.g. лѝто for лѐто 'summer'). The various systems may be summarised, with Avanesov, in tabular form, and the key-words for each stressed vowel may be лѝпа (*i*) 'lime-tree', лѐто (*ẹ*), клен (*e*) 'sycamore', кот (*ọ*) 'tom-cat', год (*o*) 'year', дуб (*u*) 'oak', and рад (*a*) 'glad'.

1	2	3	4	5
i	*i*	*i*	*i*	*i*
ẹ	*ẹ*	*ẹ*		
			e	
e	*e*	*e*		*e*
ọ	*ọ*			
		o	*o*	*o*
o	*o*			
u	*u*	*u*	*u*	*u*
a	*a*	*a*	*a*	*a*

Type 1, which shows these vowels evenly spaced, may be taken as standard. In types 2–5 клен becomes клён, i.e. *e* becomes *o* before a hard consonant. Avanesov adds a sixth type to his table (2 a), which has the vowel-system of type 4, but retains words of the клен-type, e.g. нес 'he carried', берёза 'birch', with original *e*. Such vowel-systems are the outcome of relatively recent analysis and have not yet been applied as criteria to differentiate dialects. The vowel criteria so far used have been the capital ones of *okan'je* (*o*-vowelling) and *akan'je* (*a*-vowelling), to distinguish North from South Russian, and the secondary ones of *jakan'je* and its corollary *ikan'je* (*i*-vowelling), to subdivide the Southern dialect. All these terms refer to the treatment of vowels in unstressed syllables. *Okan'je* means the pronunciation of unstressed written o as an *o*-sound, which normally does not distinguish degrees of openness (e.g. городá—goro'da 'towns'). In contrast to *okan'je* the South Russian (and White Russian) characteristic of *akan'je* involves the use of *a* for written o in the first pretonic syllable. Two kinds of *akan'je* are recognised, viz. non-dissimilative and dissimilative: the former is the more common and occurs in the Central Russian area as well as in the South Russian area, except in its western parts, and the latter is peculiar to White Russian dialects and to the adjoining South Russian types. Non-dissimilative *akan'je* shows *a* in the first pretonic and *shva* (ə) in the other unstressed syllables (e.g. городá—gəra'da 'towns'). Dissimilative *akan'je* embodies the influence of the stressed vowel: pretonic *a* appears only if the stressed syllable contains any vowel other than *a* (cf. nom. sing. cохá—sə'xa 'plough' with coхи́—sa'xi). *Akan'je* and *okan'je* may be shown diagrammatically as follows:

Akan'je			Okan'je		
Pretonic	Stressed	Post-tonic	Pretonic	Stressed	Post-tonic
a	ǫ/o	ə	o	ǫ/o	o

Miscegenation between the two types has been observed, for instance, in the Moscow province and shows assimilative features: thus nominative na'ga 'leg; foot' is opposed to genitive no'g̣i, dative no'g̣ε, i.e. stressed *a* gives rise exceptionally to *akan'je*.

The phonetic peculiarities which have just been reviewed are conditioned by hard unstressed syllables (e.g. ногá). The presence of a soft consonant naturally affects the quality of the following vowel, and we get the parallel phonetic phenomena of *jokan'je* (*jo*-vowelling), *ikan'je*, and *jakan'je*. *Jokan'je* involves the pronunciation of jo for written ë in the first pretonic syllable before a hard consonant (e.g. я нёсу́ for я несу́ 'I carry') and is characteristic of many North Russian dialect types. *Ikan'je*, a feature of Literary Russian as well as of other Central Russian and of some South Russian types of speech, shows i for written e/я in the first pretonic syllable (e.g. нису́ for несу́). Of the three soft vowellings the most intricate is *jakan'je*. This, as we have seen, characterises South Russian, in which straightforward as well as

Types of Jakan'je[1]

Strong	Moderate	Dissimilative (Archaic)	Assimilative	*Ikan'je*	Stressed syllable
		First Pretonic Syllable			
a	*a*	*a*	*i*	*i*	*i*
a	*i*	*a*	*i*	*i*	
a	*a*	*a*	*i*	*i*	*u*
a	*i*	*a*	*i*	*i*	
a	*a*	*a*	*i*	*i*	*ǫ*
a	*i*	*a*	*i*	*i*	
a	*a*	*i*	*i*	*i*	*o*
a	*i*	*i*	*i*	—	
a	—	*a*	*i*	*i*	*ę*
a	*i*	*a*	*i*	*i*	
—	—	—	—	—	*e* (*'o*)
a	*i*	*i*	*i*	*i*	
a	*a*	*i*	*a*	*i*	*a*
a	*i*	*i*	*a*	*i*	

[1] The upper letter in each square, where there are two, is the vowel before a hard consonant, the lower letter the vowel before a soft one. A prevocalic apostrophe indicates a preceding soft consonant. In all cases the vowel of the first pretonic syllable is preceded by a soft consonant.

subtle varieties of the phenomenon occur. Of the recognised types of *jakan'je*—dissimilative (five varieties), moderate, and strong, the dissimilative and moderate types may be complicated by elements of assimilation, and an assimilative *jakan'je* and a full *ikan'je* add to the chaos of the phonetic picture. A certain order may be introduced into this chaos by resort to diagrammatic notation. If we regard strong *jakan'je* as one extreme and *ikan'je* as the other, we may arrange the remaining types of *jakan'je*, isolated by Avanesov, between these as the intermediate members of a scale (see Table on p. 95).

It will be observed that the pattern of dissimilative *jakan'je* in the foregoing table represents the Archaic variety. There are two subdivisions of this, viz. the Obojan' (south of Kursk) and the Zadonsk (north of Voronež), but the difference between these two types is exceedingly small, consisting as it does in the use of pretonic *e* in the Zadonsk *jakan'je* for the Obojan' *i* (e.g. ļɛˡsok for ļiˡsok 'spinney'). The other four varieties of dissimilative *jakan'je* are known as the Sudža, Don, Ščigry, and Žizdra varieties. The first two of these, like the Archaic variety, belong to the southern (more properly south-western) dialect of South Russian, and the Žizdra variety is characteristically White Russian. The geography of all these varieties of *jakan'je* is rather complicated, and the complication is increased by the presence of *akan'je* near Orjol and of strong *jakan'je*, exceptionally, round Tula. Phonetically the difference between the five varieties of dissimilative *jakan'je* may be illustrated as follows: while the Obojan'-Zadonsk varieties have *i/e* before stressed *o*, *e('o)*, and *a*, i.e. before the more open vowels, the Sudža variety has *i* before stressed *ę*, *e('o)*, and *a*, the Don variety has *i* before all stressed vowels, except close *i* and *u*, the Ščigry variety reverses this and has *a* before all stressed vowels, except *e('o)* and *a*, which are preceded by *i*, and the Žizdra variety has *i* before stressed *a*, and *a* before all other vowels. The scale of dissimilative *jakan'je* between the termini of *ikan'je* and strong *jakan'je* is Don-Archaic-Sudža-Ščigry-Žizdra. The Archaic and Sudža varieties are similar in the number of pretonic *i*-sounds, but they differ in their distribution, the former having *i/e* before *o*, the latter *i* before *e*. Assimilative *jakan'je* (an incomplete *ikan'je*) resembles the Don variety of dissimilative *jakan'je*, except that it has *a* before stressed *a* and *i* before stressed *i* and *u*. Like *ikan'je* and strong *jakan'je*, it has a regularised pattern, though it lacks their absolute quality. A similar regularised pattern occurs in the assimilative-dissimilative *jakan'je* of the Novosel'sk variety, where we find pretonic *a* before all stressed vowels, except *e('o)*, which requires *i*. Assimilative-moderate *jakan'je* shows a curious parallelism of *a* before hard and *i* before soft consonants, unless the stressed syllable contains *a*.

We have so far been concerned with the vowels of the stressed and of the first pretonic syllable. These are the two 'strong' positions in Russian. All other syllables, both pretonic and post-tonic, are 'weak', and the vowels in these syllables vary in quality according to the hardness or softness of adjacent consonants and according to the prevalence of *okan'je* or *akan'je*. Where the former prevails unmodified, the vowel of the spelling is preserved, but when there is either modified *okan'je* or pure *akan'je*, the central vowel ə is normally substituted (e.g. сторона́ 'side': ok. storoˈna; mod. ok. stəroˈna; ak. stəraˈna). The post-tonic vocalism exhibits the same dichotomy into *okan'je* and *akan'je* (e.g. вы́нос 'carrying out': ok. ˈvinos; ak. ˈvinəs), which may now be summarised as the differentiation of pure vowels in unstressed syllables and their 'reduction' to a few unstressed types (a, ə, u) respectively. *Okan'je* is a kind of spelling pronunciation, but this view overlooks its historical side, for it existed before the spelling was devised. *Akan'je* represents a later development in the written language, but it may very well have existed in the spoken 'from the beginning'.

3

The treatment of consonants shows fewer acute deviations between North and South Russian. The most outstanding of them has been referred to in passing, viz. the phonetic interpretation of r. North and Central Russian interpret it as a plosive (cf. English g in 'go'); South Russian interprets it as a fricative, like Modern Greek ɣ, i.e. the voiced counterpart of German or Scotch x (e.g. in Sc. 'loch'). This means that the plosive pair k/g occurs only in North and Central Russian, and the corresponding fricative pair x/ɣ only in South Russian. The paired occlusives (e.g. p/b) have palatalised correlates (e.g. p̡/b̡) as separate phonemes, except k/g, which in some dialects, for instance in the Moscow pronunciation of Literary Russian, combine hard and soft in one phoneme. The nasals, 'liquids', and fricatives, except ʃ/ʒ and j, the palatal consonant *par excellence*, also generally have a parallel soft series (e.g. m̡, l̡, s̡/z̡), and some dialects, notably Moscow Russian, have long hush-sibilants (viz. ʃʃ/ʒʒ in щи—ʃʃi 'cabbage soup', and вóжжи—ˈvoʒʒi 'reins'). The two affricates tʃ and ts are single phonemes, the first soft, the second hard, and it is these which show considerable dialectal variation, known to Russians as *cokan'je* (c-articulation) and *čokan'je* (č-articulation).[1] These phenomena refer to the confusion of *c* (ts) and *č* (tʃ) in one phoneme. Where this takes place the phoneme is normally ts (e.g. molˈtsi for Lit. R.молчú!—molˈtʃi! 'be quiet!'), but it may occasionally be tʃ (e.g. tʃiˈna for Lit. R. ценá—tsəˈna 'price') or an intermediate sound like Polish *ć* (e.g. *spać* 'to sleep'). *Cokan'je* characterises many varieties of North Russian, but is also found sporadically in the other two dialect areas. Other consonants, which can serve as criteria of dialectal differentiation are f, v, long ʃ/ʒ, l, and r. The f-sound is replaced mainly in South Russian, as in White Russian, by xv or x (e.g. xvunt for Lit. R. фунт—funt 'pound' and ˈxabrikə for ˈfabrikə 'factory'). Long ʃ and ʒ appear in the following variants:

$$ш — ʃtʃ — ʃtʃ̬ — ʃʃ — ʃt̬ — ʃʃ$$
$$жж — ʒdʒ — ʒ̬dʒ̬ — ʒʒ — ʒ̬d̬ — ʒʒ$$

These are distributed irregularly among various dialects, and even the same dialect, for instance Moscow Russian, may distinguish two types by using soft ʃʃ for щ and hard ʃʃ for morphematic junctions, i.e. where 'words' join (e.g. сшúла 'she has

---

[1] The rarer *čakan'je* is used by some investigators, for instance Bogorodickij (see Classified Bibliography, III), to avoid confusion with *čokan'je* 'clinking (of glasses)'.

sewn' < с + шйла). In parts of the Vologda and Kirov provinces and in some South Russian dialects the European 'clear' l is used for the normal Russian velar sound, and velar l sometimes becomes w in both North and South Russian (e.g. on p̡i¹ʃow for Lit. R. on p̡i¹ʃol 'he came'). The vibrant r shows local variations, being a 'multivibrant' (*raskatistyj r*), of Scotch type in certain Volga, Siberian, and South Russian dialects in opposition to the more usual 'univibrant' of the literary language.

All the foregoing are isolative phonetic phenomena, i.e. they are not due to the influence of adjacent sounds. Combinative, or assimilative, phenomena include the palatalisation of k after soft consonants (e.g. ¹dotʃk̡ə 'daughter'). This is a South Russian feature, and its western boundary almost coincides with that of South Russian on the one hand and of White Russian and Ukrainian on the other.

4

The morphological peculiarities of Russian dialects are less distinctive than the phonetic. Among them we may list the treatment of the pronominal and adjectival ending -oro/-ero, found in the masculine and neuter genitive singular, which is generally pronounced -ovo/-(j)evo in North Russian, -oɣə/-(j)iɣə in South Russian, though both g and ɣ may be heard in some North Russian subdialects, for instance the Maritime and the Olonecian. Other differentiating factors of more or less extended application are: confusion of case-endings (e.g. dat. and instr. plur. in N.R.), the oblique case-forms of the personal pronouns я 'I' and ты 'thou' (cf. S.R. мене́ with N.R. меня́ 'me'), the infinitive ending -чи, the ending of the 3rd person present indicative, both singular and plural (-т in N.R., -ть in S.R.), peculiarities of stressing, and the use of a postpositive article (in N.R.). Syntactic criteria of dialectal differentiation include the case of the object with the infinitive, which is nominative in some types of North Russian, and the use of participial for finite forms (e.g. вы́пивши for вы́пил 'he drank up'). Lexical differences between North and South Russian are numerous enough and comprise chiefly diverse nouns for the same object or action (cf. N.R. изба́ 'cottage' with S.R. хáта; N.R. орáть 'to plough' with S.R. пахáть).

Such differences occur also inside a single dialectal group. The western and Olonecian types of North Russian share certain words with the transitional Pskov area, the western type of South Russian shows affinities with White Russian and Ukrainian, and the Siberian dialects have developed vocabularies different from those of their North Russian cognates. In the various Russian dialects, taken as a whole, we discover certain peculiarities familiar to the linguist, viz. a wealth of special terms and the occasional absence of the general term which could be their focus and substitute. Thus corresponding to Literary Russian сноп 'sheaf', the dialects present a large number of words denoting varieties of sheaves (e.g. кубáч 'large straw-sheaf', головá 'heavy sheaf topping a stook', гóрстка 'small sheaf'). Synonyms are very common: thus городьбá, зáгородка, огорóд, плетéнь, тын, слéги, and частокóл all mean 'fence'. As agriculture is the basis of peasant economy, the agricultural vocabulary is well developed (e.g. цéлыжень 'virgin soil', зáлежь or вётошь 'fallow', óрка 'ploughland', сукú 'clearing'). Fishing, too, has an extensive and detailed vocabulary as may be seen, for instance, from the number of words designating the bottom of river or lake (e.g. мя́коть 'lake bottom', нальё 'stony bottom', креж 'hole in river bed'). The presence and character of forests over extensive tracts of the Russian-speaking territory is reflected in the multitude of synonyms for лес 'forest' (e.g. бор 'coniferous forest', сузём or лядúна 'dense forest', дубрóва 'deciduous forest', шéлеп 'spinney'). Dairy-farming provides a plethora of petty discriminations (e.g. a name for each year of a horse's early life: сосýн 'foal', стригýн 'yearling', бороноволóк 'two-year-old', борóнка 'three-year-old').

Besides such special vocabularies, there are, in the dialects, numerous historically attested words and expressions which have not survived in Literary Russian. These embrace nearly all parts of speech (e.g. поздóль for вдоль 'along'; кóмонь for конь 'horse'; вобáть for подбирáть 'to peck'; лю́дно for мнóго 'many'; пы́лко for óчень 'very').

5

We are now in a position to name the principal characteristics of the three major Russian dialects. North Russian has various degrees of *okan'je* from complete to partial. The imperfect types are due to miscegenation with South Russian and are found, for instance, in the divergent Vladimir-Volga subdivision. Similar degrees characterise the parallel phenomenon of *jokan'je*, which in its imperfect varieties, alternates with *jekan'je* (*je*-vowelling), as in тенý—t͡sᴵnu 'I drag' (for Lit.R. тянý), in contrast to нёсý—ŋoᴵsu 'I carry' (for Lit.R. несý). Plosive g and the lapse (syncope) of intervocalic j (e.g. игрáт for игрáет 'plays') are the main consonantal features of North Russian. The outstanding morphological characteristics of this dialect are the genitive-accusative forms of the personal and reflexive pronouns in -я (e.g. меня 'me', тебя 'thee', себя 'self'), which recur in Literary Russian, and the preponderance of the hard -*t* ending of the 3rd persons of verbs in the present tense (e.g. он несёт 'he carries', они несýт 'they carry'). All the characteristics we have just specified, both phonetic and morphological, are peculiar to North Russian as a whole, but there are others which, though widespread, are more limited. Chief of these are: stressed *e* for *a* (æ) between palatalised consonants (e.g. зеть for зять 'son-in-law'), *cokan'je*, the existence of the pure *f*-phoneme (e.g. фунт 'pound', торф 'peat'), palatalised *s* (ş) in the nominal suffixes -*sk*- and -*stv*- (e.g. женьськóй for жéнский 'female', балосьвó for баловствó 'indulgence'), assimilations involving the nasals (e.g. дамнó for давнó 'long ago', оммáн for обмáн 'deception', fem. оннá for однá 'one'), fusion of the dative and instrumental plural forms of noun and adjective (e.g. свóим глазáм for свóими глазáми 'with one's own eyes'), an infinitive form in -чи with -*k*/-*g*-stem verbs (e.g. печи́ or пекчи́ 'to bake', мочи́ or могчи́ 'to be able'), mobility of stress in the declension of feminine nouns in -*a* (e.g. nom. рукá 'hand; arm', acc. рýку), and the use of a postpositive article (e.g. дóм-от 'the house', избá-та 'the cottage', сёлó-то 'the village'), which, unlike the parallel Bulgarian article, can be inflected for case (e.g. acc. sing. женý-ту 'the wife') and therefore resembles the declined article of German rather than the invariable article of English.

The territorial grouping of the North Russian subdialects has been described, but their interrelations still remain to be considered. The Vladimir-Volga type differs in a great many ways from the rest, which show a greater family likeness. Among the other types, the most divergent mutually are the Maritime and the eastern. The Olonecian and the western lie somewhere between these, but the western type, in some of its dialectal constituents, shows traces of the influence of Central Russian. The treatment of historical stressed *ě* (ѣ) is a useful criterion in effecting this fivefold classification. Its reflexes vary from *e* (as in Literary Russian) in the Vladimir-Volga subdialect to *ę* in the Olonecian, *i* in the western, and diphthongal *ie* in the eastern. Lexically the Vladimir-Volga subdialect also shows affinities with Central Russian (e.g. the use of лóшадь for конь 'horse'), which, in its turn, shares part of its vocabulary with South Russian.

6

From the historical standpoint, the Central Russian dialect is, as we have seen, a mixture of Northern and Southern, so that we are prepared to discover a compromise between certain antithetic features of both. Thus Central Russian combines the stress-dominated South Russian vowel-system with the North Russian plosive value of r. The *jakan'je* which it has taken over from South Russian is of the moderate type. Many varieties of Central Russian also show palatal plosives (c/ɉ) for palatalised ķ/ǥ (e.g. masc. nom. sing. ˈcisļij 'sour' for Lit. R. кислый). Of the two subdialects of Central Russian, western and eastern (i.e. divisions of Ušakov's Group B),[1] the first, for geographical reasons, is closer to North Russian, the second to South Russian. Thus lapse of intervocalic j prevails in the first, and the second uses fricative ɣ, and has w for v/f (e.g. дéўка for дéвка 'wench'). The last is peculiar to the western subdialect of South Russian as well as to White Russian. The western subdialect of Central Russian also resembles the Pskov type of transitional dialects (Ušakov's

---

[1] See Classified Bibliography, IV.

Group A), which possesses White Russian characteristics (e.g. злый for злой 'evil', дзёци for дёти 'children', дерёўня for дерёвня 'village').

7

The substitution of **w** for **v**/**f** is a phonetic feature with a tendency, in terms of mapping, to horizontal mobility. Its source and focus appear to be in the west, and it has encroached on South Russian territory in its western portions, for its easternmost limits are marked by a sinuous line running from Kaluga, on the Oka, to Bobrov, near the Don, and from there on, along the southern and eastern boundaries of strong *jakan'je*, to Stalingrad. Another horizontally mobile feature, viz. *k′* (ḱ) after palatalised consonants, extends from an easterly centre westwards into the linguistic march between Russian and White Russian, so as to enclose Brjansk and Žizdra. This line forms the frontier between South Russian on the one hand and White Russian and Ukrainian on the other. The northern frontier between South and Central Russian is that of the southernmost extension of plosive **g**. Within these frontiers lies the populous area of South Russian, whose chief characteristics, phonetic and morphological, are *akan'je*, *jakan'je* in several varieties, fricative **ɣ**, genitive-accusative forms of the personal and reflexive pronouns in stressed -*e* (e.g. менё, тебё, себё), and palatalised *t′* (ţ) as the index of the 3rd person, singular and plural, of verbs in the present tense (e.g. он несёть 'he carries', анй несуть 'they carry'). Apart from these universal features, there are others peculiar to restricted areas. Many South Russian dialects have **x(v)** for **f**, a fixed stress in the paradigm of feminine nouns in -*a* (e.g. nom. sing. рукá 'hand', acc. руку́), ḱ after a palatalised consonant, and hard long **ʃ/з** (e.g. ᵗʃʃukə 'pike', ᵛvoззɨ 'reins'). Other localised characteristics are: the relative infrequency of the change of *je* into *jo* before hard consonants (cf. gen.-acc. sing. eё for Lit.R. eё 'her'), the extension of the newer masculine plural ending -*á* to feminines (e.g. nom. plur. степя́ for стёпи 'steppes'), and the confusion of the unstressed endings of the 1st and the 2nd conjugation of verbs (e.g. лю́бют for лю́бят 'they love').

The classification of the various types of South Russian is determined, as we have learnt, by the varieties of *jakan'je*, which fluctuate between the extremes of strong *jakan'je* and *ikan'je*. Another criterion of classification is *akan'je*, and this can be either dissimilative (e.g. nom. vəˈda 'water', gen. vaˈdɨ) or non-dissimilative (e.g. vaˈda/vaˈdɨ). Then there are the reflexes of 'original' *ě*, the quality of final written *v*, viz. f and w, the hardness or softness of final labials (e.g. сем or семь 'seven'), the disintegration of *c* (ц) and *č* (ч), which sometimes become ş and ʃ respectively, and the elimination of the historical apophony *k/č* in conjugation (e.g. пяку́ 'I bake', пекёшь 'thou bakest' for Lit.R. пеку́, печёшь). Of the three recognised varieties of South Russian, the western (Avanesov calls it 'northern'), or Kaluga type, is very chequered and in some respects approaches the Central Russian of the Moscow province. The southern (Kursk-Orjol) and especially the eastern (Rjazan') variety are more uniform and distinct, and could be regarded as more 'typical', the former with its subtleties of dissimilative *jakan'je*, the latter with its forthright strong *jakan'je*.

8

The colonial dialects of Russian are scattered over the immensities of Siberia. Historical record shows that Russian adventurers crossed the rampart of the Urals at the end of the sixteenth century and were on the Pacific littoral less than a century later. It appears that these and the Russians who followed them—soldiers, administrators, and settlers—came from the North Russian dialect-area, and accordingly North Russian is, as it were, the foundation, or 'substratum', of later dialectal developments. These involved the influence of the indigenous vernaculars, Uralian, Palaeoasiatic, and chiefly Altaic, as well as inter-mixture with Central and South Russian dialects and with the allied White Russian and Ukrainian. A. M. Seliščev[1] is inclined to exaggerate the importance of the non-Slavonic element and to discover it not only in the vocabulary, but in the phonematic system of certain forms of Siberian Russian. Inter-Slavonic dialectal miscegenation began when speakers of Central and

[1] See Classified Bibliography, IV.

South Russian as well as White Russians and Ukrainians arrived in Siberia in the eighteenth century, and it has continued with the rising tide of immigration which accompanied the opening of railway communication in the 1890's and especially the exploitation of mineral deposits in Siberia since 1917. To-day the dialects of the 'natives' (*starožily*) may still be distinguished from those of the later colonists, who easily outnumber them. The 'natives' now include the Old Believer communities (*semejskije*), which settled in Siberia in the second half of the eighteenth century, as well as those descendants of the pioneers of the sixteenth and seventeenth centuries who were not absorbed into their non-Russian linguistic environment by perceptible stages. One of these, incidentally,—a precarious bilingualism—is represented by the hero of V. G. Korolenko's story *Makar's Dream* (1885).

We may study, as typically Siberian Russian, the dialects of the oldest layer of the Russian-speaking population and note their mainly North Russian characteristics, among which the most prominent is *okan'je*, either complete or partial. But even the latter and some types of *akan'je* have an *o*-dialect basis. The speech of the Old Believers, on the other hand, is of the *a*-type. It would seem that the majority of 'Siberians' (*sibirjaki*) to-day speak a Russian in which *akan'je* preponderates, so that the *okan'je-akan'je* dichotomy, characteristic of European Russian, no longer applies to Siberian. This is due not merely to the presence of Central and South Russian speakers in very considerable numbers, but to the levelling effects of Literary Russian. A curious feature of the speech of both the *starožily* and the *semejskije* is the diphthongal uo in stressed position (e.g. *sem.* харашуо́ 'good', тюо́тка 'auntie'), which, incidentally, is reflected in Yakut (Altaic) borrowings (e.g. *uzuor* < узор 'design'). Siberians pronounce r as a plosive and the ending -oro/-ero with intervocalic v. Other characteristics of North Russian pronunciation are instances of syllabic contraction (e.g. ду́мат for ду́мает 'thinks'), the presence of *cokan'je*, a liking for f instead of x (e.g. в юрта́ф for в юрта́х 'in cottages'), and assimilation of oral to nasal consonants (e.g. ла́нно for ла́дно 'very well'). In morphology and vocabulary the North Russian element is equally marked: чо? is used for Literary Russian что? 'what?', the declined postpositive article occurs, the 3rd singular and 3rd plural of the present tense end in hard -t, and there is an abundance and variety of North Russian dialect words (e.g. изба́ 'cottage', квашня́ 'kneading trough'). South Russian, for instance in the speech of the Old Believers, is represented by *akan'je* and *jakan'je-ikan'je*, the fricative ɣ, x for ſ, bilabial w for v and velar l, and ķ after palatalised consonants, as well as by such morphological features as хто? for кто? 'who?', the genitive-accusative case singular of the personal and reflexive pronouns with the ending -*e* (e.g. мине́ 'me'), soft -ţ in the 3rd singular and plural forms of the present tense, and words like бу́льба 'potato', гной 'manure', and masculine singular ма́рный 'dark'.

Distinct from both North Russian and South Russian are certain characteristically Siberian developments such as 'glycolalia' (*sladkojazyčije*), which is found chiefly among women and consists in the displacement of the 'liquids' by j (e.g. гойова́ for голова́ 'head', хойошо́ for хорошо́ 'good'). As this phonetic phenomenon occurs in dialects influenced by the Palaeoasiatic languages Yukagir (Odul), Koryak (Nganasan), and Chukcha (Luoravetlan) on the lower Kolyma, investigators like Seliščev and P. Černych[1] regard it as of alien origin. Such an origin can certainly be attributed to part of the great wealth of regional words which make the vocabulary of Siberian Russian almost as distinctive as that of American English. If words like ба́ско 'fine', лони́сь 'last year', ту́нно 'in vain', има́ть 'to catch', and губа́ 'mushroom' are obviously of Russian origin, words like ча́ут 'lariat', куль 'devil', адали́ 'as if', мерге́нь 'hunter', and жары́н 'sorry' are as obviously loans from other languages. Alien influences have also been noted in the 'singing intonation' of Siberian Russian and especially in the sharp, emphatic rising tone used in Western Siberia to express intense emotion. The same influences may also account, at least in part, for the marked variations in stressing which may be heard in Siberian dialects (e.g. дочка́ for до́чка 'daughter', опасно́ for опа́сно 'dangerous', со́сна for сосна́ 'pine').

[1] See Classified Bibliography, IV.

PART II

THE DEVELOPMENT OF RUSSIAN

CHAPTER VI

CONJECTURE AND RECORD

I

By collating the linguistic forms found in the oldest records of the various Slavonic languages with those found in existing ones it has been possible to study these languages in the perspective of time and to observe the substitution of sounds and the accompanying changes of form which have taken place. This constitutes the known history of a language, but, as we shall see presently, it can be no more than selective, for the quantity of written material is always relatively restricted, especially in the early stages, and the choice represented by these materials is fortuitous and haphazard. Nevertheless, a picture of development does emerge, and this, though inevitably distorted, is founded on recorded fact. But human ingenuity has not been content with historical evidence only. It has attempted, with apparent success on the conjectural plane, to establish prehistoric relationships between the various known languages of Indo-European type (not to mention other linguistic types here) by reducing them to intermediate and final unities. Thus, by abstracting from the materials of the Slavonic languages, it has been possible to set up a hypothetical Common Slavonic (Proto-Slavonic) language, described, for instance, by J. J. Mikkola and A. Meillet,[1] from which the modern Slavonic languages are conceived to have been derived by a process of dialectal differentiation. Beyond the Common Slavonic stage a remote unity is envisaged in the still more vague and tenuous Balto-Slavonic language, which embodies the characteristics of the present-day Baltic (viz. Latvian and Lithuanian) and Slavonic languages. Balto-Slavonic, in its turn, is regarded as having emerged from the 'ultimate' source of the Indo-European languages—Common

---

[1] J. J. Mikkola, *Urslavische Grammatik*, I–II (Heidelberg, 1911–50); A. Meillet, *Le slave commun*[2] (Paris, 1934).

Indo-European, a language which is an even more recondite complex of linguistic formulas than Balto-Slavonic and Common Slavonic. It is obvious to a little thought on this subject that we are dealing here with abstractions, which lack the validity of mathematical formulas. They represent merely a set of relations, phonetic and morphological, between recorded forms of Slavonic, Baltic, Germanic, Celtic, Italic, Greek, Albanian, Armenian, Indic (Indo-Aryan), and Iranian, though these forms, unfortunately for plausibility, present the various languages at different periods of time and make it impossible to treat Indo-European linguistics synchronically. The comparatively recent discovery of two types of Tocharian (A and B) and the still more recent discovery of Hittite and its cognates have naturally led to a revision of some of the hypothetical, or 'starred' forms, and E. H. Sturtevant[1] goes so far as to postulate an even earlier unity than Indo-European, to which he has given the name 'Indo-Hittite'. The possibility of such radical reconstructions of the protoglossa (Ger. *Ursprache*) shows how entirely dependent orthodox 'comparative-historical' linguistics is on chance discoveries, and this and the involuntary choice of temporally disparate forms, representing the most varied stages of linguistic development, are sufficient in themselves to invalidate the protoglossa, or parent-language, theory as an adequate explanation of the unrecorded past. The theory, however, has had its uses, not the least of which is the value of the 'starred' forms, if cautiously delimited, as a mnemonic device summarising existing relationships between cognate languages. Thus a posited Indo-European root $*g^uher$- $*g^uhor$- may be used as a label for the juxtaposition of Sanskrit *gharmáḥ* 'heat', Ancient Greek θερμός 'hot', Latin *formus* 'warm', Old Irish *guirim* 'I heat', Gothic *warmjan* 'to warm', Albanian *zjarm* 'fire', Armenian *jerm* 'warm', Old Prussian *gorme* 'heat', and Old Church Slavonic *gorĕti* 'to burn' (cf. R. горѣть). This illustration helps to indicate the lexical relationship of Russian with several of the other Indo-European languages and particularly the closeness of this relationship with Old Church Slavonic.

---

[1] *Introduction to Linguistic Science* (New Haven, 1947).

2

Old Church Slavonic,[1] the oldest recorded Slavonic language, whose earliest surviving monuments go back to the latter part of the tenth century, is at the literary origins of Russian or, more properly, East Slavonic. It is essentially a written language and could hardly have been spoken in the form in which we have it, except in the received and unchanging formulas of homily and liturgy. The living Slavonic language which provided it with its phonetic and grammatical framework was a Macedonian dialect of Bulgarian spoken in the vicinity of Thessalonica (Salonica), where the apostles of the Orthodox Slavs St Cyril (Constantine) and St Methodius were born into a cultured Greek family. Both brothers took part in semipolitical missionary activities in Moravia from 863 onwards, and St Cyril is said to have devised the first Slavonic alphabet. As two alphabets, Glagolitic and Cyrillic, are used in Slavonic MSS. from the tenth century onwards, it is not definitely known which of them was St Cyril's invention, but a consensus of scholarly opinion believes that it must have been the Glagolitic, in which case Cyrillic (now used in Russian in a modernised form) is a later development from Greek uncials, or capital letters. It was this Cyrillic alphabet and a literature, both sacred and profane, translated into Old Church Slavonic mainly from Byzantine originals, which were brought to the principality of Kijev at the end of the tenth century, when the Grand Prince Vladimir was baptised as Vasilij, and Christianity became the official religion. As Old Russian and Old Church Slavonic were very similar, though distinct, languages, it was not difficult to fit the Cyrillic letters to Russian sounds and to absorb the Old Church Slavonic literature, both translated and original, by copying and recopying it over the centuries with a diminishing accuracy that spelt the increasing encroachment of Old Russian speech.

Before the coming of the alphabet and the alien literature

[1] See my articles, 'The Old Bulgarian Language-Type' (*Archivum Linguisticum*, I, 2; Glasgow, 1949), and 'Sources of Old Church Slavonic' (*The Slavonic and East European Review*, xxviii, 71; London, 1950).

which illustrated its use, the East Slavonic principalities probably used their own dialects for public as well as for domestic intercourse, notwithstanding that there is no vestige of a written form. The existence of twelfth-century treaties as well as other secular documents couched in a noticeably different language and style from those of the mainly ecclesiastical literature which Christianity brought with it from Bulgaria suggests that Russian had had some degree of oral cultivation before it was reduced to writing. In fact Old Russian MSS. of the eleventh and twelfth centuries are of three kinds from the standpoint of their language, viz. (i) ecclesiastical works which are predominantly Old Church Slavonic, (ii) secular works which are almost entirely Old Russian, and (iii) works representing a varying mixture of the two elements, alien and vernacular. Thus the Metropolitan Ilarion's homily (*slovo*) 'The Law and Grace' is largely Old Church Slavonic, making due allowance for the lateness of its earliest extant MS. (sixteenth century), the Old Russian code of law *Russkaja Pravda* is largely Russian, and Prince Vladimir Monomach's 'Instruction' (*Poučenije*) and 'The Lay of Igor'' (*Slovo o polku Igoreve*), if this is not an eighteenth-century forgery, as A. Mazon[1] thinks, occupy linguistically intermediate positions, the first nearer to Old Church Slavonic, the second to Old Russian.

Our study of the historical development of Russian must be preceded by an account of its earliest recorded form, which from the eleventh century to the end of the seventeenth is generally known as Old Russian, though there is unavoidably a considerable disparity between the language, say, of the sixteenth and seventeenth centuries and that of the eleventh and twelfth. Some investigators have suggested the application of the term 'Middle Russian' to the former on the model of 'Middle English' and *Mittelhochdeutsch*, but a translation of the French distinction between *le vieux français* and *le français moderne* has been generally preferred. In the present study we shall content ourselves with

[1] *Le Slovo d'Igor* (Paris, 1940). For a spirited and scholarly defence of the traditional view, see H. Grégoire, R. Jakobson et M. Szeftel, *La geste du prince Igor'* (New York, 1948).

presenting Russian as a structure at its two extremes of time, Old and Modern,[1] and we shall divide the account of its development into historical periods, beginning with those of Kijev and the 'Interregnum' (tenth to the fourteenth centuries), and of Moscow (fifteenth to the seventeenth centuries), and ending with the formal tripartite division of the Modern Age into the eighteenth, nineteenth, and twentieth centuries.

3

The adaptation of the Cyrillic alphabet to the system of Old Russian (Old East Slavonic) sounds led to a considerable amount of redundancy in the use of characters (e.g. оу, ȣ, у, ѫ, all represent u), for Old Russian had discarded its nasal vowels, preserved in Old Church Slavonic, and *jer'* (ь) and *jer* (ъ) had lapsed in unstressed medial and final positions, simultaneously closing the originally open syllables: thus the dissyllabic O.C.S. пѫть 'way' and пать 'five' were interpreted as the monosyllabic O.R. путь and пять, although at least one of the nasal symbols (*jusy*) was frequently used not only in the earliest MSS., but down to the seventeenth century. The phonetic value of O.R. *jat'* (ѣ) is not altogether certain,[2] as it is represented in Slavonic languages to-day by sounds ranging from close i in Ukrainian to open a in Polish (cf. O.C.S. лѣсъ 'forest' with Ukr. ліс, R. лес, Pol. *las*). The use of O.R. ѣ (*ě*) and ꙗ (Mod. R. я) as phonetic equivalents in both Old Church Slavonic and Old Russian MSS. suggests that ѣ stood for an open rather than a close sound, and may have been pronounced like English æ in 'that' (cf. O.R. грѣхъ 'sin' with the Latvian loan-word *grēks*, pronounced græːks), though there is also cogent evidence to show that it was not differentiated from e in Old Russian. Another view of *jat'*, held for instance by G. O. Vinokur,[3] is that this letter symbolised, according to context, either close *e* or diphthongal *ie*. The remaining vowels—*i*, *e*, *a*, *o*, *u*, *y*—were all probably pronounced in much the same way

---

[1] This has already been described in Pt I.
[2] See my article 'The Phonetic Value of *Jat'* in Old Russian' (*Slavistična Revija*, III, 3–4; Ljubljana, 1950).   [3] See Classified Bibliography, V.

as they are now, and the so-called 'surds' (*gluchije*), or 'reduced' vowels, ь, ъ, which later became respectively *e* and *o* in stressed position, were probably ι and ə(< ɔ) wherever they were pronounced. This gives us the following triangular distribution of Old Russian vowels:

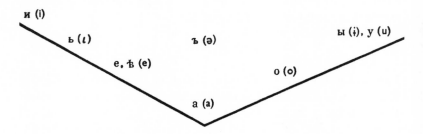

и (i)

ь (ι)   ъ (ə)   ы (i), y (u)

e, ѣ (e)   o (o)

a (a)

The Old Russian consonantal system no doubt partly resembled that of Old Church Slavonic, but there were considerable differences. The hard-soft parallelism, which is such an out-

	П б	—	Т Д	—	—	К Г
Plosives	p b p̦ b̦	—	t d ț d̦	—	—	k g —
	м	—	н	—	—	—
Nasals	m m̦	—	n n̦	—	—	—
	—	ф в	с з	ш ж	(й)	х
Fricatives	—	f v f̦ v̦	s z ș z̦	— ʃ ӡ	j —	x x̦
Affricates	—	—	ц ts	ч tʃ	—	—
Laterals	—	—	—	л l l̦	—	—
Vibrants	—	—	—	p r r̦	—	—

114

standing feature of Modern Russian, would appear to have existed in the eleventh century, except that the present hard hush-sibilants ш (ʃ) and ж (ʒ) and the hard affricate ц (ts) were all three pronounced soft. Accordingly we may postulate for Old Russian the table of consonants given on page 114.

As in Old Church Slavonic, j was represented at first in Old Russian by means of the undotted iota with a ligature (e.g. ꙗ, ѥ, ю), but subsequently the letters я (< the nasal ѧ), plain e, and ю, which embodied it when used initially or after a vowel, became the customary 'suggestions' of its presence. It was also the second element, or 'terminus', of the only kind of diphthongs that occurred in Old Russian (e.g. краи—kraj 'verge; land').

A glance at the foregoing arrangement of consonantal phonemes shows that, as in Modern Russian, some of the fricatives and affricates occur singly, not having corresponding hard or voiced correlates: thus x and tʃ want their respective voiced counterparts ɣ and ʤ. The letter щ, as now in Literary Russian, except its Moscow variety, was pronounced ʃtʃ, i.e. as a consonantal compound.[1]

4

The grouping of the phonemes, which have just been enumerated, into words and word-complexes, or syntagmas, reveals certain idiosyncrasies, only part of which have survived to the present time. Some of them are East Slavonic and help to discriminate between this linguistic group and its Southern and Western congeners. The most salient features, shared by Russian with White Russian and Ukrainian, are phonetic, viz. (i) 'pleophony', or full vowelling (*polnoglasije*), which opposes the groups -*oro*-, -*olo*-, -*ere*- (e.g. O.R. го́родъ 'town', го́лодъ 'hunger', пе́редъ 'before') to the South and West Slavonic monosyllables -*ra*-, -*la*-, -*rě*-, and their variants (e.g. O.C.S. градъ, гладъ, прѣдъ; Czech *hrad, hlad, před*), and (ii) *č*, *ž*, derived from conjectured **tj*, **dj* and contrasting with O.C.S. *št*, *žd* (cf. O.R. свѣча́ 'candle' and са́жа 'soot' with O.C.S. свѣща, сажда). These,

---

[1] For a fuller and documented account of the Old Russian system of phonemes, see my article, 'The Pronunciation of Medieval Russian' (*The Slavonic and East European Review*, XXIX, 73; London, 1951).

along with y and я/ѣ corresponding to the Old Church Slavonic
nasal vowels ѫ and ѧ respectively, are the commonly cited
criteria for dividing the Slavonic languages into three major
groups (see ch. I). The term 'pleophony' covers two primary
sets of phonetic phenomena, which represent a peculiar development of syllabic liquids associated with two sorts of
vowels. The first and the second pleophony may be illustrated
in Russian by the words го́род 'town' and верёвка (< O.R.
вьрвь) 'string' respectively. Only the first of them is 'prehistoric', i.e. earlier than the middle of the eleventh century,
to which the first dated Russian text belongs. It forms part of
the Old Russian phonetic heritage, which included, among other
features, the palatalisation of consonants before all front vowels,
the substitution of initial o for e (cf. R. о́зеро 'lake' with O.C.S.
ѥзеро), and the sporadic lapse of initial j (e.g. унъ for юнъ
'young'). Old Russian phonetic developments of which we
have record constitute a further complex of divergences from
Old Church Slavonic. Among them we may note: (i) the loss
of the unstressed 'surds', which is attested by documents as early
as the eleventh century; (ii) the already mentioned change of
stressed ь and ъ into e and o, which began in the second half of
the twelfth century and gave rise to the modern vocalic alterna-
tions o/ё/e/zero (e.g. сон < O.R. сънъ 'sleep; dream', gen. сна;
лён < O.R. льнъ 'flax', gen. льна; пень < O.R. пьнь 'stump',
gen. пня); (iii) the second pleophony (from the thirteenth
century); (iv) the change of i into the asyllabic semivowel j after
vowel sounds (e.g. твои < твой 'thy'); (v) the 'reduction' of i
to ь in weak position (e.g. судия < судья 'judge'); (vi) the
development of epenthetic, or interpolated, vowels (e.g. gen.
plur. чисел < O.R.числъ 'of numbers'); (vii) the loss (apocope)
of final l after a consonant (e.g. нёс < O.R. неслъ 'he carried');
(viii) the hardening of final labials in the fourteenth century
(e.g. дам < O.R. дамь 'I shall give'), and various kinds of assimilation (e.g. где? < O.R. къдѣ? 'where?'). It will be noticed from
a perusal of these transformations that many of them emanate
from the twofold development of the 'surds' (ь, ъ), viz. 'lower-
ing' to e/o in strong syllables and lapse in weak.

5

The Old Russian (Old East Slavonic) morphological and syntactic patterns, like the phonological, differed in a multitude of ways from the grammatical system of the modern language. The contrasted paradigms of declension and conjugation were noticeably more involved than they are to-day, so that the juxtaposition of Old Russian and Modern Russian flexion allows us to infer that the main tendency in the development of Russian is a slow and gradual simplification by a process of levelling. The slowness of the process may be seen by comparing the history of Russian with that of English, and the structure of eleventh-century Old Russian with that of the far less conservative seventh-century Old English (Anglo-Saxon).[1]

Old Russian declension, like its modern counterpart, distinguished a nominal from a pronominal type, but, unlike Modern Russian, it had three numbers, including a dual for paired objects, and seven cases, including a vocative. Further complications were introduced by a greater diversity of stems. Thus there were, among others, masculine *o*- and *ъ*-stems, which may be studied by confronting their paradigms.

	Singular			*Dual*				*Plural*	
	('clan')	('son')							
Nom.	ро́дъ	сы́нъ	Nom.⎫			Nom.⎫		ро́ди	сыно́ве
Voc.	ро́де	сы́ну	Voc.⎬ ро́да	сы́ны	Voc.⎭				
Gen.	ро́да	сы́ну	Acc.⎭			Gen.	ро́дъ	сыно́въ	
Dat.	ро́ду	сы́нови	Gen.⎫ ро́ду	сыно́ву	Dat.	ро́домъ	сынъ́мъ		
Acc.	ро́дъ	сы́нъ	Loc.⎭			Acc.	ро́ды	сыны́	
Instr.	ро́домь	сы́нъмь	Dat.⎫ ро́дома	сынъма́	Instr.	ро́ды	сынъми́		
Loc.	ро́дѣ	сыну́	Instr.⎭			Loc.	ро́дѣхъ	сынѣхъ	

The *ъ*-stem nouns were restricted in number and were later absorbed into the preponderant *o*-stem paradigm, as will be seen from the declension of the foregoing two words in the modern language (see p. 118).

Simplification and standardisation of type is illustrated by a comparison of the old and the modern paradigms, but at the

---

[1] See ch. I, p. 14.

same time the curious complexity introduced into the declension of сын in the plural will not escape notice.

	Singular		Plural	
Nom.⎫ Voc.⎭	род	сын	роды́	сыновья́
Gen.	ро́да	сы́на	родо́в	сынове́й
Dat.	ро́ду	сы́ну	рода́м	сыновья́м
Acc.	род	сы́на	роды́	сынове́й
Instr.	ро́дом	сы́ном	рода́ми	сыновья́ми
Loc.	ро́де	сы́не	рода́х	сыновья́х

Besides the hard masculine *o-* and *ъ-*stems, there were the corresponding soft *jo-* and *ь-*stems (e.g. конь 'horse' and путь 'way'), for the phonetic parallelism of hard and soft runs through the entire system of Russian flexion and derivation, i.e. it has its morphological reflexes. Thus the hard case-endings -а, -ы, -у, -омь/-ъмь have soft counterparts in -я, -ѣ, -ю, -емь/-ьмь. This gives four types of masculine vowel-stem declensions, to which we may add the consonant stems represented by дьнь 'day' (gen. дьне) and камы 'stone' (gen. ка́мене) and the mixed types represented by горожя́нинъ 'townsman' and учи́тель 'teacher', which have a singular paradigm of the *o-*stem type and plural one of the consonant-stem type (e.g. nom. plur. горожя́не, учи́теле), but no recorded dual forms. The complexity of the masculine paradigms is counterbalanced by the simplicity of the neuter, which has only the antithetic *o-* and *jo-*stems (e.g. село́ 'village', по́ле 'field'), and three types of consonant stems, viz. -*n-* (e.g. и́мя 'name', gen. и́мене), -*s-* (e.g. чю́до 'miracle', gen. чюдесе́), and -*t-* (теля́ 'calf', gen. теля́те). Feminine nouns hold an intermediate position with their paired *a-* and *ja-*stems (e.g. жена́ 'woman', gen. жены́ and земля́ 'earth', gen. землѣ́), the *ū-* and *ь-*stems (e.g. цьркы 'church', gen. цьркъве and ночь 'night', gen. но́чи) and one consonant stem in -*r-* (e.g. дъчи 'daughter', gen. дъчере). Like the masculine, the neuter and feminine nouns show an impoverished dual system, with only three distinct forms and a 'zero', or uninflected, form in the genitive plural. In the neuter the nominative, vocative, and accusative tend to be morphologically identical in all three numbers, and in the feminine it is only the *a-/ja-*types which distinguish a vocative form (e.g. жёно, зёмле). Even the variant of the *ja*-stem, with a nominative singular in -*i* (e.g. богы́ни 'goddess'), has the same form for nominative and vocative. It is not surprising then that the analogy and cumulative influence of the neuter and most of the feminine paradigms led to the ultimate loss of the vocative case in Russian. The identity of nominative and accusative, both singular and plural, in the feminine and neuter conditioned the removal of their formal disparity in the masculine, and the example of the feminine plural forms of the dative, instrumental, and locative (e.g. женáмъ, женáми, женáхъ) introduced uniformity into the modern plural paradigm. The survival of gender in present-day Russian helps to maintain the existing diversity in nominal declension, but there appears to be a tendency to eliminate the neuter. South Russian has moved a long way in that direction, and, in view of this, it is not impossible to visualise the Russian generic system as ultimately reduced to the binary type of, say, French, Hindi, or Lithuanian.

Old Russian declension differed from that of Modern Russian in having two distinct paradigms for the adjective, the short and the long. The modern language has only the latter, which is conceived from the synchronic point of view as typically adjectival. As a matter of fact the short adjective, which survives as a predicative form to-day, is the original type, and the long was formed from it by suffixing the personal pronoun, whose original nominative form (e.g. и 'he', я 'she', e 'it') has been lost. The short adjective (e.g. nom. sing. добръ, добрá, добрó 'kind; good') was declined like the corresponding noun stem (e.g. добръ like родъ, синь 'blue' like конь). The long, or 'articulate' form (e.g. masc. nom. sing. дóбрыи < добръ + и), so called because the suffixed pronoun functioned like the definite article in other languages, represents, in its oblique cases, an attempt to decline both parts of the compound (e.g. masc. gen. sing. дóброго is a 'blurred' form of дóбра + егó). This is seen much more clearly in Old Church Slavonic, where we find such forms as добраѥго and добрааго. In Old Russian then the long adjective was already a formal unit, and this enabled it subsequently to usurp the main function of the adjective.

The other members of the nominal category—comparative adjective, participle, and numeral—also had a more complicated declension in Old Russian. As in the modern language, all these systems have common features as well as idiosyncrasies. The comparative adjective (e.g. nom. sing. хýжии, хýжьши, хýже 'worse') and the declinable active participles (e.g. pres. несá, несýчи, несá 'carrying'; past несъ, нéсъши, несъ 'carried') have this in common that the 'feminine' suffix *č* or *š* reappears in all the oblique cases (e.g. masc. nom. sing. несá, gen. несýчя, dat. несýчю; nom. несъ, gen. нéсъшя, dat. нéсъшю). The passive participles (e.g. pres. несóмъ, несóма, несóмо 'being carried', past несéнъ, несенá, несенó 'carried') decline like the hard-stem nouns and short adjectives (e.g. masc. nom. sing. несóмъ, gen. несóма), and the active past participle with the suffix -*l*- is indeclinable and lends itself to use in compound past tenses (e.g. неслá есть 'she has carried'). The declension of Old Russian numerals is even more varied than it is in the modern language. Generic distinctions affect only the first four cardinals (e.g. одúнъ, однá, одинó 'one'; дъва, дъвѣ 'two'; трие, три 'three'; четы́ре, четы́ри 'four'), but only 'one' recognises all three genders and has a full paradigm, both singular and plural (e.g. nom. plur. masc. однúú, fem. одны́, neut. однá). 'Two' opposes a masc. form (дъва) to a common feminine and neuter form (дъвѣ) and declines only in the dual. 'Three' and 'four', like 'two', have the masculine/non-masculine formal antithesis, but a plural-type paradigm. The cardinals from 'five' (пять) upwards know nothing of gender: those from 'five' to 'nine' inclusive decline like feminine singular ь-stems, and 'ten' (дéсять) has dual and plural as well as singular forms. The remaining decades, which contain дéсять, naturally follow 'ten'. Сóрокъ, known from the fourteenth century and synonymous with четы́редесяте (40), is a noun which originally meant a sack containing the forty sable pelts needed to make a fur coat (*šuba*). Девянóсто (90), attested in the fourteenth century for дéвятьдесятъ, and съто (100) follow the neuter noun paradigms, and ты́сячя (1000) is feminine.

Pronominal declension, intrusive in the long adjective, may

be seen in its variety by collating the personal with the non-personal types. Variety of form, as will be seen, is restricted very largely to the singular. The identity of the genitive and accusative forms will also be noted in the personal pronoun and a *rapprochement* between them in the demonstrative singular.

Singular			*Dual*		*Plural*	
Nom. я(зъ) 'I'	тъ 'that'	Nom. ⎫			Nom. мы 'we'	ти 'those'
Gen. менé	тогó	Acc. ⎬ вѣ	та	Gen. насъ	тѣхъ
Dat. мънѣ, ми	тому́	Gen. ⎫		Dat. намъ, ны	тѣмъ
Acc. менé, мя	тъ, тогó	Loc. ⎬ наю, на	тóю	Acc. насъ, ны	ты
Instr. мънóю	тѣмь	Dat. ⎫		Instr. нáми	тѣми
Loc. мънѣ	томь	Instr. ⎬ нáма, на	тѣма	Loc. насъ	тѣхъ

Complete formal identity between the two cases is illustrated by the paradigm of the interrogative къто? 'who?', in contrast to which that of чьто? 'what?' shows the presence of the same form in the nominative and accusative, like all other neuters.

Nom.	къто	чьто
Gen.	когó	чегó, чьсó
Dat.	кому́	чему́
Acc.	когó	чьто
Instr.	цѣмь	чимь
Loc.	комь	чемь

Formal differences between these two paradigms point the dichotomy of animate and inanimate gender. This is the source of the choice of the genitive for the accusative to express animate, as distinct from sex, gender in the Modern Russian masculine singular noun and in the epicene plural (e.g. nom. sing. конь 'horse', gen.-acc. коня́, nom. plur. кóни, gen.-acc. конéй). In Old Russian animate gender, which appears to be 'personal' and masculine in origin, was only in its embryonic stage, because the accusative of animate nouns was mostly like the nominative and not like the genitive in form (e.g. nom.-acc. рабъ 'slave', конь 'horse').

The Old Russian verbal system bears the same relation to that of the modern language as its system of declension does to that of the latter. In both cases there has been considerable simplification and reconstruction, but the initial complexity has not been anything like so radically modified as the Anglo-Saxon flexional system has in present-day English. The contemporary Russian nominal and verbal systems are still comparable to the 'synthetic' Latin type rather than to the mainly 'analytic' French and English types.[1] But there is a great difference between the changes undergone by the Old Russian verb and those of the Old Russian noun. The system of Old Russian declension has been mainly levelled out, the system of the Old Russian verb has been largely recast. This verbal system, like that of Old Church Slavonic, is dominated by the category of tense, which expresses itself in a formal contrast between present and past time, and into which the notion of aspect enters as a differentiating factor, assuming such special paradigms as the imperfect, to express the durative aspect, and the aorist, to express the perfective. The present-tense form is contrasted with two simple forms in the past tense, viz. imperfect and aorist, and two compound forms, viz. perfect and pluperfect, which combine the present and aorist forms of the auxiliary verb бы́ти 'to be' with the indeclinable participle in -l-. The future-tense form of the same verb (e.g. 1st–3rd pers. sing. бу́ду, бу́деши, бу́деть) also combines with this participle to form the future perfect (e.g. бу́ду нес́лъ 'I shall have carried'). The simple future, on the contrary, combines this auxiliary, as in Modern Russian, with the infinitive (e.g. бу́ду нести́ 'I shall carry'). All these tense-paradigms belong to the indicative mood, which, in Old Russian, is contrasted with the conditional (optative, subjunctive) and the imperative. The conditional uses the entire aorist paradigm of бы́ти in conjunction with the -l-participle (e.g. нес́лъ быхъ 'I should carry'), and the imperative is complicated by formal distinctions unknown to Modern Russian. The dual number is present in the finite verb, as in the participles, and invariably opposes a 1st person form to a common form for the 2nd and 3rd persons (e.g. несéвѣ 'we two carry', несéта 'you/they two carry'). Another Old Russian feature which has disappeared from the modern language is the dichotomy of infinitive and supine (cf. нести́ 'to carry' with нестъ 'in order to carry'), which are both interpreted historically as petrified case-forms of the same paradigm. The supine expressed purpose, and its place was subsequently taken by the

[1] See ch. i, pp. 15–16.

morphologically analogous infinitive. The other two verbal categories—voice and aspect—are represented, as in Modern Russian, by special forms. Voice is confined to the participle, where it combines with tense and invests the declensional system of both the short and the long adjective. Here, as in the other declinable parts of speech, there is formal opposition between masculine and neuter on the one hand and feminine on the other. Aspect permeates the entire system of Old Russian conjugation, but does not dominate it. Its presence is felt not only in the contrast between the imperfect and the aorist, which is that between French *imparfait* and *passé défini* (e.g. *je portais* and *je portai*) or between our own progressive and simple preterite (e.g. 'I was carrying' and 'I carried'), but also in the aspective force of verbal affixes. Modern Russian, as we have learnt, exploits these to make up for the loss of imperfect and aorist in the ruin of the Old Russian temporal conjugation. As a specimen and summary of the formal inventory of the Old Russian verb we may present the following finite paradigms, which do not include compound forms.

		Indicative		
	Present	Imperfect	Aorist	Imperative
Sing.				
1st	несу́	неся́хъ	несо́хъ	—
2nd	несе́ши	неся́ше	несе́	неси́
3rd	несе́ть	неся́ше	несе́	неси́
Dual				
1st	несе́вѣ	неся́ховѣ	несо́ховѣ	несѣвѣ
2nd–3rd	несе́та	неся́ста	несо́ста	несѣта
Plur.				
1st	несе́мъ	неся́хомъ	несо́хомъ	несѣмъ
2nd	несе́те	неся́сте	несо́сте	несѣте
3rd	несу́ть	неся́ху	несо́шя	—

All that survives of this in Modern Russian are the modified conjugations of the present tense and the imperative, viz. pres. tense несу́, несёшь, несёт, несём, несёте, несу́т; imper. неси́, неси́те.

Syntactically, Old Russian in its specifically Russian, as distinct from its Church Slavonic, style, for instance that of the writs (*gramoty*) and the *Russkaja Pravda*, was inclined to prefer the short sentence to the period, to emphasise co-ordination rather than subordination, and to bind its short sentences with a limited number of copulative conjunctions, notably и 'and'. In styles more influenced by the syntax of Old Church Slavonic, which will unimaginatively reproduce that of Byzantine Greek almost 'without remainder', the period, subordination, participial ellipses, appositions, absolute constructions (but with the 'logical' subject in the dative case), neuter plurals as abstract collectives, and a multitude of conjunctions and 'modal words' are all in evidence. Two quotations will illustrate the difference of style. These may be regarded as 'marginal' and therefore as delimiting the scale of styles in Old Russian literature, which depends on the relative admixture of Old Russian and Old Church Slavonic elements. As an instance of paratactic (co-ordinative) simplicity we may take a few sentences from the passage in the 'Primary Chronicle', or 'Tale of Bygone Years' (*Povest' vremennych let*), describing the single combat between the Russian prince Mstislav Vladimirovič of T'mutorokan' and the Circassian (Kasog) prince Rededja, viz.

И рече́ Реде́дя къ Мьстисла́ву: ‚не ору́жьемь ся бье́вѣ, но борьбо́ю.‘ И я́ста ся боро́ти крѣ́пко... и рече́ Мьстисла́въ: ‚о Пречи́стая Богоро́дице! помози́ ми; а́ще бо одолѣ́ю сему́, съзи́жу це́рковь во и́мя твое́.‘ И се рекъ уда́ри имъ о́ землю, и вынзе́ ножь, и зарѣ́за Реде́дю.[1]

And Rededja said to Mstislav: 'Let us not fight with weapons, but wrestle.' And they started to wrestle strongly...And Mstislav said: 'O Blessed Virgin, help me; for if I overcome him I shall build a church to thy name.' And saying this he struck him to the ground, and stabbed him with his knife, and killed Rededja.

This passage, like all other Old Russian writing, is not entirely free from Old Church Slavonic influence, as will be seen in the smooth use of conjunctions (e.g. бо 'for') and in participial ellipse (e.g. и се рекъ уда́ри имъ 'and saying this he struck (with) him'). One of the omitted portions illustrates the dative ab-

---

[1] See Н. К. Гудзий, *Хрестоматия по древней русской литературе XI–XVII веков*[4] (Москва, 1947).

solute, a parallel formation semantically to the Latin ablative absolute and the Old Greek genitive absolute. This will now appear in a specimen of the periodic style, which exhibits the full measure of alien penetration. It comes from the 'Life of St Feodosij of the Kijev Crypt Monastery' (*Žitije Feodosija Pečerskogo*).

Бысть же роди́телема блаже́наго пересели́ти ся в инъ градъ, Курьскъ нарица́емыи, кня́зю та́ко повелѣ́въшю (dat. absol.), па́че же реку́, Бо́гу си́це изво́ливъшю (dat. absol.), да и та́мо до́бляаго о́трока житие́ просия́еть, намъ же, я́ко же есть лѣ́по, отъ въсто́ка дьньни́ца възиде́ть, събира́ющи (pres. part.) о́крьстъ себе́ ины́ мно́гы звѣ́зды, ожида́ющи (pres. part.) сѣ́лнца пра́вьдьнааго, Христа́ Бо́га (apposit.), и глаго́люща: ,се азъ, влады́ко, и дѣ́ти, я́же въспита́хъ духо́вьнымь твоимь бра́шьнъмь, и се, Го́споди, ученйци мой, се бо сия́ ти приведо́хъ, йже научи́хъ вся жити́иская (neut. plur.) през-рѣ́ти, и тебе́, еди́ного Бо́га и Го́спода, възлюби́ти.'[1]

The parents of the blessed one had to migrate to another town called Kursk at the command of the prince, or I should say rather, because it was God's will, so that there too the life of this fine youth should give lustre, and that for us, as is fitting, the morning star should rise, gathering many other stars about it in expectation of the sun of righteousness, Christ, our God, and saying: 'Behold me, Lord, and the children I have nurtured on Thy heavenly food and taught to despise the things of this life and to love Thee, the only Lord and God.'

[1] See В. В. Сиповский, *Историческая хрестоматия по истории русской словесности*, I, 2[10] (Петроград, 1916).

CHAPTER VII

THE KIJEV AND TARTAR PERIODS
(ELEVENTH TO THE FOURTEENTH CENTURIES)

I

Recorded Russian—and we may include White Russian and Ukrainian here, for all three, as we know, can be traced back to a common, though hardly uniform, East Slavonic 'source'—is no older than the eleventh century, which gives it a history extending over less than a millennium. The medieval language already exhibited dialectal differentiation (e.g. North Russian *cokan'je-čokan'je*), although perhaps not quite so marked as it was to become later, especially from the fourteenth century onwards, and according to the chronicles it was used by a group of tribes occupying the basin of the middle and upper Dnieper and the upper valleys of the Western Dvina and Volga. By the eleventh century these tribes had been moulded politically and economically into a system which recent Russian historians (e.g. B. D. Grekov[1]) insist on describing, not altogether accurately, as 'feudal'. The adoption of a settled mode of life had made agriculture the chief source of wealth and ownership of land the chief source of political power. This was concentrated in the hands of princes, with the Grand Prince (Prince Paramount) of Kijev, a descendant of the ninth-century Varangian invader Rjurik (Hrörekr), as *primus inter pares*. From the latter part of the tenth century onwards Varangian Russia (Rus') became a province of Byzantine religion and culture. In the eleventh century, after the death of Jaroslav the Wise (978–1054), who was in some respects the Russian counterpart of Alfred the Great, the authority of the princes of Kijev rapidly declined and ultimately vanished in the ruinous passion of internecine strife. By the twelfth century the number of disunited principalities, which varied considerably

---

[1] *Киевская Русь*[5] (Москва-Ленинград, 1949).

in size and population, had risen to twelve, and this loose political patchwork was further weakened by the process of subdivision characteristic of the appanage system of inheritance. The thirteenth century saw a 'divine visitation' in the shape of the most formidable invasion of Russian territory that had ever been undertaken from the eastern steppe, and for the next two centuries the 'Tartar' steppe dominated the eastern principalities of the forest zone, and the 'feudal' disintegration of the country reached its utmost limits. Out of this political chaos Russia was gradually 'redeemed' by the centralising activities of the princes of the originally second-rate appanage Moscow, and after that the North (Moscow and later St Petersburg), and not the South (Kijev), was arbiter of Russian history.

Within the time limits we have drawn here the Russian language passed through the first period of its recorded development. The statements of chroniclers make it evident that at the time of the creation of the Russian state in the ninth century there was considerable tribal differentiation, which would naturally involve a differentiation of speech. Šachmatov,[1] approaching the problem of the origins of East Slavonic *a posteriori*, groups the tribal dialects, of which, it must be admitted, we have no written monuments, into a northern, a southern, and an eastern division. The speakers of the northern dialect, he tells us, were the Slovene of the Lake Il'men' area and the Kriviči (cf. Latv. *krievi* 'Russians') of the upper Western Dvina; those of the southern dialect, whose territory took in the middle and lower Dnieper and the associated Bug and Dniester, the Poljane, Derevljane, Severjane, Duleby (Bužane), Velynjane, Chorvaty, Uliči, and Tivercy; and those of the eastern dialect the Vjatiči of the Oka, a southerly affluent of the Volga. Between the speakers of the northern and southern forms of Old Russian, Šachmatov places the Radimiči, to whom he gives a West Slavonic affiliation to explain some of the 'Polish' characteristics of modern White Russian (e.g. *cekan'je* and *dzekan'je*; cf. R. тёплый 'warm', день 'day' with W.R. цёплы, дзень). This view,

---

[1] *Очерк древнейшего периода истории русского языка* (Энц. Слав. Фил. xi, 1; Петроград, 1915.)

however, is not generally supported by scholarly opinion. On the other hand his theory of tribal intermixture as the source of dialectal differentiation has attained the status of a principle. Accordingly the source of modern Literary Russian as a spoken language is sought in the mixed dialects created by the conjectured interpenetration of northern and eastern types. The written language, however, had a much more complicated past, and it is this that must now engage our attention.

2

The Cyrillic alphabet and the Old Church Slavonic literature of translations and imitations of Hellenistic and Byzantine prototypes reached the Eastern Slavs along with Christian doctrine in the course of the tenth century. By the end of that century Christianity had become the official religion of the Kijev principality, and the Old Church Slavonic literary language, in a Russian recension, not only its exclusive repository, but a widely accepted medium of official communication. We find specimens of this language in inscriptions on coins (e.g. Владиміръ на столѣ 'Vladimir on (his) throne' on a gold coin struck between 972 and 1015) and in copies of Old Church Slavonic MSS. and codices, of which the best known is the illuminated Ostromir Gospels (1056–7), an *evangelistarium*, or collection of Gospel extracts, executed in bold and beautiful uncial characters for Ostromir, governor (*posadnik*) of Novgorod, by the deacon Grigorij. The inscriptions are far too short to give an adequate idea of the earliest literary language, but the substantial Gospel text shows that it was not a pure Old Bulgarian, for though the language is of the archaic (possibly Cyrillo-Methodian) pattern, its details disclose the intrusion of what must have been Old Russian phonetic practice, notably pleophony and the substitution of lowered (mid-level) vowels for the 'surds'. The presence of Russian phonetic elements is increasingly observable in the later MSS., both dated and undated, and we are warranted in describing their language as a Russian form of Old Church Slavonic. The characteristic system of the latter is naturally plainest in versions of the Scriptures and generally in ecclesiastical literature (exegetic writings, homilies, hagiography), and it tends to yield more and more to the Old Russian spoken language as the subject-matter of the mainly anonymous authors becomes more secular and more familiar. We can therefore distinguish two extremes of literary Old Russian, viz. an ecclesiastical language only slightly distinguishable from Old Church Slavonic, and a secular language which is predominantly, but not purely Old Russian. In between these, as we have seen, there was a scale of intermediate types, some tending towards Old Church Slavonic, others towards Old Russian. For purposes of classification it is expedient, in discussing the literary language of the Kijev period, to admit the co-existence of three styles of writing: (i) ecclesiastical, (ii) 'literary', and (iii) administrative (*delovoj stil'*), and to recognise each by the relative proportion of Old Church Slavonic ingredients. The extreme styles also represent two types of spoken language, viz. the ecclesiastical, an Old Church Slavonic and Old Russian hybrid speech found at its purest in the liturgy, and the colloquial, largely the everyday Russian of gentle and simple alike. The first type was scarcely a spoken language as commonly understood.

Original composition in one or other of the foregoing styles would obviously not begin quite so early as the mere copying of alien material, but we must not overlook the text of the Russo-Byzantine treaties of 912 and 945, and, if genuine, inscriptions like the sentence on the T'mutorokan' Stone of 1068, which tells how Prince Gleb Svjatoslavič measured the frozen sea across the Kerch narrows of the Sea of Azov. We shall accordingly find, in compiling our catalogue of Old Russian literature in the widest acceptation of the word, that translated material at first exceeds imitative, not to mention original, works. In the eleventh century this literature could not have been very considerable, though no doubt only a fraction of it survives, viz. some dozen MSS., but if we take into account the period from the eleventh to the fourteenth century we shall discover that it is reflected in about 180 inscriptions and in over a thousand MSS. The former are found carved in stone or on coins and domestic utensils (e.g. goblets), the latter engrossed mostly on parchment (vellum), though occasionally on paper, which becomes the customary medium in the fifteenth century. The parchment leaves are either left unbound as *chartae* (*gramoty*) or bound together as 'books' (*knigi*), and the writing on them may be in one of three kinds of script—uncial, semi-uncial, and cursive. The uncial characters are used to the exclusion of the other two in the oldest monuments, the semi-uncials appear about the fourteenth century as an innovation emanating from the Balkans, and the beginnings of the cursive hand belong to the next century. The difference between the cursive and the other scripts resides in its use of ligatures as against isolated symbols, and this makes the cursive script less clear than the others and generally much more difficult to decipher.

The oldest manuscript material goes back to the eleventh century, though we may assume *a priori* that there were tenth-century MSS. which have not survived. Even a great deal of the eleventh-century material is known only in much later transcripts: thus the oldest existing chronicles, notably the Laurentian (Laurentine), are no older than the fourteenth (1377). All the eleventh-century MSS. are copies of Old Church Slavonic prototypes. Apart from the already mentioned 'Ostromir Gospels' (a massive book of 294 leaves) there are the rather later 'Svjatoslav Miscellanies' (*izborniki*) of 1073 and 1076, which contain various examples of Byzantine didactic literature translated for the enlightened Bulgarian tsar Simeon (tenth century), whose patronage of Old Church Slavonic literature served as model and inspiration to the Russian princes Vladimir and Jaroslav and to some of their descendants down to Vladimir Monomach (1053–1125), all of whom, like Alfred the Great, were both men of action and lovers of letters. The other eleventh-century monuments are Scriptural and liturgical translations (e.g. the 'Archangel Gospels', 1092, and the 'Novgorod Liturgical Menaea', 1095), into which phonetic features of North Russian (e.g. письчь for письць 'scribe', личе for лице 'face') have intruded. In the twelfth century, Ukrainian features appear in the 'Galič Gospels' (1144) and the 'Dobrilo Gospels' (1164).

And among the more numerous MSS. of this century (*c.* fifty) we already have original as well as translated literature. The latter is still ecclesiastical in character (e.g. the 'Mstislav Gospels', 1171); the former includes materials of documentary as well as literary interest in the guise of two bequests (*darstvennyje zapisi*) to monasteries and copies of legends of Russian saints, for instance, 'The Legend (*skazanije*) of Boris and Gleb', the oldest version of this popular hagiographical work, which, in its simple way, is as touching as the ingenuous Anglo-Saxon 'Life of St Edmund' (ninth century).

The thirteenth and fourteenth centuries, the period of feudal discord and Tartar hegemony, add considerably to the total number of ancient MSS., the fourteenth century accounting for about half the material inherited from the first four centuries of Old Russian literature. At this time Russian writing is no longer concentrated in the two major ecclesiastical and political centres, Kijev and Novgorod, but distributed among these and a great many others, viz. Galič (Halyč), Smolensk, Pskov, Polock, Tver', Rostov, Suzdal', Moscow, and Rjazan', where, as elsewhere, monasteries were the foci of literary activity and authority. It was in these, for instance, that the extant copies of the chronicles, themselves primarily of monastic origin, were made. The core of the chronicles—'The Tale of Bygone Times'[1] —is supposed to have been begun in Kijev not later than the eleventh century. Other chronicles mostly bear local names, for instance the 'Novgorod Chronicle', extant in a thirteenth-century copy, and the fourteenth-century 'Suzdal' Chronicle', which continues the Laurentian MS. of the 'Primary Chronicle'. But the chronicles are only one of several species of writing attested by MSS. of the thirteenth and fourteenth centuries, and most of them have a linguistic and historical, rather than a literary, value. The brief and mostly stereotyped writs, emanating from Smolensk, Tver', and Novgorod, go back to the thirteenth century, and others from Polock, Pskov, Moscow, and Rjazan' to the fourteenth. The legal codex *Russkaja Pravda*, in its earliest form, is dated 1282. Both this and the treaties, as mainly

[1] See Pt III, no. 3, also p. 124.

Old Russian in subject and vocabulary, present a linguistic interest, though of limited extent, as the texts consist largely of variations on a relatively small number of syntactic patterns. Besides the chronicles and legal documents, the thirteenth- and fourteenth-century MSS. bring us versions of Byzantine prototypes (e.g. the universal history of the ninth-century chronicler Georgios Hamartolos) and original works of the order and merit of the homilies of Kiril, Bishop of Turov. It is here that we can speak of the existence of a literature in terms of aesthetic canons, but naturally this literature, even in its more secular forms, cannot be strictly described as Old Russian. Kiril's homilies, which scholarship traces back to the twelfth century, are largely of Byzantine inspiration and in the Byzantine style, and their wording is closely modelled on the idiom and grammar of Old Church Slavonic. The century separating the composition and the oldest existing copy of these homilies is a relatively short period compared with the distance between the origin and MSS. of certain other works of Old Russian literature. The celebrated homily of the Metropolitan Ilarion[1] is thought to have been delivered towards the middle of the eleventh century (1037–50); Vladimir Monomach's equally renowned 'Instruction'[2] belongs either to the end of that century or to the beginning of the twelfth, and the 'Lay of Igor'' (*Slovo o polku Igoreve*),[3] whose authenticity has been recently impugned,[4] as it was by O. I. Senkovskij ('Baron Brambeus') and others well over 100 years ago, is still regarded by a majority of serious opinion as having been written *c.* 1187–8. But in all these cases the work, as we know it, belongs to a much later period. The text of the 'Instruction' is contained in a fourteenth-century MS. of the 'Primary Chronicle', Ilarion's 'The Law and Grace' in a sixteenth-century recension, and 'The Lay of Igor'' has not even manuscript support and takes the form of a book printed in 1800 and of a variant and even faultier transcript of what is supposed to have been a fifteenth- or sixteenth-century MS., which perished in the Moscow fire of 1812. The original literature of the thirteenth and fourteenth

[1] See Pt III, no. 1. [2] See Pt III, no. 2.
[3] See Pt III, no. 4. [4] See A. Mazon, *op. cit.*

centuries comprises material exhibiting a nascent consciousness of style on the part of the author, although it still remains predominantly anonymous. The thirteenth-century 'Supplication (*molenije*) of Daniil the Captive'[1] initiates a series of exercises in inflated rhetoric, with manner counting for more than matter, which culminate in the hagiographic fantasies of the sixteenth. At this time too the Tartar invasion provides more immediate and absorbing themes, and these dominate both the chronicle story (e.g. 'The Coming of Batu') and the earliest 'military narratives' (*voinskije povesti*), whose more elaborate specimens (e.g. *Zadonščina*, or 'Exploits beyond the Don')[2] belong to the early fifteenth century. The religious preoccupations of the age find expression, (i) in the homilies of Serapion, Bishop of Vladimir, the author of an ornate style which contrasts with the relative simplicity of Ilarion, Kliment Smoljatič, and Kiril of Turov, and especially with the homeliness of Luka Židjata (early eleventh century); (ii) in the 'Epistle of Vasilij of Novgorod to Polikarp';[3] and (iii) even in the 'Life of Prince Aleksandr of the Neva',[4] where, as in the fifteenth-century 'Life of Prince Dmitrij of the Don', we are confronted with the idealised portrait of a Christian hero.

3

The language reflected in the foregoing works, which cover the period from the eleventh to the fourteenth century, is naturally not uniform, whether in contemporary or in historical perspective, and the study of it is complicated by the preponderance of later copies of early material, which makes the dating of particular linguistic phenomena a matter of pure conjecture. Already in the eleventh century, as we have seen, the Russian copies of Old Church Slavonic material contain errors which involuntarily betray characteristics of the copyists' mother tongue. Such pleophonic forms as Володи́мира for O.C.S. Влади́мира in the Ostromir Gospels and хорони́ти 'to preserve' for храни́ти and поло́нъ 'captivity' for плѣ́нъ in the 'Svjatoslav Miscellany'

[1] See Pt III, no. 5.   [2] See Pt III, no. 8.
[3] See Pt III, no. 7.   [4] See Pt III, no. 6.

(1073) are demonstrably Russian, and these earliest dated codices illustrate many other details, phonetic and morphological, which mar the pattern of the Old Church Slavonic original and simultaneously preserve echoes of contemporary speech. The 'Ostromir Gospels', for instance, has Russian пръже 'before' for O.C.S. прѣжде, and вълкъ 'wolf' for влькъ, and the 'Svjatoslav Miscellany' (1073) illustrates the extension of the genitive-accusative form with animates (e.g. рабъ господи́на своего́ сла́вить 'the servant praises his master') and intermixture of the masculine *o*- and ъ-paradigms (e.g. отъ льну 'from flax' for отъ льна). Even the very brief inscription on the T'mutorokan' Stone shows the characteristic Russian omission of the auxiliary in the perfect tense (e.g. мѣрилъ 'measured' for мѣрилъ есть).

The twelfth-century linguistic material illustrates both the conservation of eleventh-century characteristics and the emergence of new ones according to place of origin. The Kijev and Novgorod MSS. ordinarily reproduce the general linguistic pattern of eleventh-century Old Russian, and those of new literary centres like Galič are marked by the presence of local phonetic idiosyncrasies (e.g. жч for жд; ѣ for e before palatalised consonants). Generally speaking certain eleventh-century trends are intensified: thus the change of ь/ъ into e/o in stressed position and perfect-tense forms without the auxiliary become more common, but the aorist survives, except in the writs.

By the thirteenth century, with the notable increase in the quantity of linguistic material, the character of Old Russian becomes clearer. For political reasons the Kijev monuments come to a sudden end after 1240, and the features associated with Kijev Russian give way by degrees to those of mainly northern types. The Novgorod dialect now predominates, and the secular matter of the numerous and geographically diverse treaties gives a fair picture of Old Russian in its dialectal articulation. The 'surds' (ь, ъ) have by this time either disappeared or changed into e/o, e followed by a hard consonant has become *jo* (e.g. купьцо́мъ for купьцѣмь < купе́ць 'merchant', Smolensk Treaty, 1284), the masculine genitive singular in -*u* has become specialised as a partitive-case index (e.g. горо́ху 'some pease',

Russkaja Pravda), and the same ending appears under stress in the locative singular (e.g. в пирý 'at a banquet', *Russkaja Pravda*). Alongside the extension of the *u*-morpheme we see that of the masculine genitive plural ending -овъ (e.g. разбóйниковъ 'of robbers', Smolensk Treaty, 1230). Dialectal features like *cokan'je* and *čokan'je* are common in the Novgorod (western) area of thirteenth-century Russian (e.g. проць for прочь 'away', Novgorod Treaty, 1270). On the contrary the eastern area of Rostov and Rjazan', though its dialect resembles that of Novgorod at many points, does not exhibit these. Other characteristic phonetic features occur in the Smolensk treaties, viz. the change of *v* into *w* before a consonant (e.g. узяти for взяти 'to take') and the hardening of the hush-sibilants (e.g. съ жонóю 'with his wife').

The fourteenth century witnesses the simplification of paradigms and the creation of a dialectal mosaic similar in many respects to the present-day distribution of dialects. The unstressed vowel-patterns begin to assume familiar features, the levelling of the system of declension approaches completion, and aorist and supine have been discarded. The Pskov dialect shows the characteristics of a transitional type between North Russian and White Russian; those of Smolensk and Polock 'prefigure' White Russian; and those of Galicia and Volynia are already obviously Ukrainian. But the Moscow dialect, which now comes under notice and naturally resembles those of the neighbouring Suzdal' and Rostov principalities, still has none of the sharp phonetic traits of the Novgorod, Smolensk, and Galič types, although its morphology already shows signs of the newer order (e.g. levelled declensions and a genitive-accusative form for animate nouns).

Over the four centuries beginning with the tenth, which saw the invasion of Old Church Slavonic and its Cyrillic alphabet, a considerable number of Old Church Slavonic words entered both the written and the spoken forms of Russian. In not a few instances this led to the creation of doublets (e.g. грáдъ/гóродъ 'town', главá/головá 'head', злáто/зóлото 'gold'). The survival of these could be assured only by semantic differentiation, and accordingly what were originally synonyms diverged by degrees in meaning (e.g. храни́ти 'to preserve'/хорони́ти 'to bury', вла́сть 'power'/во́лость 'canton'). Where the recognition of *nuances* was for some reason impossible, one of the paired forms disappeared (e.g. воро́гъ, the O.R. term for врагъ 'enemy'). But even Old Church Slavonic had its synonyms, which were taken over into Old Russian (e.g. пра́вьда/ и́стина 'truth'; женьчю́гъ/би́сьръ 'pearl'), and some of these have survived in Russian to this day by acquiring distinct shades of meaning (cf. лобъ/чело́ with E. 'forehead/brow'). In a number of cases the Old Russian and Old Church Slavonic words were phonetically identical, though different in meaning (e.g. сѣно O.C.S. 'grass', O.R. 'hay'; страда́ти O.C.S. 'to suffer', O.R. 'to work'). This gave rise to homonyms, i.e. the 'same' word came to stand for two often diverse meanings (e.g. живо́тъ 'property; life'). Quite apart from such words, Old Russian had its own particular regional vocabulary, inevitably unknown to Old Church Slavonic. The essentially Russian terminology may be classified as vernacular terms of cultural significance (e.g. поса́дьникъ 'governor', гри́вьна 'mark', кожю́хъ 'fur coat'), loans of similar import (e.g. плугъ 'plough', шелкъ 'silk', тиу́нъ 'bailiff'), and names of places and peoples (e.g. Ко́рчевъ 'Kerch', мур-ма́нинъ 'Northman', обе́зъ[1] 'Georgian').

Like the Old Russian vocabulary, Old Russian syntax reveals the same fusion of an alien with a native principle. The Old Church Slavonic sentence-structure, modelled as it was un-critically on Byzantine writing, was hypotactic and periodic and therefore inherently complex. In contrast to this, literary Old Russian has the brevity, baldness, and paratactic inconse-quence of a spoken language. Potebnja describes Old Russian constructions as lacking in 'syntactic perspective', and others speak of their peculiar 'untidiness' (*neskladica*), which reveals itself in an incoherent (Vinokur has 'chaotic') word-order, in asyndeton, or in the overworking of a few particles (e.g. и, же). These characteristics are to be found especially in those forms of

---

[1] This looks like Abkhaz. To-day the Abkhaz people are neighbours of both the Circassians to the north and the Georgians to the south.

literary Old Russian which contain a substantial proportion of the native element. As a case in point we may observe the absence of *oratio obliqua* (e.g. и повелѣ́ осѣдла́ти конь, а то ви́жю ко́сти его́, lit. 'and he ordered his horse to be saddled, so that I may see its bones', i.e. so that he might ride out to view the bones of his dead horse), which recalls the modern Hindi and Urdu use of direct speech after *ki* 'that' (e.g. *us ne mujh se kahā ki ghar jāo* 'he told me to go home', lit. 'him-by me-to was said that home go'). Nevertheless, the same literary language will use purely literary absolute constructions, both dative and nominative, the latter no doubt also inspired by Old Church Slavonic example (e.g. а вы плóтници сýще, а пристáвимъ вы хорóмъ рубúти 'as you are carpenters we shall set you to build a house').[1]

---

[1] А. Н. Насонов, *Новгородская первая летопись старшего и младшего изводов* (Москва-Ленинград, 1950), p. 15.

CHAPTER VIII

THE MOSCOW PERIOD

(FIFTEENTH TO THE SEVENTEENTH CENTURIES)

I

The Tartar 'interregnum' in Russian history, which began in the early thirteenth century and extended to the fifteenth, lies between the Kijev civilisation and that of Moscow. With protective forests in front and behind it and with its general lack of cultural values, Moscow was much less vulnerable and desirable than Kijev, which was exposed to the steppe and lay almost on the 'highroad' from Central Asia to Central Europe. When Kijev fell to the Tartars, Moscow inherited from the older capital its name (Russia) and literary culture as well as its Byzantine tradition, which was to generate the imperialistic idea of Moscow as the Third Rome, and when the Tartar power ultimately collapsed, its rulers could set about their self-imposed task of 'collecting' the Russian-speaking lands into a centralised Russian state. This had already become a reality towards the end of the fifteenth century, which saw the first conquests of Ivan III, and was firmly established by the end of the sixteenth, which saw those of Ivan IV.

The core of the Muscovite state was essentially northern. The princes of Moscow had inherited the title of 'Grand Prince of Vladimir' in 1328, and their appanage was less than a century older, having been detached from the larger domain of Rostov-Suzdal' in 1260. Even the conquests that were to make Muscovy a territorially imposing state were also almost exclusively northern. By the beginning of the sixteenth century the territories of Muscovy and of the Russian language (as distinct from White Russian and Ukrainian) were already identical, and the literature produced on this territory, unlike that of the preceding period, was focused in a single centre. This state of things was the inevitable consequence of the attractive force of politically centralised power. Unlike the feudal literature of Kijev, which had been cultivated at scattered princely centres, both northern and southern, and expressed in this variety the decentralising tendencies of the age, the centralised literature of Moscow imposed its *cachet* and colour on literary creation throughout the whole of Muscovy from the sixteenth century onwards. But till then there was still considerable local diversity.

2

The literature of the Moscow period, mainly ecclesiastical at first, reveals the steady penetration of secular and foreign influences and numbers among its original creations such diverse works as the warlike *Zadonščina*,[1] regarded as a *pastiche* of the 'Lay of Igor'' by some scholars and as its prototype by others, Afanasij Nikitin's 'Itinerary beyond Three Seas' (*Choženije za tri morja*) with its naïve pictures of medieval India,[2] the verbose and polemical correspondence of Prince Andrej Kurbskij with his master Ivan IV,[3] the vivid historical memoirs of Grigorij Kotošichin (1667), and the writings of the militant and courageous Old Believer, Archpriest Avvakum.[4] From a linguistic point of view the 'Household Book' (*Domostroj*, sixteenth century), the 'Book of a Hundred Headings' (*Stoglav*, 1551), and the 'Code of Tsar Alexis' (*Uloženije*, 1649), as well as the translated literature of the seventeenth century, are at least of equal value. All these works are preserved in a mostly contemporary form either as MSS. or as books. The latter are later than the middle of the sixteenth century, for printing came to Moscow in 1563, and a secular printed literature appears nearly a century after that, for it was only in 1648 that the first non-ecclesiastical work, viz. a Church Slavonic grammar, was printed.

An unfortunate revival of South Slavonic influence associated with the immigration of Balkan refugees led to the 'correction' of Scriptural and liturgical texts according to the orthographic canons in force among the Southern Slavs. The influx of the

[1] See Pt III, no. 8. [2] See Pt III, no. 10.
[3] See Pt III, nos. 12 and 13. [4] See Pt III, no. 16.

Southern Slav bookmen was the direct outcome of the Turkish conquest of the Balkans, which had begun in the second half of the fourteenth century with the Serbian defeat on Kosovo Field (1389). They found welcome and asylum in Muscovy, and their 'reactionary' spelling reform helped to bolster up the idea of Moscow as the political heir of Byzantium. The reforms, however, were not exclusively orthographical and they were not confined to ecclesiastical literature, for the second wave of South Slavonic influence resulted not only in the restoration of discarded letters (s, oy, ѫ), the substitution of features of Serbian Church Slavonic for Russian Church Slavonic spelling (e.g. ы for ъı) as well as the elimination of Russian pleophonic forms (e.g. городъ 'town' gave way to градъ, хóлодъ 'cold' to хладъ), and the introduction of a plethora of superscript signs, but in the use and dissemination of a grandiloquent, loquacious, and archaic manner of writing (*pletenije sloves*), which reinforced the native passion for rhetoric, already noticeable in Daniil's thirteenth-century *Supplication*. It was in this style that Jepifanij the Most Wise, for instance, wrote his lives of St Stefan of Perm'[1] and St Sergij of Radonež in the fifteenth century. But the style is essentially literary and largely ecclesiastical, and therefore does not affect the plain idiom of Nikitin's *Itinerary* and of the 'military narratives', or relieve the dry savour of the plain administrative, or 'chancery', style (*prikaznyj stil'*), which intrudes in varying degrees into both non-literary works like Sil'vestr's *Household Book*, Avvakum's *Autobiography*, and Koto-šichin's *Memoirs* and literary works like the anonymous picaresque romances (e.g. *Frol Skobejev*) and the equally anonymous satires (e.g. *Jorš Jeršovič*). It was chiefly the fifteenth century which felt the impact of South Slavonic rhetorical writing as practised and popularised by the Serbian publicist Pachomij Logofet. The next century still shows obvious traces of its influence, notably in the Kurbskij-Ivan IV correspondence, but by that time Polish and West European secular influences, percolating in part through White Russia and the Ukraine, which since the time of the Tartar inroads had gravitated to the Polish-Lithuanian political focus,

[1] See Pt III, no. 9.

had arrived to neutralise that of the Church Slavonic literary tradition and to reinforce that of the spoken language. In the seventeenth century the spoken language is even more evident in literary composition of the more popular kinds, but more serious writing remains within the pale of Church Slavonic. We may still distinguish two extremes of style: (i) the Church Slavonic, used mainly in ecclesiastical works, and (ii) the administrative, as used in the chanceries and for diplomatic and private correspondence. These two styles figure also as the inevitable ingredients of a variety of literary 'manners'. The Church Slavonic style was obviously the more archaic, and apparently the difficulty of following it led to the compilation of grammars and glossaries from the sixteenth century onwards. The former came from medieval Serbia and present the facts of the Serbian recension of Old Church Slavonic (e.g. the fourteenth-century treatise *Concerning the Eight Parts of Speech* and the fifteenth-century 'Compendium'—*Slovesa vkratcě izbranna*—based on the work of the Bulgarian Konstantin the Philosopher). Unfortunately, the terminology of these grammars is often too vague and obscure to serve as a reliable guide, and this explains to some extent the motley character of fifteenth- and sixteenth-century MSS. in point of spelling. The vocabularies too have a non-Muscovite origin. One of them was compiled in Novgorod (1431), where there was a lexicographical tradition. Lavrentij Zizanij (Tustanovskij) and Pamva Berynda, late sixteenth and early seventeenth-century lexicographers who are known by name, both belonged to the western, non-Russian areas, where Church Slavonic scholarship ranked higher than in Moscow. The ecclesiastical style, to which these grammars and vocabularies furnish a key, was farthest removed from colloquial speech, mainly because its basis was alien to Russian. The administrative style, on the other hand, drew on Russian speech and was tinged at first with local colour, which reflects the phonological and grammatical systems of the Novgorod, Rjazan', and Moscow dialects (e.g. the confusion of ѣ/e and ц/ч in Novgorod, *akan'je* in Rjazan', and the absence of all these in Moscow) as well as their vocabularies, which point to a diversity of contacts with the outside world (e.g. Novg. бýса 'ship', Mosc. армя́къ 'peasant's coat'). To what extent the structure of spoken Moscow Russian, the leading dialect, is mirrored in the administrative language of Muscovy, it is difficult to say precisely, but the very considerable disparity between this and the ecclesiastical style suggests that the vernacular ingredient, like that of the medieval writs, was an important element in its constitution. Yet even the administrative style is essentially a written one, undetachable from parchment and paper and the atmosphere of officialdom. By contrast to it the style of popular literature, which came into existence in the later seventeenth century under Western influences, shows itself, especially in dialogue, to be much nearer to contemporary speech, and this nearness becomes emphatic if we compare such dialogues with, say, those contained in H. W. Ludolf's *Grammatica Russica* (Oxford, 1696).

The language used in writing, whatever its tradition and colour, had inevitably to submit in varying measure to the confusing 'amelioration' to which Russian spelling was subjected from the fifteenth century onwards. Naturally the church books felt it most and popular literature least. The South Slavonic spelling-reformers of the fifteenth century were succeeded early in the sixteenth by Maksim the Greek, a monk from Mt Athos, who 'improved' some of the liturgical books by collating them with his Greek originals. In the middle of the century (1550) the 'Centicapital' Synod (*Stoglavyj sobor*) emphasised the need of further grammatical and orthographical reforms, and even a century later Jepifanij Slavineckij was invited over from Kijev to complete the work of Pachomij Logofet and Maksim the Greek. He was only one of many Ukrainian and White Russian scholars who came to Moscow in the course of the seventeenth century and helped not only to raise its standard of scholarship, but to create its early imaginative literature. It was in the later seventeenth century too that the Ukrainian and White Russian lands were drawn into the political orbit of Muscovy and the literary communication between north and south characteristic of Medieval Russia was renewed. The vehicle of intercourse was a 'neutral' form of Church Slavonic, from which local Ukrainian and White Russian elements had been expunged. It is characteristic of the ascendancy of Moscow in culture as well as in politics that such distinguished non-Russian preachers as Ioannikij Goljatovskij, Dmitrij Rostovskij, Simeon Polockij, Stefan Javorskij, and Feofan Prokopovič, should have made concessions to Russian by not only avoiding the characteristic features of their own languages, but giving preference to those of Russian even in their private correspondence. For the same reason also the Moscow edition (1648) of the 'normative' Church Slavonic grammar by the Ukrainian Meletij Smotrickij (Vil'na, 1619) contains morphological concessions to spoken Russian. But some alien influence was bound to be exerted on the character of Moscow Russian in view of the considerable number of immigrants from the other East Slavonic territories and from Central and Western Europe. The presence of the plosive ɣ in certain, mainly ecclesiastical words as pronounced by many Russians to this day (e.g. gen. Бо́га 'God'; Госпо́дь 'Lord'; masc. nom. sing. бога́тый 'rich') is probably a legacy of Ukrainian and White Russian influence rather than a feature of South Russian, which, incidentally, had, in the course of the seventeenth century, changed the vocalic basis of the Moscow dialect by substituting *akan'je* for the *okan'je* that had prevailed till then. This change, Vinokur thinks, was due to social upheavals in the Troubled Times (*smutnoje vremja*). A decree of Tsar Alexis (Aleksej Michajlovič) in the second half of the seventeenth century declares that *akan'je*, if it appears in spelling is not longer to be deemed 'dishonourable', and indeed the same tsar's private correspondence suggests that *akan'je* had by that time invaded the speech of royalty and presumably therefore of the ruling classes.

European influence on Russian is noticeable particularly in the many loan-words with which Russians familiarised themselves chiefly from translations of West European narratives and the mainly anonymous imitations of these (e.g. *The Story of the Russian Sailor Vasilij Kariotskij* and *The Story of the Russian Gentleman Aleksandr*). This literary vocabulary and the technical expressions that accompanied the introduction of new objects and ideas into Muscovy helped to leaven the administrative language and to render it more flexible and accommodating to literary expression. At the same time the spoken language penetrated into writing chiefly through reported dialogue and plain narrative (cf. Avvakum's *Autobiography*), and a third, 'intermediate', style, which was to become the literary κοινή, was gradually evolved out of these varied elements. With emancipation from ecclesiastical tutelage, to which the West European secular literature effectively contributed, the ecclesiastical style came to be regarded as a distinct written language, to which the name 'Slavonic' (*slavenskij jazyk*) was given, in contrast to the administrative language, which was regarded as 'Russian' (*rossijskij*). It was this new attitude that determined the reform of Russian spelling undertaken by Peter the Great at the end of the century by the institution of the simplified 'civil alphabet' (*graždanka*), which was later taken over for secular publications by all the other Orthodox Slavs. Yet in spite of this, Church Slavonic in its Russian development still remained the background of Russian grammatical study: Smotrickij's Church Slavonic manual, republished five times by 1723, was the standard work on Russian grammar till it was displaced by Lomonosov's greater authority in the second half of the eighteenth century. It naturally took time for the impact of West European secular literature to make itself widely felt, and it was only in the eighteenth century that Russian literature was released from the pressure of Byzantine and South Slavonic example and ideology and became a province of European Classicism.

3

Linguistically the period from the fifteenth to the seventeenth century inclusive saw the gradual emergence of Moscow Russian, a dialectal type which geography and history were to endow with both North and South Russian characteristics. In the fifteenth century the Moscow dialect appears to have been predominantly Northern in its phonological system, except that, then as now, it was not characterised by the confusion of $c/č$ peculiar to Novgorod Russian. Accordingly it shared the phonetic and grammatical features of the contemporary

Vladimir and Rostov-Suzdal' types of Russian, which to this day, as constituents of the Vladimir-Volga subdialect of North Russian, diverge in certain important particulars from the other four subdialects as a group. The changes in the system of Russian sounds in the Moscow period mainly affect the quality of unstressed vowels (*akan'je*), but they also include the restored pronunciation of *e* before hard consonants in the 'ecclesiastical style', the complete coincidence of e and ѣ, and the sporadic use of ɣ for g in a small number of words. In the domain of the morpheme, where phonology and grammar meet, we have the analogical substitution of *k/g/ch* for *c/z/s* in the feminine dative-locative singular (e.g. руцѣ, нозѣ > рукѣ, ногѣ; cf. nom. рукá 'hand', ногá 'leg'; foot') and in the masculine nominative-accusative plural (e.g. вóлци, бóзи, дýси > вóлки, бóги, дýхи 'wolves; gods; spirits'), i.e. the effacement of the 'second palatalisation' of velars, which had been caused by -*ĕ* and -*i* of diphthongal origin. Of the grammatical categories of Old Russian, the dual number and the vocative case, the aorist and the imperfect, became obsolete in this period, so much so that the two latter were frequently confused by copyists. These features were now associated with archaic and Church Slavonic speech. Other changes in the language, however, involved not loss, but gain: the animate-inanimate dichotomy in the noun, expressed in the formal identification of genitive and accusative, both singular and plural, was systematised in the sixteenth century after having been known as personal (masculine/non-masculine) gender to Old Russian; the collective-singulative antithesis was formally developed by pluralising the first term (e.g. брáтья as the plural form of брáтъ 'brother'); the short form of the adjective attained its modern vestigial condition; the comparative adjective became adverbialised and invariable; the system of numerals came to differ little from the modern; and the compound past tense, which had functioned for the aorist in non-ecclesiastical Old Russian, was generalised as a simple expression of past time by suppressing the auxiliary (e.g. 3rd sing. былъ 'was' for былъ есть).

Both the Church Slavonic and the Russian elements are present in force in the vocabulary of the ecclesiastical style and in such secular styles as have experienced its influence. This results in the use of doublets, the non-pleophonic tending to preponderate in these styles as opposed to the pleophonic, which characterise the administrative language and especially colloquial speech. It is significant that Prince I. M. Katyrev-Rostovskij, who deliberately chooses an ecclesiastical style for the narrative of his 'Chronicle Book' (*Letopisnaja kniga*, 1626),[1] has ten to twelve times as many non-pleophonic forms as pleophonic, preferring, as he does, градъ to го́родъ 'town', глава́ to голова́ 'head', even мразъ to моро́зъ 'frost'. Such non-Russian forms were felt even then as 'slavonicisms', and their use had been perpetuated in literature by the introduction of printing in the sixteenth century. Some of them (e.g. глава́) have survived to this day by semantic specialisation, others (e.g. мразъ) have become as obsolete as the dual or the aorist. Other additions to the Russian vocabulary were mainly West European culture-terms, which were borrowed in large numbers, especially under Peter the Great (e.g. табаке́рка 'snuff-box', бо́мба 'bomb', шпале́ры 'espalier'). The earliest had come during the long years of largely hostile contact with Poland (e.g. ры́нокъ 'market'<*rynek*; по́чта 'post' <*poczta*). Of the more specifically West European vocabulary, Dutch words led the way, mostly in the domain of seafaring and marine architecture (e.g. крейсеръ < *kruiser*, шки́перъ < *schipper*, га́вань < *haven*, гарпу́нъ < *harpoen*, вы́мпелъ < *wimpel*, рейдъ < *reede*, шлю́пка < *sloep*, шлю́зы < *sluis*). Some of these forms (e.g. шлю́пка), like loans from English in the same period (e.g. фальшки́ль 'false keel'), have alien phonetic features and probably entered Russian through a foreign, chiefly German, medium. German loans are older than either Dutch or English ones and go back to the thirteenth-century contacts between the Hansa and the north-western Russian states (e.g. шпи́льманъ < *Spielmann*; фо́готъ < *Vogt*). During the three centuries from the fifteenth to the seventeenth the following words, among many others, were admitted: бунтъ 'revolt', стулъ 'chair', шля́па 'hat', я́рманка (later я́рмарка) 'fair'.

---

[1] The authorship of this book, also known as *The Origins of the Reigning City of Moscow*, is disputed. S. F. Platanov ascribes it to Katyrev-Rostovskij.

In the eighteenth century German loans were to become particularly numerous, only to be ousted in a number of cases at the turn of the century by loans from French. Like the German loans, which represent the impact of European culture, the loans from Turkic languages, especially from Kazan′ Tartar, which represent the impact of the eastern steppe, begin in the Middle Ages. The Tartar domination of south-eastern Russia gave тамга́ 'tribute', улу́съ 'settlement', карау́лъ 'sentry', де́ньга 'coin', башма́къ 'shoe', and later contacts between Russian and Tartar (sixteenth and seventeenth centuries) added колпа́къ 'night-cap', каба́къ 'tavern', колча́нъ 'quiver', and бары́шъ 'profit'. Such common words as ло́шадь 'horse', хозя́инъ 'master', арка́нъ 'lariat', балага́нъ 'booth', бирю́къ 'wolf', сунду́къ 'trunk', and изю́мъ 'raisin(s)' (the last six, like all others of this type, now written without ъ) are also of Turkic origin, and some of them fall into the period under review.

CHAPTER IX

THE EIGHTEENTH CENTURY

I

The last few years of the seventeenth century and the first quarter of the eighteenth coincide with the reign of Peter the Great, which marks a turning-point in the Russian language as it does in Russian history. The territorial aggrandisement of Muscovy was, as we have learnt, achieved mainly at the end of the fifteenth and in the course of the sixteenth century. The Gulf of Finland, the White Sea, and the Caspian had all been reached, and some of the West Russian territories recovered from Poland-Lithuania. By the seventeenth century the Sea of Okhotsk and the Pacific Ocean were known, and part of Siberia had been annexed. In the early eighteenth century Peter the Great acquired the Baltic Provinces and built St Petersburg on the Neva marshes as his new capital. The choice of this site was dictated by a consistent policy of *rapprochement* with the West. It was the 'window on to Europe' and became in the course of the eighteenth century a centre of cosmopolitan learning and fashion. By the end of the century it was the capital of a considerably enlarged empire, which included the Russian share of the last partition of Poland, the Black Sea coast, and the northern fringe of Central Asia. The construction of this empire had engaged the energies of a succession of sovereigns, who followed the 'directives' of geography and Peter's aggressive example. The royal power remained absolute and was reinforced by a civil service founded on Peter's 'table of ranks'. The first eight of these were almost the monopoly of the landed gentry (*dvorjanstvo*), which had gradually superseded the old nobility (boyars) as the most influential social group. The slow growth of industry, however, had created a middle class by the middle of the eighteenth century. But the sources of power were still agrarian, flowing, as they did, from the ownership of land and serfs, and this power, in the guise of an imperial autocracy, shaken to some extent by the French Revolution and its repercussions, was inherited by the nineteenth. Within the overgrown limits of the linguistically heterogeneous Russian empire of the eighteenth century the language of the numerically largest nationality remained paramount. At the beginning of the century, however, it had reached a crisis, which had been brought on by the rapid tempo of political development. For this Peter the Great was in part personally responsible, and it was left to his successors, the leaders of Russian science and literature, from Lomonosov to Karamzin, to solve in a manner acceptable to succeeding generations.

2

Although Peter the Great had subordinated Church to State and encouraged secular education, Russian literacy continued to be based on knowledge of Church Slavonic grammar, which had come to Moscow as a system in Smotrickij's seventeenth-century work and was taught in all theological seminaries, whose alumni still constituted the majority of the cultured *élite*. In the middle of the century even Russian secular scholarship in the illustrious person of M. V. Lomonosov (1711–65) commended it as the key to the understanding of Russian grammatical usage. Lomonosov's *Dissertation on the Utility of Church Books to the Russian Language* (1748), which reproduces ideas familiar to Quintilian and Aulus Gellius, contains, among other things, a theory of three literary styles (*štili*)—the high, the middle (intermediate), and the low—defined in terms of the Russian vocabulary. To Lomonosov this vocabulary consists of three categories of words, both Church Slavonic and Russian, viz. (i) words common to both languages (e.g. Богъ 'God', рука́ 'hand', сла́ва 'glory', ны́не 'now', почита́ю 'I respect'); (ii) Church Slavonic words little used in colloquial Russian, but understandable to the educated (e.g. отверза́ю 'I open'; masc. nom. sing. госпо́день 'Dominical', насажде́нный 'planted'; взыва́ю 'I invoke'); and (iii) Russian words unknown to Church Slavonic (e.g. говорю́ 'I speak', руче́й 'brook', кото́рый 'which', лишь 'only'). The last category also includes the 'contemptible' (vulgar) words that are fit only for use in 'low comedy'. By combining words of the listed categories in different ways the writer is able to construct one or other of the three styles. The high style combines words of the first two categories and should be used for 'heroic verse, odes, and discourses in prose on important matters'. The middle style, which is adapted for use in 'theatrical composition, verse epistles, satires, eclogues, elegies, and historical and scientific works', draws largely on the first category of words, but admits discretely selected words from the other two. The low style is made up of words of the third category and, like the middle style, can take from the other two vocabularies according to the exigencies of the theme. It is particularly suitable for 'comedies, epigrams, songs, familiar correspondence, and accounts of ordinary matters'. Lomonosov was aware of the danger that lay in the abuse of the extreme categories. His own good taste enabled him to steer clear of it and, as his pupil N. N. Popovskij believed, 'to introduce into Russia a pure style in prose and verse'. In his *Russian Grammar* (1755),[1] which was to become a classical reference-book to several generations of Russians till displaced by more modern compilations in the first half of the nineteenth century, Lomonosov tried to apply to his mother tongue the terminology and rules culled from Smotrickij. His grammar, however, is not merely a modernisation of his predecessor's, but contains individual elements, especially his treatment of the verb in terms of tense rather than aspect. It represents a selection and synthesis of Church Slavonic and Russian grammatical data (e.g. the Russian verbal system, the Church Slavonic participles, *akan'je*, morphological spelling, and adherence to Latin and German prototypes in syntax).

Lomonosov, like Puškin after him, arrived at a personal and eclectic solution of the problem of style, which did not satisfy some of his contemporaries. Of these, the russianised Rumanian prince, Antioch Cantemir (1708–44), cultivated verse and followed Boileau's example in his satires, whose metrical principle is syllabic, as in French or Polish and in the seventeenth-

---

[1] See Pt III, no. 18.

century attempts to write Russian verse (see Simeon Polockij's *The Maiden*, Pt III, no. 17). In contrast to Cantemir, Lomonosov had followed Günther and introduced the principle of tonic (accentual) versification, which was more in accord with the phonetic character of Russian. It received sublime interpretation in his odes and 'meditations' and represents the earliest Russian verse with a modern rhythm. Lomonosov's example influenced his progressive, but pedantic opponent, V. K. Tred'jakovskij (1703–69), whose French training had induced him at first to exploit the syllabic principle. In his prose too Tred'jakovskij followed French models by translating novels of Paul Tallement and Fénelon into a style that may be defined, with Lomonosov, as 'middle'. Though he used Church Slavonic words, he had no feeling for them and was generally hostile to the ecclesiastical language, which he described as 'obscure' and 'hard on the ear'. Tred'jakovskij's pedantry and eccentricity appear in his critical prose, which includes a disquisition on metre and elaborates a phonetic system of spelling. Opposition to Lomonosov came also from A. P. Sumarokov (1718–77), whose facile and prolific pen tried all *genres*, and whose activity falls partly into the reign of Catherine II. By this time French influence had become widespread in language as well as in general culture and had reached a point bordering on mania.[1] A French manner of writing characterises the work of even those who were consciously opposed to it: thus D. I. Fonvizin (1745–92) jeers at contemporary gallicisms in his comedy *The Brigadier* (1769) and himself makes use of them (e.g. дéлать дóлжность '*faire son devoir*', взять отстáвку '*prendre congé*', рáдуюсь сдéлать вáше знакóмство '*je suis heureux de faire votre connaissance*'). Others, however, went much further than this and displayed a veritable frenzy for French words and turns of phrase, which made their speech and writing a Russo-French jargon. Sumarokov gives an example of this in the curious sentence: ,я в дистрáкции и дезеспéре, амáнта моя сдéлала мне инфиделитé, а я ку сюр прóтив ривáля своегó бýду реванжúроваться' ('I am distraught and in despair. My beloved has been unfaithful to me,

[1] See E. Haumant, *La culture française en Russie (1700–1900)*; Paris, 1910.

and I will certainly be avenged on my rival'). But these represent an extreme development, like the homilies and addresses of eighteenth-century churchmen from Feofan Prokopovič, who pronounced the funeral oration on Peter the Great, to the archimandrite Kiril Florinskij, who in 1741 greeted the anniversary of the birth of the Empress Elizabeth. The course of development of literary Russian lay between such extremes and is best exemplified in Catherine's Russia by the language of the periodical press (e.g. *Vsjakaja Vsjačina*, 'This, That, and the Other'), to which Catherine herself contributed. This middle style reappears too in contemporary translations (e.g. V. Levšin's of Marmontel's *Merveilles de la nature*, 1788) and in the memoirs of Princess N. B. Dolgorukaja, and shows the erudite and the colloquial elements of the language in a state of almost perfect equilibrium.

The end of the eighteenth and the beginning of the nineteenth century saw the solution of the problem of a Russian literary style, which the Russian Classicists had posed and could not solve. But Classicism was by no means a hidebound movement. How far Russian poetical style had advanced may be seen by comparing the achievements of G. R. Deržavin (1743–1816) with those of Lomonosov, and the progress of Russian prose may be measured by comparing Karamzin's with Lomonosov's. By Karamzin's time Sentimentalism had reached Russia—indeed he himself was its chief exponent in *Letters of a Russian Traveller* (1797) and in lachrymose short stories (e.g. *Poor Liza*, 1792) modelled on Sterne. The more individualistic Romanticism too was becoming more widely known. These two literary fashions used and encouraged the use of the middle style, and it was this that Karamzin's practice brought to a personal perfection. By reducing the number of Church Slavonic terms, as Deržavin had done in his less formal verse and the publicist N.I. Novikov in prose, and by following Catherine's practice of avoiding foreign loans, of which there are not a few in the *Letters*, Karamzin was able to focus attention on the purely Russian element and to evolve a mode of literary expression which was close enough to everyday educated speech not to seem stilted and bookish. This he was able to do all the more easily with the aid of his syntactic reforms. Instead of cultivating a periodic Latin-German style of the Lomonosov pattern, he followed French literary example and imitated the short sentences and word order of colloquial Russian. Puškin, who was to use a similar syntax later, said of Karamzin that he had liberated Russian from a foreign yoke and 'converted it into a living spring of national speech'. This statement, however, may be misleading, as it can incline us to imagine that Karamzin's middle style drew exclusively on a Russian vocabulary. By the end of the eighteenth century the middle style, whose hesitant beginnings we have observed as far back as the origins of Russian authorship, and especially in the seventeenth century with its copious versions of Western romances of chivalry, had absorbed a considerable number of foreign words as well as something of the Church Slavonic idiom, and these ingredients are not absent in Karamzin's writings. But neither they nor even the gallicisms he permitted himself are too obvious in a style which possesses a delicacy and lightness, a personal organising rhythm, and a vocabulary that looks largely Russian, because of its skilful and 'convincing' loan-translations in the 'creative' manner of Lomonosov (e.g. влияние 'influence', человечный 'humane', промышленность 'industry', совершенствовать 'to perfect'). Karamzin helped substantially to mould the prose of Russian Romanticism as well as its verse. His own poetry drew its themes and metrical forms from German, as Žukovskij's was to do later.

We have dwelt on Karamzin and shall have more to say about him in the next chapter because of the capital importance of his contribution to the history of Russian literary style. But Karamzin represents merely the initial phase in the evolution of the middle style in the eighteenth century. Awareness of its existence and possibilities must be ascribed, in the first instance, to Lomonosov, who clearly distinguished between the Slavonic and the vernacular element in Russian and regarded literary Russian as an amalgam of these. In contrast to him, his rival Tred'jakovskij essayed to reproduce in his mother tongue what he found in French, but failed, because in his time there was no generally accepted norm of educated Russian on which to base a literary style. The literary style had to create the norm, and this became possible only towards the end of the century with the growth of a native literary tradition and the impact of foreign literary fashions. By the end of the eighteenth century the differentiation between the Slavonic and Russian elements on the one hand and their fusion in the middle style on the other may be considered to have been accomplished. Yet the champions of the high style and of Church Slavonic did not give ground without a last desperate struggle. This took place in the early years of the nineteenth century, and Karamzin was actually involved in it.

3

Phonetically and morphologically Russian had assumed, by the beginning of the eighteenth century, a form little different from what it is at present, so that the evolution of the language, which we have to trace in the course of the next two and a half centuries, consists mainly of changes in syntax and especially in vocabulary. Peter the Great's private letters reflect the condition of a form of the written language at this time. They show how rapidly the language was absorbing, if not completely digesting, a European vocabulary, and to what extent the living speech had found its way into writing. The European loan-words are a measure and mirror of Russian policy, which still gravitated towards Western Europe, as it was beginning to do at the end of the sixteenth century. In this policy a notable part was played by Peter himself, who had personal experience of several West European countries and was ardently intent on adapting his own, if necessary by main force, to Western standards of society and culture. Like his predecessor Ivan IV, he encouraged the settlement of Europeans in Russia, and the Foreign Quarter (*Nemeckaja sloboda*) of Moscow flourished under his patronage, which took the form of frequent visits there. This intercourse with Europeans at home and the contacts made by Russians sent out to study in Western Europe materially contributed to the expansion of intellectual horizons and the enrichment of the native vocabulary with new terms and expressions. A still more prolific source of these were the translations of technical treatises and imaginative literature. Word statistics show that by the time of Peter's death (1725) some 3000 foreign loan-words had become part and parcel of the new Russian. A quarter of these belong to the administrative terminology (e.g. арестова́ть 'to arrest', бухга́лтер 'book-keeper', губерна́тор 'governor', меда́ль 'medal', на́ция 'nation', ра́туша 'town hall') and were taken over from German either directly or, as the verbal suffix *-ova-* shows, through Polish. Another quarter belongs to seafaring and derives from Dutch, English, French, and Italian as well as German (e.g. э́ллинг 'stocks', ли́мберс 'limbers', аборда́ж 'boarding', бриганти́на 'brigantine'). We have already observed the influx of these terms in the second half of the seventeenth century. The remaining fifty per cent of European loan-words consist of military and scientific terms which were borrowed from German and French. The German terms have sometimes a Polish appearance (e.g. вербова́ть 'to recruit', штурмова́ть 'to storm'), and the French a German one (e.g. паке́т 'packet', президе́нт 'president', генералите́т 'general staff'). But in a number of cases the loans were made direct from the source (e.g. F. барье́р 'barrier'; It. аба́ка 'abacus'). The predominance of German appears not only in the forms of 'international' words, but in the large number of words of purely German origin (e.g. ло́зунг 'slogan', шла́фрок 'dressing gown', штибле́ты 'boots'). German was to yield in the course of the century to French as a source of borrowing, in spite of the fact that Peter's most talented successor, Catherine II, was a German princess. This was due to the ascendancy of France in European culture and to the dictates of Classicism, which was largely a French creation. Even with the emergence of English Sentimentalism and German Romanticism at the close of the eighteenth century, and notwithstanding the negative impact of the French Revolution and the Napoleonic wars, which penetrated to the heart of Russia and burnt Moscow, French influence remained the predominant foreign influence, and French syntax helped to modify Russian syntax.

But before all this took place a considerable change in the use of literary Russian had had to be accomplished. As we have seen, Peter the Great was largely instrumental in producing a crisis in the development of his mother tongue by encouraging an unchecked intake of foreign words. These naturally appeared primarily in the administrative and diplomatic language, as well as in translations of technical treatises, and helped to differentiate the two styles—official and literary—from the ecclesiastical, which held doggedly aloof from linguistic innovations and even insisted on eliminating from Church Slavonic orthography the Ukrainian element introduced by influential southern scholars after the annexation of the Ukraine in 1654. The Ukrainians themselves, we already know, sought to adapt their kind of Church Slavonic to Russian usage, and their efforts were so successful that a uniform Russian type was eventually evolved. The centralising tendency present here was echoed in Peter's injunction to the Academy of Sciences in 1724 to cultivate only 'one kind of language and spelling' within its precincts. Peter was also responsible for drawing the line between 'Slavonic' and Russian elements in the secular literary language. In 1715, for instance, he ordered Konon Zotov to procure books on navigation and 'to translate them into our style of Slavonic'. The tsar seems to have meant a Church Slavonic modified by the usage of the administrative language. A sidelight on this may be obtained from an expression used by Count I. A. Musin-Puškin in passing orders from the emperor to the lexicographer F. Polikarpov, who had an antiquarian's passion for Church Slavonic. Polikarpov was to revise his version of Varenius's geography as well as to compile a Latin-Slavonic lexicon 'not in high terms, but in simple Russian by using the vocabulary of the Foreign, or so-called Ambassadors', Office (*Posol'skij prikaz*)'. The spelling reform, involving the introduction of the *graždanka*, pursued the same policy of differentiation. By the end of Peter's reign the written language had not, indeed, ceased to illustrate the traditional extremes of Church Slavonic and official Russian, but the still hesitant middle style was slowly assuming definite shape as a compromise between the two and exhibiting a character of its own, derived from a mingling of West European vocabulary and literary practice with the idiosyncrasies of colloquial speech. This extraordinary conglomerate had acquired a certain pliancy, which emerges quite clearly from a comparison of Russian translations with their European originals and more particularly from a perusal of the original Russian 'romances' (e.g. *The Story of the Russian Gentleman Aleksandr*) and the first Russian newspapers (e.g. *Russkije Vedomosti*, 'Russian News', 1703, and *Peterburgskije Vedomosti*, 'St Petersburg News', 1711), where we discover both a certain conversational ease and a European flavour.

CHAPTER X

THE NINETEENTH CENTURY AND AFTER

I

The eighteenth century had been for Russia an age of victory abroad, celebrated in the odes of Lomonosov and Cheraskov, and of the rumblings of domestic discontent, expressed actively in the Pugačov revolt under Catherine II and in the career and writings of A. N. Radiščev (1749–1802), which, in some sort, are a reverberation of the French Revolution in Russia. In the nineteenth century and the early twentieth Imperial Russia nearly reached the limits of its external conquests, which took her to the present-day frontiers of Turkey, Persia, and Afghanistan, and enabled her at a number of points to violate Chinese sovereignty. All this increased the non-Russian elements in the empire, though it did not affect the leading position of Russian, which naturally became the official *lingua franca* of the annexed areas and steadily encroached on the regional languages in the course of the century as the result of a deliberate policy of russification supported by school and Church.

But the nineteenth-century victories were marred by defeats. The beginning of the century witnessed the Napoleonic invasion, the middle the Crimean reverse, and the beginning of the twentieth century abject defeat at Japanese hands. In each case there was revolt at home, which, though suppressed by force, led to social and political concessions and contributed to the progressive decay of state authority till it finally collapsed in the turmoil of the First World War. With the growth of industrialism and international trade, wealth and influence passed from the landowners to the industrialists and merchants, and a vigorous new class of heterogeneous origin was interposed between aristocracy and peasantry. The class distinctions, however, were not rigid, and in the intellectual and literary fields, where the cultivation of language was paramount, they ceased to be discernible as the century wore on. The eighteenth century had produced a largely, but not exclusively aristocratic literature, as it had in Western Europe. The nineteenth-century literature on the other hand was created jointly by the aristocracy and the commonalty (*raznočincy*), and the latter predominated in the early twentieth and became the almost exclusive purveyors of literature after the 1917 Revolution.

2

The phonetically and grammatically modern type of Russian must be sought in the early part of the eighteenth century. Since then the development of the language has been not so much phonetic and morphological as lexical and syntactic. The history of Russian in the eighteenth century is largely a history of the absorption of a West European vocabulary, the gradual ascendancy of the middle style in prose, and the creation of a standard syllabo-tonic system of versification. The work of the reformers from Lomonosov to Karamzin, however, was not to pass unchallenged, and it was even modified to some extent by the challenge. Thus Tred'jakovskij's propaganda for a literary style modelled on French example helped Lomonosov's middle style to final victory over the high style, of which Lomonosov was such an adept, and Karamzin's practice was challenged in the early years of the nineteenth century by champions of the Church Slavonic tradition and the high style, and yielded to their strictures by a more determined pursuit of a Russian free from the distorting pressure of foreign influence.

The conflict between the Old and the New Styles at the onset of the nineteenth century resolved itself essentially into one between the adherents of Admiral A. S. Šiškov and those of Karamzin. Šiškov had viewed Karamzin's stylistic reforms with disquiet and disapproval, and in 1803 he published his *Dissertation on the Old and the New Style in Russian*, which appeared in a second edition in 1818 and left some impression on his more thoughtful contemporaries. He wished not only to reinstate Lomonosov's three styles, but to substitute unadulterated Church Slavonic for the high style, or slavonicised Russian. Although it was pointed

159

out to Šiškov that the two languages were distinct, he obstinately refused to regard Church Slavonic as anything but a stylistic variant of Russian and complained that even the clergy were beginning to neglect it. It is obvious that this attitude had no foundation in reality. Nor had some of his criticisms of the New Style any relevance, for not a few of the many words he pilloried have since become an essential part of the cultured vocabulary (e.g. эпóха 'epoch', развúтие 'development', трóгательный 'touching', сосредотóчить 'to concentrate'). A form like развúтие, for which Karamzin was responsible, is constructed on the Church Slavonic, and not on the Russian, model with the neuter morpheme -ие (-*ije*) and shows in its manner of formation an awareness of the Church Slavonic element in the literary language. It was the awareness of this element as of the other two, viz. the colloquial and the West European, that Karamzin passed on to later writers. These included a group of poets— I. I. Dmitrijev, Batjuškov, Žukovskij, Prince P. A. Vjazemskij, Baratynskij, and especially Puškin, as well as prose authors like Zagoskin and Bestužev-Marlinskij. Even self-confessed adherents of Šiškov's, like Küchelbecker, followed Karamzin, who had examples of style to offer, rather than Šiškov, who offered mainly criticism.

The eclectic art of Puškin, who drew extensively on both predecessors and contemporaries and found the literary style, in verse and in prose alike, already elaborated at the outset of his career and requiring only the touch of a master, represents an easily discernible peak in the history of Russian literature. It was his mastery of direct and elegant expression and the variety of his talents as author that led to his elevation in the minds of later generations of his compatriots to the pedestal of a literary genius. Puškin summarised in his work the results of a century of literary development and at the same time pointed out the way along which this development was to proceed. His art and its significance were, we might say, Janus-headed. It is an error to assert, as is often done, that Russian culminated in him. This is merely an expression of the adulation mingled with national sentiment that has been his posthumous heritage.

Puškin's language, like Karamzin's, represents a new and peculiar synthesis of existing elements. The difference between the two writers lies not only in an inevitable difference of literary talent, but between an earlier and a later point of view. The latter obviously gives a clearer perspective and enables the 'reformer' to profit by his predecessor's shortcomings. This Puškin did by striking a balance between the literary and the colloquial idiom, the latter suggested partly by Krylov's and Dmitrijev's fables in verse, and by condensing the three lexical ingredients of the language—Church Slavonic, West European, and vernacular— into a more effective unity than Karamzin's.[1] Puškin began his literary career as 'the Frenchman', as an admirer and imitator of French Classical models, and attained by degrees to an enlightened nationalism not unlike his predecessor's. His mature conception of literary Russian was in terms of history as understood by the philosophical Romanticism of the 1820's and 1830's. A discreet and harmonious synthesis of the three ingredients into which his historical approach analysed the Russian vocabulary, was the substance of the literary manner, which, within the limits imposed by the lucidity and precision of eighteenth-century French syntax, he applied to a diversity of *genres*. But this manner was not a mere paper style in Puškin's conception: it was to draw sustenance from the cultured speech of an intellectual *élite* which was still mainly aristocratic, as it had been in the eighteenth century.

Puškin's brilliant example was followed in both verse and prose by Lermontov, and the Ukrainian Gogol''s extremely original manner revealed the startling possibilities of the literary Russian that had taken shape in the 1830's. Puškin and Gogol' represent extremes of prose style—the Classical and the baroque —evolving in the atmosphere of an increasingly realistic ideology associated with, and in part deriving from, the influx of the commonalty, or democratic elements, into journalism and literature. Lermontov's prose presents a spontaneous and happy 'mean' between the two, and he and Puškin were closely followed by such style-conscious realists of the second half of

[1] В. В. Виноградов, *Язык Пушкина* (Москва-Ленинград, 1935).

the century as Turgenev and Lev Tolstoj. Lermontov and Gogol'
were also influences in the rather untidy Russian of the commoner
Belinskij, from whom modern Russian criticism, both social and
literary, takes its militant origin. Gogol''s influence alone may
be traced in Dostojevskij and in the twentieth-century developments of extreme individualism in Russian prose style (e.g.
Andrej Belyj's). But on the whole the prevailing literary manner
of the second half of the nineteenth century—the great age
of Russian prose, which now overshadowed Russian verse—
exhibited a solid and 'democratic' uniformity reflecting the
predominance of realism in Russian criticism. The difference
between literary and non-literary composition, as may be seen,
for example,. by comparing Herzen's publicistic works with his
imaginative prose, was not so acute as it had been in the Romantic
age and in the eighteenth century, for literature had soon adapted
itself to the requirements of social criticism, and this was rooted
in material reality.

The language of the publicist, for instance Belinskij's, had been
affected since the period from the 1820's to the 1840's by extensive
developments in the vocabulary of philosophy and the sciences.
It had enriched itself with a formidable array of abstract words
(e.g. проявление 'manifestation', мировоззрение 'conception
of reality', действительность 'reality', целесообразный 'expedient'), and this vocabulary was considerably extended in
the second half of the century (e.g. крепостничество 'serfdom',
среда 'milieu', впечатлительный 'impressionable'). In the
development of publicistic styles an important part was played
by Dobroljubov, Černyševskij, and Saltykov-Ščedrin, the last
showing himself to be particularly good at inventing 'winged
words' (e.g. административный восторг 'administrative rap-
ture', головотяпы благоглупости 'blessed dolts'). The multi-
plication of loan-translations from West European languages was
so considerable that the Church Slavonic element in Russian was
noticeably diminished. In the literary style the influence of
vernacular turns of speech made itself increasingly felt, and the
bulk of these was assembled in V. I. Dahl's *Explanatory Dictionary
of Current Great Russian* (1868). It was the widespread study of

social habits (*byt*) that led to the reinforcement of the vernacular in literature, and the way for this had been paved by the individualistic art of Gogol'. We see it figuring largely in Saltykov-Ščedrin, A. N. Ostrovskij, Lev Tolstoj, and Leskov, and in the writings of the young Maksim Gor'kij. As for the spoken idiom and vocabulary of the *intelligentsia*, they are given due prominence in Čechov's plays, and we observe that they are almost identical in essentials with the language of Tolstoj's gentry.

3

The Church Slavonic tradition, maintained by the alumni of theological seminaries, still commanded respect in the nineteenth century, as it had in the later eighteenth, when the archpriest Pjotr Aleksejev published his *Ecclesiastical Dictionary, or Elucidation of Ancient Slavonic Locutions* (1794). Interest in language at this period led Russian scholarship, primed by West European example, to focus attention not only on Russian, but on the cognate Church Slavonic, with which its ties had been so close over the centuries. For the first time the two languages were studied in a spirit of conscious inquiry and their earliest forms revealed free from the accumulated errors of later years. The researches of A. Ch. Vostokov (Osteneck), who incidentally hit on an acceptable interpretation of the *jusy* (Ѫ, Ѧ) and *jery* (ь, ъ), inaugurated a long period of fruitful grammatical study, which scarcely suffered interruption even in the revolutionary years (1917–21). It was Vostokov's *Russian Grammar* that in 1831 replaced Lomonosov's (1755) and came to serve as a prototype for subsequent grammars, which have followed one another at frequent intervals down to the present time. In the century and nearly two decades under consideration we may distinguish two periods of grammatical research in Russia, with the turning-point in the years 1870–80, when the Neogrammarian movement reached the apex of its influence. From 1800 to 1870 we have a comprehensive and documented study of every facet of Russian—structure, vocabulary, dialects, history—which after 1870 came to be investigated separately as special subjects. The decade

1870–80 was marked by an intense curiosity in the details of the language and by the emergence of a group of linguists, who belonged to two distinct camps according to the general linguistic principles, either Formalist or Psychological, which they professed. The Formalist school of F. F. Fortunatov (Moscow) approached language from the outside, i.e. from its forms; the Psychological School of Jan Baudouin de Courtenay (Kazan'-St Petersburg) approached it from the inside, i.e. from the notions, or concepts, expressed by the forms. Neither school was specifically interested in Russian, and it remained for others to apply these modes of approach to the language. The outstanding names here are those of A. A. Potebnja (Char'kov), A. I. Sobolevskij (St Petersburg), and A. A. Šachmatov (Moscow), a pupil of Fortunatov's. The Ukrainian Potebnja, whose ideas were moulded by Humboldt's and Steinthal's, was probably the most original thinker of them all. Sobolevskij's formalism had a strong historical bias. And Šachmatov, who in some ways resembled Sweet, combined theoretical with practical interest and was primarily an historian of language. These three grammarians and their contemporaries, viz. D. N. Ovsjaniko-Kulikovskij and A. M. Peškovskij, who were both interested in syntax, and V. A. Bogorodickij and L. V. Ščerba, whose main interests were phonetic, raised the study of Russian to a European level and laid foundations on which it has continued to build since the Revolution. The importance of Potebnja's researches resides in their linguistic philosophy, that of Sobolevskij's and Šachmatov's in their 'historicity'. None of these scholars wrote a systematic descriptive grammar of the Russian literary language, though parts of such a grammar and two volumes on aspects of Russian syntax by Šachmatov appeared after his death (1920).

Normative grammars, summarising the contemporary state of Literary Russian and reflecting the nature of contemporary grammatical research, were published in both the first half of the nineteenth century (e.g. Vostokov's, N. I. Greč's, and F. I. Buslajev's) and in the second half (e.g. K. S. Aksakov's), and these as well as others like them served as a framework and foundation for compilers of school grammars at various levels. Examination of such works shows how little Russian has changed in structure since Puškin's time. The main differences appear inevitably to be phonetic and lexical. Puškin's rhymes, for instance, often show that he used *e* for *jo* (e.g. instr. sing. алтарéм < алтáрь 'altar', рев 'roar', полéт 'flight'), and that his stressing of certain loans as well as native words was different from what it is to-day (e.g. музы́ка for му́зыка 'music', кружи́т for кру́жит 'turns'). Inevitably the most striking divergences occur in his vocabulary, which contains not only words reflecting the pattern of contemporary culture, but words derived from his eighteenth-century predecessors. It is this vocabulary, so different from that of to-day, and the ideas and fashions it stands for, which reveal most clearly the social shifts that have taken place in Russia in the course of four generations of living.

CHAPTER XI

THE POST-REVOLUTIONARY PERIOD

I

The marked difference between modern Russia and Puškin's referred to above was emphasised by the radical changes which came in the wake of the Revolution of 1917. The First World War, which had made it possible, had been a defeat for Russia, and the defeat was partly due to the Revolution. There were German invasion and Allied intervention, there was complete social unheaval, followed by enormous loss of life through civil war, and when Russia ultimately emerged as the U.S.S.R. from her political and social catastrophe she was the poorer by a zone of territory on both the western and the eastern fringes of her empire. The territorial losses were relatively small, but they involved a reduction in the total number of diverse languages spoken in the U.S.S.R. Loss of these strengthened the position of the *lingua franca* at home, especially as the seceding languages included Baltic German and Polish, both of which had served as intermediaries between Russian and the West in the past. In one respect, however, it seemed to Western observers, for instance to A. Meillet,[1] that Russian had suffered eclipse. A wise line in the policy of the new government towards the non-Russian nationalities had been the granting and encouragement of regional autonomy in speech. This was expressed not only by the establishment of autonomous republics, provinces, and areas, but by the use of local languages as vehicles of instruction in schools, at least at the elementary level. In some of the constituent republics, notably in the federal ones (e.g. Ukrainian, White Russian, Armenian, and Georgian), the languages are now studied at higher levels and used even for administrative purposes. This linguistic decentralisation was inevitable in the early and more liberal days of the Revolution, serving, as it

[1] *Les langues dans l'Europe nouvelle*[1] (Paris, 1918).

did, to win the sympathies of the subject peoples for the central government. But we can hardly forget that Russian remained the auxiliary language taught in all schools. Moreover, by far the largest of the constituent republics of the U.S.S.R. was, significantly enough, the Russian Federal Republic, which, though parcelled into various autonomous, ethnographically delimited areas, possessed an immense Russian-speaking majority and controlled both the modern capitals with their administrative departments and multiplicity of educational and cultural establishments, including the Academy of Sciences and most of the universities. This naturally left Russian with the position it had held before the Revolution, viz. as the *lingua franca* of a vast and linguistically heterogeneous geographical area. Meillet's fear that the creation of a diversity of literary languages —some of these, incidentally, were not newly created, but, like Armenian and Georgian, had literary traditions even older than Russian—would diminish the prestige of the language as an international medium of intercourse was entirely unfounded[1] and, moreover, the unhampered cultivation of the non-Russian languages of the U.S.S.R. has provided an enrichment to general culture and a valuable asset to Soviet linguistics.

2

Some of the leading writers of the pre-Revolutionary period survived to influence the literature that followed the Revolution. Among their names that of Maksim Gor'kij (A. M. Peškov, 1868–1936) looms largest. Abandoning the romantic realism of his early stories, he became a publicist, a literary legislator, and the propagandist of Socialist Realism, which since the 1930's has been the Soviet literary creed, though both verse and prose still give modest scope to personal expression. There is a striking contrast between the variety and colour of the literature produced in the first decade after the Revolution and the relative uniformity and monotony of the literature written since about 1930. That first decade was still aware of the literary brilliance of the early

[1] *Op. cit.* See also my *Languages of the U.S.S.R.* (Cambridge, 1951).

nineteenth century and even open to its irradiation, for it had not yet been regimented by a criticism subservient to political directives. Its connection with the exiled Russian literature which was cultivated at various European centres (e.g. Paris and Berlin) had not been completely broken off, and we find several prominent authors (e.g. A. Belyj and A. Tolstoj) returning home after a more or less protracted sojourn abroad. It was this earlier period of Soviet literature that witnessed notable contributions to poetry and the pursuit of unorthodox metrical experiments, which go back to pre-Revolutionary Symbolism and especially to Futurism, and represent perhaps the most considerable deviation from the ordered lucidity of the Puškin tradition. Nevertheless, even in this period there are already signs of uniformity, notably in the choice and treatment of the Civil War theme. But with the approach of the 1930's, heralded by the inauguration of the first Five Year plan (1928) and especially by the formation of a writers' union (1932), with its own press (*Sovetskij Pisatel'*, 'The Soviet Author'), Socialist Realism becomes the leading principle in Russian literary doctrine and practice and remains in force to this day, in spite of the disastrous interlude of the Second World War, which brought patriotic fervour and human personality to the fore in the years of greatest suffering.

Compared with the literary styles characteristic of the pre-Revolutionary period and its revolutionary aftermath, the styles prevalent to-day show considerable similarity. The language too in both its imaginative and its publicistic aspect is substantially the same, and its cultivation illustrates a predilection for the same weaknesses. Lenin, who was distinctly better as orator than as writer, complained, like Fonvizin a century earlier, of the proclivity of some of his contemporaries for a foreign terminology (*inostranščina*) and yet made lavish use of it himself, seeking cover in his schoolmasterly habit of elucidation, which is more suited to spoken than to written languages (e.g. организа́- ция, т.е. объедине́ние, сою́з, мирово́го крестья́нства колосса́- льна, т.е. огро́мна, необъя́тна 'the organisation, i.e. unification, union, of the world's peasantry is colossal, i.e. enormous, unbounded'). The jargon of the Russian pamphleteer and journalist is still permeated with latinity, still prefers the 'international' to the simpler and more comprehensive vernacular word. Its vocabulary has also quite naturally found its way into the literary language where this deals with the fashionable social and 'Socialist' themes. Away from these, its simplicity is occasionally vitiated by an effervescent, immature desire to be clever and 'different', which generally assumes the form of exploiting provincialisms, vulgarisms, and idiosyncrasies of expression. The impact of the subtle juggleries of Andrej Belyj, whose art is beyond imitation, Remizov, Zamjatin, Pasternak, and Tichonov has not been completely outlived, in spite of the wise admonitions of Gor'kij, who exercised his considerable influence as an author to maintain the purity and clarity of the mother tongue.

The official language of Soviet Russia, for all its vagaries, is still the lineal descendant of the language of the nineteenth century—of Turgenev and Lev Tolstoj, whom Lenin professed to admire, if not of Puškin. And this tie has not been weakened by the change in spelling, which was imposed by authority on contemporary practice in 1917. The change meant, as we know, the initial removal of only five letters (viz. i, ъ, ѣ, θ, v) and the subsequent restoration of one of them (ъ). The introduction of a Latin-style alphabet would have given the language another 'face', as it did to the many Soviet languages which adopted it from 1922 onwards, but the mask would not, naturally, have affected the structure. And indeed we can well imagine that 'latinisation', which Lenin approved for other languages, would ultimately have yielded, as it has in those languages, to the habit and pressure of the traditional Cyrillic.

3

The changes brought about in Russian by the Revolution have been far-reaching, but they have not materially affected the character of the written language, which preserves the form it had assumed at the end of the nineteenth century and displays the same relatively small differences between the publicistic and the purely literary style. For the more fundamental changes we must turn to the phonetics and vocabulary of the spoken language. The elimination of a substantial part of the middle class and of the gentry and the influx of a motley variety of dialect-speakers into the two capitals, as well as the growth of literacy have all led to the decline of the Moscow-style 'standard' Russian and the ascendancy of a conservative spelling pronunciation more in harmony with that of Leningrad. The characteristics of the Moscow style of pronunciation still linger on the Russian stage and among the older generation of teachers in schools and at universities (e.g. the pronunciation of щ as ʃʃ, жж as ʒʒ; a palatalised r̩ in masc. nom. sing. пе́рвый 'first', верх 'top', четве́рг 'Thursday'; ʃn for чн in such common words as коне́чно 'of course', скучно 'boring', masc. nom. sing. кори́чневый 'brown'; ij or əj in the long adjectival endings -кий, -гий, -хий and in the verbal endings -кивать, -гивать, -хивать; -s for the reflexive ending -сь; and -jut for the unaccented verbal ending -ят). Attempts have been made by these conservative forces to maintain the old 'standard', and the more pedantic and less tolerant have insisted on them as exclusively correct. A more enlightened attitude to changes in pronunciation has been that of the compilers of an 'orthoepic' (normative) dictionary, which is still due to appear. They sent round to numerous representatives of Literary Russian a questionnaire containing lists of debatable words and asked them to indicate the way they pronounced and stressed these words. The statistics based on a sifting of the answers to the questionnaire will determine the pronunciation of a social *élite*, and this pronunciation will be recommended to the rest. Such a course, however, is hardly an adequate way of establishing a standard. It is obvious that the questionnaire, being merely selective, must be incomplete, and however widely circulated it may have been, it cannot achieve more than an approximation to 'standard' practice. A further difficulty presents itself in the recognised fact that the pronunciation of the same person varies in the course of his lifetime, and its idiosyncrasies depend in part on the changing character of his speech environment, which it is bound to reflect to some extent. This raises the issues of age and profession as well as of schooling and origin. In the last resort the statistically determined 'standard', based, as it is, on limited data, will represent the 'composite' and 'abstract' dialect of a small minority.

The lexical changes which have perceptibly modified contemporary Russian are associated with the influence of the Revolution, the Civil War, and the new order, political and social, which was established after them. The Revolution broke down barriers, extirpated the ruling class and a large part of the educated element, gave free scope to the idiom of the uneducated, and, by evoking a series of rapid changes, furnished the objective data of linguistic (mainly semantic) creation. But its contribution to the total stock of new words and expressions, like the contribution of the war that had preceded it, had been anticipated to a notable extent by the 1905 revolution and the Russo-Japanese war (e.g. шрапнéль 'shrapnel', пулемёт 'machine-gun', райóн 'area', саботáж 'sabotage', большевѝзм 'Bolshevism', буржýй 'bourgeois'). Both Russian revolutions moreover inevitably derived much of their political terminology from that of the French Revolution.

Analysis of the vocabulary acquired during the 1917 revolution shows that the new words fall into the following types: (i) old words with specialised meanings (e.g. клáсс 'class', фронт 'front', товáрищ 'comrade'); (ii) West European loans (e.g. интервéнция 'intervention', спекуля́нт 'speculator', милиционéр 'policeman'); (iii) loan-translations (e.g. сознáтельный Fr. *conscient*); (iv) contractions (e.g. коминтéрн 'Comintern', спец 'specialist', политрýк 'political officer'); and (v) slang (e.g. стенолéз 'vodka', хамовóз 'motor-car', шáмать 'to gorge'). So far we have considered mainly the words of full meaning, but, besides these, the new linguistic material includes morphemes distributed between the two principal parts of speech, noun and verb, with the balance well in favour of the first. A curious, but understandable feature is the use of a number of loan-morphemes in the formation of nouns and adjectives (e.g. -изм in царѝзм 'tsarism', -аж in пилотáж 'piloting', анти- in masc. nom. sing. антисовéтский 'anti-Soviet'). We observe from these few typical instances that while the noun morphemes are exclusively suffixes, the adjectival morphemes are exclusively prefixes. In the verbs the foreign element is in the stem (e.g. реквизи́ровать 'to requisition', буржу́йствовать 'to play the bourgeois', блефну́ть 'to bluff'). All this imposes the inference that the system of conjugation is more conservative and less susceptible to outside influence than the system of declension, which is the first to lapse where a language undergoes a radical shift in development (cf. English, French, Bulgarian, and Persian).

The changes in Russian brought about by the Second World War were merely additions to the vocabulary. Some of these, as in the First World War and in the wars preceding it, were merely ephemeral, having been bred by the evil passions of the hour (e.g. фаши́стский зверь 'Fascist beast'), but others were of a more enduring character (e.g. ка́дровый in the sense of 'select'). We see the same word-formations, the same slang-element, the mixture of soldier-words (бомбёжка 'bombing attack') from the front line and publicist's jargon developed in the rear (e.g. захва́тчик 'aggressor'), and, as in previous wars, no fundamental alteration of the structure of the language. There is only a semantic reflection of changed conditions. Structural changes, as we have seen, are of very slow growth and infinitesimal, except when, over long periods, they have become cumulative.

The study of Russian since the Revolution has continued the traditions established by Potebnja and Šachmatov, the two figures, who, except during the recent short-lived revival of the 'new linguistic theory', advanced by N. J. Marr as a counterblast to the Indo-European 'ethnocentric' (racial) dogma of the protoglossa, or parent-language,[1] have been the most admired, and whose views have received the most publicity. There has been a shift of emphasis, however, from the study of Old Russian documents to the investigation of the contemporary literary language and the modern dialects. Contributions to Russian descriptive grammar have been made by D. N. Ušakov, V. I. Cernyšov, V. V. Vinogradov, and R. I. Avanesov. The last, along with A. M. Seliščev, B. A. Larin, N. P. Grinkova, and

[1] See my article 'The Soviet Contribution to Linguistic Thought' (*Archivum Linguisticum*, II, 1–2; Glasgow, 1950).

F. P. Filin, has studied Russian dialects and is perhaps the most prominent member of the new Moscow school of phonology, which goes back through Ščerba to Baudouin de Courtenay.[1] Russian phonetics is best represented by Ščerba. The history of the language has been covered more or less satisfactorily by N. N. Durnovo, S. P. Obnorskij, G. O. Vinokur, and the Ukrainian L. A. Bulachovskij. A great deal of attention has been paid to the study of style (*stilistika*), and many articles have been devoted to this subject in both the *Bulletin* of the Academy and the periodical *Russian in School*. Nor has lexicography been neglected, for the last two decades have seen the publication of Ušakov's *Explanatory Dictionary of Russian* (Moscow, 1934–40) and the beginnings of the great Academy dictionary, some of whose fifteen volumes have already appeared.

[1] The paramount influence of Prince N. S. Trubetzkoy on Soviet phonology is inevitable and undeniable, though it is minimised even by those who are critical of the Moscow school. Cf. S. K. Šaumjan, *Проблема фонемы* (Изв. Акад. Наук. Отд. лит. и яз. ix, 4; Москва, 1952).

PART III

SPECIMENS

A SELECTION OF
PASSAGES FROM RUSSIAN LITERATURE
WITH ENGLISH VERSIONS

1

Похвалимъ же и мы, по силѣ нашей, малыми похвалами великаа и дивнаа сътворьшаго нашего учителя и наставника, великаго кагана нашеа земли Владимера, внука стараго Игоря, сына же славнаго Святослава, иже, въ своя лѣта владычствующа, мужствомъ же и храбърьствомь прослуша в странахъ многахъ и побѣдами и крѣпостію поминаются нынѣ и словутъ. Не в худѣ бо и не въ нѣвѣдомѣ земли владычьствовашя, но в Русской, яже вѣдома и слышима есть всѣми концы земли.

(Митрополит Иларион, *О законе и благодати*)

2

А се в Черниговѣ дѣялъ есмъ: конь дикихъ свойма руками связалъ есмь в пушахъ 10 и 20 живыхъ конь, а кромѣ того же, по ровни ѣздя,ималъ есмъ свойма руками тѣже кони дикиѣ. Тура мя 2 метала на розѣхъ и с конемъ, олень одинъ мя болъ, а 2 лоси, одинъ ногами топталъ, а другый рогома болъ: вепрь ми на бедрѣ мечь оттялъ, медвѣдь ми у колѣна подъклада укусилъ, лютый звѣрь скочилъ ко мнѣ на бедры и конь со мною поверже: и богъ неврежена мя съблюде.

(Вел. князь Владимир Мономах, *Поучение*)

И приспѣ осень, и помяну Олегъ конь свой, иже бѣ поставилъ кормити и не вседати на нь, бѣ бо въпрашалъ волъхвовъ и кудесникъ: ‚отъ чего ми есть умрети?‘ и рече ему кудесникъ одинъ: ‚княже! конь, егоже любиши и ѣздиши на немъ, отъ того ти умрети‘. Олегъ же приймъ въ умѣ си, рече: ‚николиже всяду на нь, ни вижу его боле того‘. (*Повесть временных лет*)

So let us also praise as best we can with meagre praise the mighty and wonderful things done by our teacher and guide, the great *kagan* (prince) of our land, Vladimir, grandson of old Igor' and son of the glorious Svjatoslav. These, ruling in their own time, won fame by their manhood and valour in many lands and are remembered and renowned to this day by their victories and fortitude. For it was in no mean land that they ruled, but in Russia, which is known and in repute at all the ends of the earth. (Metropolitan Ilarion, *The Law and Grace*)

(Early eleventh century; MS. sixteenth century)

2

And this is what I did in Černigov. With my own hands I bound wild horses on the plains, ten to twenty of them alive. Moreover, riding about the land, I have caught the same kind of wild horses. Two bisons tossed me on their horns, horse and all; a stag gored me; and of two elks, one trampled me underfoot, the other gored me with its horns. A wild boar wrenched the sword from my hip; a bear bit through the saddle-cloth at my knee; a wild beast (panther) pounced on my hips and tumbled me with my horse; and yet God preserved me unharmed. (Prince Vladimir Monomach, *Instruction*)

(Eleventh–twelfth centuries; MS. fourteenth century)

3

Then the autumn came, and Oleg remembered the horse he had given orders to feed and had never mounted. For he had asked sorcerers and magicians: 'What shall be the cause of my death?' And a magician had said to him: 'Prince you shall die through the horse you love and are riding on.' Oleg, mindful of this, had said: 'I shall never mount him and see him again.'

(*The Tale of Bygone Years*)

(Twelfth century; MS. fourteenth century)

4

На Дунáи Ярослáвнынъ гласъ ся слы́шитъ; зегзи́цею незнáема рáно кы́четь. ‚Полечю́, — речé, — зегзи́цею по Дунáеви, омочю́ бебря́нъ рукáвъ въ Кая́лѣ рѣцѣ, утрý кня́зю кровáвыя егó рáны на жестóцѣмъ егó тѣлѣ!‘ Ярослáвна рáно плáчетъ въ Пути́влѣ на забрáлѣ, а ркýчи: ‚О, вѣтрѣ, вѣтри́ло! Чемý, господи́не, наси́льно вѣеши? Чемý мы́чеши хинóвьскыя стрѣлкы на своéю нетрýдною крилцю́ на моéя лáды вóи? Мáло ли ти бя́шетъ горѣ подъ óблакы вѣяти, лелѣючи корабли́ на си́нѣ мóрѣ?‘

(Слóво о полкý И́гореве)

5

Орéл пти́ца царь надо всѣми пти́цами, а осéтръ над ры́бами, а лев над звермú, а ты, кня́же, над переслáвцы. Левъ ры́кнетъ, кто не устраши́тся; а ты, кня́же, речéши, кто не убои́тся? Яко же бо змии стрáшенъ свистáниемъ свои́мъ, тáко и ты, кня́же нашь, грóзенъ мнóжеством вои. Злáто красотá женáм, а ты, кня́же, людéмъ свои́мъ. Тѣло крепи́тся жи́лами а мы, кня́же, твоéю держáвою.

(Дании́л Затóчник, Молéние)

6

Бѣ же тогдá день субóтный, восходя́щу сóлнцу, сступи́шася обóим, и бысть сѣча зла и трускъ отъ кóпей и ломлéніе и звукъ отъ мéчнаго сечéніа, я́кожь мóрю мéрзшу дви́гнутися; не бѣ ви́дѣти лéду, покры́лося бя́ше крóвію. Се же слы́шавъ отъ самови́дца, речé: ви́дехомъ полкъ бóжій на вóздусе, пришéдши на пóмощь Алексáндру Ярослáвичю. И побѣди́ я пóмощью бóжіею, и въдáша рáтніи плéщи своá.

(Житиé кня́зя Алексáндра Нéвского)

4

Jaroslavna's[1] voice is heard on the Dunaj, crying lonely as a cuckoo in the morning. 'I will fly', she says, 'like a cuckoo down the Dunaj. I will wet my beaver sleeve in the river Kajala. I will wipe the bleeding wounds on my prince's strong body.' Jaroslavna weeps on the walls of Putivl' in the morning, saying: 'O wind, dear wind, why, my lord, do you blow so hard? Why do you carry the Hunnish arrows on your careless wings against my love's warriors? Was it not enough for you to blow on high under the clouds and to rock the ships on the blue sea?' (*The Lay of Prince Igor'*)
(Late twelfth century; first published 1800)

5

The eagle is lord of all birds, the sturgeon of fishes, the lion of beasts, and you, my prince, are lord of the people of Perejaslavl'. When the lion roars, who is not terrified? And when you speak, my prince, who is not afraid? As the serpent is terrible because of its hissing, so you, my prince, are terrible because of the multitude of your warriors. Gold is an adornment to women, and you, my prince, are an adornment to your people. The body is strong because of its sinews, and we, my prince, are strong because of your power. (Daniil the Captive, *Supplication*)
(Early thirteenth century; MS. sixteenth century)

6

It was then the Sabbath day, and as the sun rose, the two sides met, and there was a fierce encounter, with a shivering and breaking of lances and a clangour of sword-strokes that was enough to shake the frozen sea. The ice could not be seen, for it was covered with blood. I heard this from an eyewitness, who said: 'We saw up in the air a divine host that had come to the aid of Prince Aleksandr Jaroslavič. And he defeated them (i.e. the Germans), and the (enemy) warriors fled.' (*Life of Prince Aleksandr of the Neva*)
(Late thirteenth century; MS. sixteenth century)

[1] Princess Jevfrosinija Jaroslavna of Galič, wife of Prince Igor' Svjato-slavič of Novgorod Seversk (1178–98).

7

То же, бра́те, не речено́ бо́гомъ ви́дѣти свята́го ра́я человѣ́комъ, а му́ки и ны́нѣ суть на за́падѣ; мно́го дѣте́й мои́хъ новгоро́дцевъ видо́ки тому́: на ды́шющемъ мо́рѣ червь не усыпа́ющій, скре́жетъ зу́бный и рѣка́ мо́лненая Моргъ, и что вода́ въхо́дить въ преиспо́дняя и па́кы исхо́дить три́жда днемъ.   (Васи́лий Новгоро́дский,
Посла́ние к Фёдору Тверско́му)

8

Ко́ни ржуть на Москвѣ́, бу́бны бьють на Коло́мнѣ, тру́бы труби́ть в Се́рпуховѣ, звени́тъ сла́ва по всей землѣ́ Ру́сской, чю́дно стя́зи стоя́ть у До́ну вели́каго на бе́резѣ, па́шутся хорю́гови бе́рчати, свѣ́тятся каланты́ри злаче́ны. Стоя́ть му́жи новгоро́дцы у святы́я Софі́и, арку́чи таково́ сло́во: ‚Уже́ намъ, бра́тія, къ вели́кому кня́зю Дми́трію Ива́новичу на посо́бь не поспѣ́ти‘.   (*Задо́нщина*)

9

Бя́ху бо въ Перми́ человѣ́цы, всегда́ жру́ще глухы́мъ куми́ромъ и бѣ́сомъ моля́хуся, волшве́ніемъ одержи́ми су́ще, вѣ́рующе въ бѣсова́ніе и въ чарова́ніе и в куде́сы. І о семъ зѣло́ съжа́лиси рабъ бо́жіи, и велми́ печа́ловаше о ихъ прелще́ніи, и разгара́шеся ду́хомъ, поне́же человѣ́цы бо́гомъ сотворени́ и бо́гомъ почте́ни су́ще, но врагу́ поработи́шася. И о семъ скорбя́ше не худѣ́, ка́ко бы ихъ исхыти́лъ из руки́ вра́жіа.
          (Епифа́ній Прему́дрый, *Житіе́ Стефа́на Пе́рмского*)

7

For God has not ordained, my brother, that man should see holy Paradise, and there are torments to this day in the West. Many of my children in Novgorod have witnessed these. An unsleeping serpent lies in a heaving sea; there is a grinding of teeth; there is Morg, the river of lightning; and water falls into the underworld and comes up again three times a day.

(Vasilij of Novgorod, *Epistle to Fjodor of Tver'*)

(Text and MS. early fourteenth century)

8

Horses are neighing in Moscow, drums beating in Kolomna, trumpets sounding in Serpuchov; glory resounds throughout the Russian land. Flags are marvellously assembled on the banks of the mighty Don, embroidered banners are fluttering, gilded mail is flashing. Novgorodians are standing round St Sophia and saying: 'It is too late, brothers, for us to help Prince Dmitrij Ivanovič.' (*Exploits beyond the Don*)

(Fourteenth–fifteenth centuries; MS. fifteenth century)

9

For there were men in Perm' who had always sacrificed to deaf idols and prayed to devils, being possessed of sorcery and believing in demonolatry, magic, and spells. And God's servant (St Stefan of Perm', d. 1396) was moved to compassion by this and was greatly distressed at their error, and burned in spirit, for they were men created and esteemed by God and had been enslaved by the Devil. And he pondered not a little how to snatch them from the Devil's hands.

(Jepifanij the Most Wise, *Life of St Stefan of Perm'*)

(Early fifteenth century; MS. fifteenth–sixteenth centuries)

10

И тутъ есть Индѣйскаа странá, и люди хóдятъ нáгы всѣ, а головá не покрыта, а грýди гóлы, а вóлосы в однý косý плетéны, а всѣ хóдятъ брюхáты, дѣти родятъ на всякый годъ а дѣтéй у нихъ мнóго, а мýжы и жéны всѣ чéрны; язъ хожý куды, инó за мнóю людéй мнóго, дивятся бѣлому человéку.

(Афанáсий Никитин, *Хожéние за три мóря*)

11

Турéцкий царь Махмéт-салтáн сам был филóсоф мýдрый по своим книгам по турéцким, а грéческие книги прочéт, и написáл слóво в слóво по турéцкии, инó великия мýдрости прибыло у царя. И он рек так сейтом и пашáм, и молнáм, и обызам: ,Пишется великая мýдрость о благовéрном цари Констянтине в филосóфских книгах: иже родися истóчник мýдрости вóинския, от мечá его вся подсóлнечная не мóжет сохранитися.'

(Ивáн Пересвéтов, *Сказáние о Магмéте Салтáне*)

12

И воздáл еси мне злые за благие и за возлюблéние моé — непримирительную нéнависть. Кровь моя, яко водá пролитая за тя, вопиéт на тя ко гóсподу моемý. Бог сердцáм врители — во умé моéм прилéжно смышлях и обличник сóвестный мой свидéтеля на ся постáвих, и искáх, и зрех мысленне и обращáяся, и не вем себя, и не наидóх ни в чем же пред тобóю согрешивша. (Князь Андрéй Кýрбский, *Эпистóлия пéрвая к царю Ивáну IV*)

10

This is the land of India, where people go about naked, their heads uncovered, breasts bare, and hair twisted into a single plait. And they (i.e. the women) all go about big-bellied and bear children every year. They have a lot of children. The men and women are all black. Wherever I go I am followed about by crowds of people astonished to see a white man.

(Afanasij Nikitin, *Itinerary beyond Three Seas*)
(Text and MS. late fifteenth century)

11

The Turkish emperor Machmet Saltan was himself an erudite philosopher versed in his Turkish books. He had read Greek books and put them word for word into Turkish and had thus acquired considerable learning. And he said to his ministers, pashas, mullas, and counsellors: 'A very wise thing is written in philosophical treatises concerning the orthodox emperor Constantine: the entire subsolar world cannot save itself from the sword of one who was born a source of military knowledge.'

(Ivan Peresvetov, *Story of Mahmet Saltan*)
(*c.* 1547; MS. sixteenth century)

12

You have requited my good with evil, my love with implacable hatred. The blood I have shed for you like water cries out to the Lord against you. As God looks into all hearts, I have searched my mind assiduously and set my accusing conscience to be a witness against me, and I have sought and seen in thought, and have turned myself over, and I do not know, nor have I found, that I have sinned against you in any way.

(Prince Andrej Kurbskij, *First Epistle to Tsar Ivan IV*)
(1563; MS. sixteenth century)

13

И ты то все забы́л, соба́цким изме́нным обы́чаем преступи́л
кре́стное целова́ние, ко врага́м христиа́нским соедини́лся еси́;
и к тому́, своея́ зло́бы не расмотря́я, си́цевыми и скудоу́м-
ными глаго́лы, я́ко на не́бо ка́мением меща́, неле́пая глаго́-
леши, и раба́ своего́ во благоче́стия не стыди́шися, и
подо́бная тому́ сотвори́ти своему́ влады́це отверга́лся еси́.

(Царь Иван IV, *Посла́ние ко кня́зю Андре́ю Ку́рбскому
про́тив его́ письма́ из гра́да Во́лмера*)

14

Царь Ива́н о́бразом неле́пым, о́чи име́я се́ры, нос протяг-
нове́н и покля́п, во́зрастом вели́к бя́ше, су́хо те́ло име́я,
пле́щи име́я высо́ки, гру́ди широ́ки, мы́шцы то́лстые. Муж
чу́дного рассужде́ния, в нау́ке кни́жного поуче́ния дово́лен и
многоречи́в зело́, ко ополче́нию де́рзостен и за свое́ оте́чество
стоя́телен; на рабы́ свои, от Бо́га да́нные ему́, жестосе́рд вель-
ми́ и на проли́тие кро́ви и на убие́ние де́рзостен и неумоли́м.

(Серге́й Куба́сов, *Написа́ние вкра́тце о царе́х моско́вских*)

15

Еще́ у мо́лотца был мил наде́жен друг —
назва́лся мо́лодцу назва́ной брат,
прелсти́л его́ реча́ми преле́сными,
зазва́л его́ на каба́цкой двор,
заве́л ево́ в ызбу́ каба́цкую,
подне́с ему́ ча́ру зелена́ вина́
и кру́шку подне́с пи́ва пья́нова;
сам говори́т таково́ сло́во:
‚Испе́й ты, бра́тец мой назва́ной,
в ра́дость себе́ и в весе́лие, и во здра́вие!
Испе́й ча́ру зелена́ вина́,
запе́й ты ча́шею ме́ду сла́дково!‘

(*По́весть о Го́ре-злоча́стии*)

13

You have forgotten everything and like a treacherous dog have broken your sacred oath and made common cause with the enemies of the Christian faith. Moreover, oblivious of your malice, you utter nonsense in such feeble words that it is like flinging stones at the sky. And you are not ashamed of yourself before your servant (Vas'ka Šibanov), who has acquitted himself honourably, and you refuse to behave like him towards your suzerain.

(Tsar Ivan IV, *Epistle in Answer to Prince Andrej's from Wolmar*)
(1564; MS. sixteenth century)

14

Tsar Ivan IV had an ugly face, grey eyes, and a long and crooked nose. He was tall and lean and had broad shoulders, a deep chest, and big muscles. He was a man of extraordinary judgement, skilled in book-lore, very voluble, harsh to his troops, and loyal to his country. Towards the servants God had given him he was extremely hard-hearted, being quick to shed blood and to kill, as well as inexorable. (Sergej Kubasov, *Sketches of the Tsars of Muscovy*)
(Early seventeenth century; MS. seventeenth century)

15

The young man also had a dear, loyal friend,
Who swore to the young man to be his sworn brother,
Flattered him with flattering words,
Coaxed him along to the tavern-yard,
Led him into the tavern-house,
Offered him a glass of rye spirits
And a mug of heady ale,
And spoke these words:
'Drink, my sworn brother,
To your joy and pleasure and health;
Drink up the glass of rye spirits
And on top of that a cup of sweet mead.'
                    (*Tale of Misery and Misfortune*)
(Mid-seventeenth century; MS. early eighteenth century)

16

Егда́ же розсвета́ло в день неде́льный, посади́ли меня́ на теле́гу и ростяну́ли ру́ки, и везли́ от патриа́рхова двора́ до Андро́ньева монастыря́ и тут на чепи́ ки́нули в те́мную пола́тку, ушла́ в зе́млю, и сиде́л три дни, ни ел, ни пил; во тме сидя́, кла́нялся на чепи́, не зна́ю — на восто́к, не зна́ю — на за́пад. Никто́ ко мне не приходи́л, то́кмо мы́ши и тарака́ны, и сверчки́ крича́т, и блох дово́льно.

(Протопо́п Авваку́м, *Житие́*)

17

Дева

Срам че́стный лице́ де́вы велми́ украша́ет,
Егда́ та ничесо́же не ле́по дерза́ет.
Зна́мя же сра́ма того́ зна́ется отту́ду,
А́ще оче́с не ме́щет сюду и ону́ду,
Но смире́нно я де́ржит ни́зу низпуще́нны
Постоя́нно, а́ки бы к земли́ пристрое́нны.
Па́ки а́ще язы́к си де́ржит за зуба́ми,
А не разширя́ет ся тще́тными слова́ми.
Ма́ло бо подоба́ет де́вам глаго́лати,
Мно́го же к чи́стым сло́вом умы́ приклоня́ти.

(Симео́н По́лоцкий)

18

Карл пя́тый Ри́мский Импера́тор гова́ривал, что Ишпа́нским языко́м с Бо́гом, Францу́зским с друзья́ми, Неме́цким с неприя́телями, Италия́нским с же́нским по́лом говори́ть прили́чно. Но е́стьли бы он Росси́йскому языку́ был иску́сен; то коне́чно к тому́ присовокупи́л бы, что им со все́ми о́ными говори́ть присто́йно. И́бо нашёл бы в нём великоле́пие Ишпа́нского, жи́вость Францу́зского, кре́пость Неме́цкого, не́жность Италия́нского, сверх того́ бога́тство и си́льную в изображе́ниях кра́ткость Гре́ческого и Лати́нского.   (М. В. Ломоно́сов, *Росси́йская грамма́тика*)

16

When Sunday came I was put on a cart with my arms stretched but and was taken from the Patriarch's residence to the Andronij Monastery, and there I was loaded with chains and thrown into a dark dungeon that went deep into the earth, and I spent three days in it, neither eating nor drinking. I made my obeisances in darkness and in chains, but whether to the east or to the west, I do not know. No one came to see me. Only mice and cockroaches (scuttled about), crickets sang, and there were plenty of fleas. (Archpriest Avvakum, *Autobiography*)

(*c.* 1672–73; MS. seventeenth century)

17
Maiden

A chaste shame greatly adorns a maiden's face
When she refrains from whatever is unbecoming.
The sign of that shame may be recognised
When she does not let her eyes roam here and there,
But in her meekness keeps them cast down
Constantly, as if they were fixed to the ground;
Also when she holds her tongue behind her teeth
And does not give vent to vain words.
It is fitting for a maiden to speak little
And to incline her mind often to chaste words.

(1679)   (Simeon Polockij)

18

The Emperor of the Holy Roman Empire, Charles V, used to say that Spanish was fitted for speech with God, French with friends, German with enemies, and Italian with women. But if he had known Russian, he would certainly have added that it was fitted for speech with all these. For he would have found in it the magnificence of Spanish, the vivacity of French, the vigour of German, the tenderness of Italian, and furthermore the abundance and forceful succinctness of expression characteristic of Greek and Latin. (M. V. Lomonosov, *Russian Grammar*)

(1755)

19

Скоти́нин. И я здесь.

Староду́м. Заче́м пожа́ловал?

Скоти́нин. За свое́й ну́ждой.

Староду́м. А чем я могу́ служи́ть?

Скоти́нин. Двумя́ слова́ми.

Староду́м. Каки́ми э́то?

Скоти́нин. Обня́в меня́ покре́пче скажи́: ‚Со́фьюшка твоя́‘.

Староду́м. Не пусто́е ль затева́ть изво́лишь? Поду́май-ка хороше́нько.

Скоти́нин. Я никогда́ не ду́маю и наперёд уве́рен, что ко́ли и ты ду́мать не ста́нешь, то Со́фьюшка моя́.

Староду́м. Э́то стра́нное де́ло! Челове́к ты, как ви́жу, не без ума́, а хо́чешь, чтоб я отда́л мою́ племя́нницу, за кого́ не зна́ю.

(Д. И. Фонви́зин, *Не́доросль*, IV, 7)

20

На тле́нность

Река́ времён в своём стремле́ньи
Уно́сит все дела́ люде́й
И то́пит в про́пасти забве́нья
Наро́ды, ца́рства и царе́й.
И е́сли что и остаётся
Чрез зву́ки ли́ры и трубы́,
То ве́чности жерло́м пожрётся
И о́бщей не уйдёт судьбы́.

(Г. Р. Держа́вин)

19

Skotinin. Here I am.

Starodum. Why have you come?

Skotinin. On my own account.

Starodum. How can I be of service to you?

Skotinin. With two words.

Starodum. What are they?

Skotinin. Embrace me warmly and say: 'Take Sof'juška.'

Starodum. Isn't this a futile undertaking? Think, man.

Skotinin. I never think, and am persuaded in advance that if you stop thinking too, Sof'juška will be mine.

Starodum. This is a queer state of things. You seem to be intelligent and yet you expect me to give my niece to a man I don't know. (D. I. Fonvizin, *Minor*, IV, 7)

(1782)

20

Transience

The river of the ages carries away
All the works of men in its course
And drowns peoples, kingdoms, and kings
In an abyss of oblivion.
And even if anything survives
Through the sounds of lyre and trumpet,
That too shall be devoured by the maw of eternity
And shall not escape the common fate.

(G. R. Deržavin)

(1816)

21

Бе́рег! бе́рег! Мы в Ду́вре, и я в А́нглии — в той земле́, кото́рую в ребя́честве своём люби́л я с таки́м жа́ром, и кото́рая по хара́ктеру жи́телей и сте́пени наро́дного просвеще́ния есть коне́чно одно́ из пе́рвых госуда́рств Евро́пы. Здесь всё друго́е: други́е до́мы, други́е у́лицы, други́е лю́ди, друга́я пи́ща — одни́м сло́вом, мне ка́жется, что я перее́хал в другу́ю часть све́та.

(Н. М. Карамзи́н, *Пи́сьма ру́сского путеше́ственника*)

22

Ту́ча

После́дняя ту́ча рассе́янной бу́ри!
Одна́ ты несёшься по я́сной лазу́ри,
Одна́ ты наво́дишь уны́лую тень,
Одна́ ты печа́лишь лику́ющий день.

Ты не́бо неда́вно круго́м облега́ла,
И мо́лния гро́зно тебя́ обвива́ла,
И ты издава́ла таи́нственный гром,
И а́лчную зе́млю пои́ла дождём.

Дово́льно, сокро́йся! Пора́ минова́лась,
Земля́ освежи́лась и бу́ря промча́лась,
И ве́тер, ласка́я листо́чки древе́с,
Тебя́ с успоко́енных го́нит небе́с.

(А. С. Пу́шкин)

21

The coast, the coast! We have reached Dover. I am in England—that country which I loved so passionately in my childhood, and which by virtue of the character of its inhabitants and the level of its public education is certainly one of the foremost countries in Europe. Everything is different here: houses, streets, people, food,—in brief, it seems to me that I have arrived in another part of the world.

(1791–92)   (N. M. Karamzin, *Letters of a Russian Traveller*)

22

Cloud

Last cloud of the scattered thunderstorm,
You alone course across the clear azure,
You alone cast a gloomy shadow,
You alone sadden the jubilant day.

A short time ago you beleaguered the sky,
And the lightning encompassed you menacingly,
And you gave utterance to mysterious thunder
And drenched the thirsty earth with rain.

Enough! Away with you! It is all over now,
The earth is refreshed, and the thunderstorm has fled,
And the wind, caressing the leaves of trees,
Is driving you from the pacified skies.

(1835)   (A. S. Puškin)

23

Лукá Лукúч. Зачéм же, Антóн Антóнович, отчегó э́то? зачéм к нам ревизóр?

Городнúчий. Зачéм! Так уж, вúдно, судьбá! (*Вздохнýв.*) До сих пор, благодарéние Бóгу, подбирáлись к другúм городáм; тепéрь пришлá óчередь к нáшему.

Аммóс Фёдорович. Я дýмаю, Антóн Антóнович, что здесь тóнкая и бóлее политúческая причúна. Э́то знáчит вот что: Россúя... да... хóчет вестú войнý, и министéрия-то, вот видúте, и подослáла чинóвника, чтóбы узнáть, нет ли где измéны.

Городнúчий. Эк кудá хватúли! Ещё ýмный человéк! В уéздном гóроде измéна! Что он, погранúчный, что ли? Да отсю́да, хоть три гóда скачú, ни до какóго госудáрства не доéдешь.   (Н. В. Гóголь, *Ревизóр*, I, I)

24

А́нгел

По небý полýночи А́нгел летéл
И тúхую пéсню он пéл;
И мéсяц и звёзды и тýчи толпóй
Внимáли той пéсне святóй.

Он пел о блажéнстве безгрéшных духóв
Под кýщами рáйских садóв,
О Бóге велúком он пел, и хвалá
Егó непритвóрна былá.

Он дýшу младýю в объя́тиях нёс
Для мúра печáли и слёз,
И звук егó пéсни в душé молодóй
Остáлся без слов, но живóй.

И дóлго на свéте томúлась онá,
Желáнием чýдным полнá;
И звýков небéс заменúть не моглú
Ей скýчные пéсни землú.   (М. Ю. Лéрмонтов)

23

Luka Lukič. What's the reason for this, Anton Antonovič? Why are we to have a visit from an inspector?

Provost. Why? Just our luck, I suppose. (*Sighing.*) So far they found their way to other towns. Now it's our turn.

Ammos Fjodorovič. I think there's a subtle, rather a political reason here, Anton Antonovič. It means this: Russia...er... wants to start a war, and the ministry, you see, has sent an official to find out whether there's any treachery about.

Provost. The idea! And you call yourself an intelligent man! Treachery in a district town! Is ours a frontier town then? Why, you can post three years from here and you won't reach another country. (N. V. Gogol', *Inspector*, I, I)

(1836)

24

Angel

The angel flew across the midnight sky
And he sang a song softly,
And the moon and the stars and the clouds in a throng
Listened to that holy song.

He sang of the bliss of sinless spirits
In the shade of the garden of Paradise;
He sang of almighty God, and his praise
Was unfeigned.

He carried in his arms a young soul
Destined for the sorrow and tears of the world,
And the sounds of his song remained
Alive, though wordless, in that young soul.

And she pined in this world for a long time,
Full of a marvellous desire,
And the dull songs of the earth
Could not replace for her the sounds of heaven.

(M. Ju. Lermontov)

(1831)

25

Когда́ смерка́лось, нас всех вводи́ли в каза́рмы, где и запира́ли на всю ночь. Мне всегда́ бы́ло тяжело́ возвраща́ться со двора́ в нашу каза́рму. Это была́ дли́нная, ни́зкая и ду́шная ко́мната, ту́скло освещённая са́льными свеча́ми, с тяжёлым, удуша́ющим за́пахом. Не понима́ю тепе́рь, как я вы́жил в ней де́сять лет. На на́рах у меня́ бы́ло три доски́: э́то бы́ло всё моё ме́сто. На э́тих же на́рах размеща́лось в одно́й на́шей ко́мнате челове́к три́дцать наро́ду.

(Ф. М. Достое́вский, *Записки из мёртвого до́ма*)

26

‚Что э́то? я па́даю? у меня́ но́ги подка́шиваются‘, поду́мал он и упа́л на́ спину. Он раскры́л глаза́, наде́ясь увида́ть, чем ко́нчилась борьба́ францу́зов с артиллери́стами, и жела́я знать, уби́т и́ли нет ры́жий артиллери́ст, взя́ты и́ли спасены́ пу́шки. Но он ничего́ не вида́л. Над ним не́ было ничего́ уже́, кро́ме не́ба — высо́кого не́ба, не я́сного, но всё-таки неизмери́мо высо́кого, с ти́хо ползу́щими по нему́ се́рыми облака́ми.

(Л. Н. Толсто́й, *Война и мир*)

27

Трофи́мов. Вся Росси́я наш сад. Земля́ велика́ и прекра́сна, есть на ней мно́го чуде́сных мест. (*Па́уза.*) Поду́майте, А́ня: ваш дед, пра́дед и все ва́ши пре́дки бы́ли крепостники́, владе́вшие живы́ми душа́ми, и неуже́ли с ка́ждой ви́шни в саду́, с ка́ждого листка́, с ка́ждого ствола́ не гляди́т на вас челове́ческие существа́, неуже́ли вы не слы́шите голосо́в... Владе́ть живы́ми душа́ми — ведь э́то разврати́ло всех вас, живу́щих ра́ньше и тепе́рь живу́щих, так что ва́ша мать, вы, дя́дя уже́ не замеча́ете, что вы живёте в долг, на чужо́й счёт, на счёт тех люде́й, кото́рых вы не пуска́ете да́льше пере́дней.

(А. П. Че́хов, *Вишнёвый сад*, II)

25

When dusk fell we were all taken into the barracks and locked up there for the night. I always found it very hard to return from out of doors to our barracks. It was a long, low, stuffy room, dimly lit with tallow candles and permeated with a strong, suffocating smell. I cannot understand now how I managed to spend ten years there. I had three boards for my bunk: it was all the space there was. The sleeping bunks in our room alone were occupied by about thirty human beings.

(1864)   (F. M. Dostojevskij, *Memoirs from a Dead House*)

26

'What's this? Am I falling? My legs are giving way', he thought, and fell on his back. He opened his eyes, hoping to see how the battle between the French and the gunners had ended, and wanting to know whether the red-haired gunner was dead and whether the guns had been taken or saved. But he saw nothing. Above him there was no longer anything but the sky— the lofty sky, not clear, but immeasurably high, with grey clouds creeping slowly over it.   (L. N. Tolstoj, *War and Peace*)

(1863–69)

27

Trofimov. All Russia is our garden. It is a large and beautiful country, and there are many lovely places in it. (*Pause.*) Think, Anja: your grandfather, great-grandfather, and all your ancestors were landowners with authority over living souls, and do you mean to say that human beings are not staring at you from every cherry-tree in the garden, every leaf, and every trunk, that you do not hear voices...Authority over living souls—why, it has corrupted you all, those of you who lived earlier and those who are living now, so that your mother, you, and your uncle do not notice that you are living in debt, at others' expense, at the expense of those people whom you do not allow to come in further than the hall.

(1903)   (A. P. Čechov, *Cherry Orchard*, II)

28

Гранит, желе́зо, де́рево, мостова́я га́вани, суда́ и лю́ди — всё ды́шит мо́щными зву́ками стра́стного ги́мна Мерку́рию. Но голоса́ люде́й, е́ле слы́шные в нём, сла́бы и смешны́. И са́ми лю́ди, первонача́льно роди́вшие э́тот шум, смешны́ и жа́лки: их фигу́рки, пы́льные, обо́рванные, ю́ркие, со́гнутые под тя́жестью това́ров, лежа́щих на их спи́нах, суетли́во бе́гают то туда́, то сюда́ в ту́чах пы́ли, в мо́ре зно́я и зву́ков; они́ ничто́жны по сравне́нию с окружа́ющими желе́зными коло́ссами, гру́дами това́ров, гремя́щими ваго́нами и всем, что они́ со́здали. Со́зданное и́ми поработи́ло и обезли́чило их. (Макси́м Го́рький, *Челка́ш*)

29
Ве́рбочки

Ма́льчики да де́вочки
Све́чечки да ве́рбочки
Понесли́ домо́й.

Огонёчки те́плятся,
Прохо́жие кре́стятся,
И пахнёт весно́й.

Ветеро́к уда́ленький,
До́ждик, до́ждик ма́ленький,
Не заду́й огня́!

В Воскресе́нье Ве́рбное
За́втра вста́ну пе́рвая
Для свято́го дня. (А. А. Блок)

28

Granite, iron, timber, the harbour paving, ships, and men—all these exhale the mighty sounds of a passionate hymn to Mercury. But the human voices, scarcely audible in it, are feeble and ridiculous. And the men themselves, who first created this din, are ridiculous and pitiable: their tiny figures, dusty, ragged, nimble, bent under the loads on their backs, run about busily here and there in clouds of dust, in a sea of heat and sound; they are insignificant compared to the steel colossi, the piles of merchandise, the thundering railway-trucks, which surround them and which they have created. Their creation has enslaved and defaced them. (Maksim Gor'kij, *Čelkaš*)
(1895)

29
Willow Catkins

Little boys and little girls
Have brought home
Little candles and willow-catkins.

Tiny icon-lights are flickering,
Passers-by are crossing themselves,
And spring is in the air.

Valiant little wind,
Tiny, tiny raindrops,
Don't put out the light.

On Palm Sunday
To-morrow I shall be the first to rise
For the holy day. (A. A. Blok)

(1909)

197

30

И такие же точно возвышались дома, и такие же серые
проходили там токи людские, и такой же стоял там зелёно-
жёлтый туман. Сосредоточенно побежали там лица; троту-
ары шептались и шаркали; растирались калошами; плыл
торжественно обывательский нос. Носы протекали во
множестве: орлиные, утиные, петушиные, зеленоватые,
белые; протекало здесь и отсуствие всякого носа. Здесь
текли одиночки, и пары, и тройки-четвёрки; и за ко-
телком котелок; котелки, перья, фуражки; фуражки,
фуражки, перья; треуголка, цилиндр, фуражка; платочек,
зонтик, перо.   (Андрей Белый, *Петербург*)

31

Легко, неслышно отворяется дверь в залу. На паркете
лежат голубоватые отражения окон. За чёрными окнами
висит луна, — большим светлым шаром. Никита влез на
ломберный столик в простенке между окнами и видит:

Вот напротив, у белой, как мел, стены качается круглый
маятник в высоком футляре часов, качается, отсвечивает
лунным светом. Над часами, на стене, в раме висит строгий
старичок с трубкой, сбоку от него — старушка, в чепце и
шали, и смотрит поджав губы. От часов до угла вдоль
стены, вытянули руки, присели, на четырёх ногах каждое,
широкие, полосатые кресла. В углу расселся раскорякой
низкий диван. Сидят они без лица, без глаз, выпучились на
луну, не шевелятся.   (А. Н. Толстой, *Детство Никиты*)

30

And the same kind of houses stood there, and the same kind of grey human currents streamed past; and there was the same kind of greenish-yellow fog. Faces ran by there intent; footpaths murmured to one another and scraped, and were scrubbed by goloshes; the Philistine nose swam by solemnly. Noses streamed past in multitudes—aquiline, duck-billed, cock-billed, greenish, white; even the complete absence of a nose streamed past. Single shapes, pairs, trios, quartets, they streamed; bowler after bowler; bowlers, feathers, peaked caps; peaked caps, peaked caps, feathers; a cocked hat, a topper, a peaked cap; a kerchief, an umbrella, a feather. (Andrej Belyj, *St Petersburg*) (1916)

31

The door into the lounge opens lightly and inaudibly. Pale bluish reflections of the windows are lying on the parquetry. Beyond the black windows hangs the moon in the shape of a large luminous sphere. Nikita has climbed on to the card-table in the space between the windows and sees there, on the opposite side, a round pendulum swinging close to the chalk-white wall, swinging in a tall clock-case and flashing moonlight. Over the clock on the wall, in a frame, hangs a severe old man with a pipe and beside him an old woman in bonnet and shawl, who stares with compressed lips. From the clock to the corner, all along the wall, wide striped armchairs, each of them on four legs, squat with outstretched arms. In the corner sprawls a low divan. They sit there without face, without eyes, goggling at the moon, and motionless. (A. N. Tolstoj, *Nikita's Childhood*) (1920)

32

Петухи́

Всю ночь вода́ труди́лась без отды́шки.
Дождь до утра́ льняно́е ма́сло жёг.
И ва́лит пар из-под лило́вой кры́шки,
Земля́ дыми́тся, сло́вно щей горшо́к.

Когда́ ж трава́, отря́хиваясь, вско́чит,
Кто мой испу́г изобрази́т росе́
В тот час, как загорла́нит пе́рвый ко́чет,
За ним друго́й, ещё за э́тим все?

Перебира́я го́ды поиме́нно,
Поочерёдно оклика́я тьму,
Они́ проро́чить ста́нут переме́ну
Дождю́, земле́, любви́ — всему́, всему́.

Б. Л. Пастерна́к

33

Неде́лю отдыха́л Ми́шка, це́лые дни проводя́ в седле́. Степь его́ покоря́ла, вла́стно принужда́ла жить первобы́тной, расти́тельной жи́знью. Коса́к ходи́л где́-нибу́дь неподалёку. Ми́шка и́ли си́дя дрема́л в седле́, и́ли, валя́сь на траве́, безду́мно следи́л, как, пасо́мые ве́тром, стра́нствуют по не́бу косяки́ опу́шенных и́зморозной бе́лью туч. Внача́ле тако́е состоя́ние отрешённости его́ удовлетворя́ло. Жизнь на отво́де, вдали́ от люде́й, ему́ да́же нра́вилось. Но к концу́ неде́ли, когда́ он уже́ осво́ился в но́вом положе́нии, просну́лся невня́тный страх.

(М. А. Шо́лохов, *Ти́хий Дон*)

32

Cocks

All night the water laboured without pause.
The rain burned linseed oil till morning.
And vapour pours from under the lilac lid;
The earth steams like a pot of cabbage soup.

When will the grass, shaking itself, leap up?
Who will describe my fright to the dew
At that moment when the first cock starts crowing,
Then another, and then all the rest.

Going over the years by name,
Calling out to the darkness in turn,
They shall prophesy change
To rain, earth, love—to everything, everything.

(1923)   B. L. Pasternak

33

Miška had a week off and spent entire days in the saddle. The steppe was mastering him, imperiously forcing him to lead a primitive, vegetative existence. A drove of horses would pass somewhere in the vicinity. Miška either dozed sitting in the saddle or, sprawling on the grass, blankly watched flocks of clouds, downed with frosty whiteness, wander across the sky, pastured by the wind. At first this state of detachment satisfied him. Life apart, away from people, even appealed to him. But towards the end of the week, when he had grown used to his new circumstances, a vague fear awoke in him.

(1928–40)   (M. A. Šolochov, *Tranquil Don*)

34

Васин. Стой! (*Выкидывает карабин.*)

Козловский (*видя, что ему не уйти*). Это свой.

Васин. Кто свой?

Козловский. Я, товарищ майор, — Василенко.

Васин (*подходя к нему и продолжая держать карабин изготовку*). Что вы здесь делаете?

Козловский. Товарищ майор... Да опустите карабин, это я. Я вам сейчас объясню...

Васин (*не обращая внимания, продолжая держать рабин*) Что вы здесь делаете?

Козловский. Да вот, пошёл проверять посты, — как и вы, евидно.

Васин. Это не ваша рота. Что вы здесь делаете?

(Константин Симонов, *Русские люди*, II, 5)

34

Vasin. Stop! (*Levelling his carbine.*)

Kozlovskij (*seeing he can't get away*). Friends.

Vasin. What friends?

Kozlovskij. It's me, Comrade Major—Vasilenko.

Vasin (*stepping up to him and still holding his carbine ready*). What are you doing here?

Kozlovskij. Comrade Major...Lower your carbine. It's me, of course. I'll explain at once.

Vasin (*taking no notice and still holding his carbine*). What are you doing here?

Kozlovskij. Why, I went out to check the sentry-posts—like you, it seems.

Vasin. This is not your company. What are you doing here?

(1942)   (Konstantin Simonov, *Russian Folk*, II, 5)

CLASSIFIED BIBLIOGRAPHY[1]

I. Phonetics and Phonology

Аванесов, Р. И., *Русское литературное произношение* (Москва, 1950).

Богородицкий, В.А., *Фонетика русского языка в свете эксперитенталь-ных данных* (Казань, 1930).

Boyanus, S. K., *Manual of Russian Pronunciation*[3] (London, 1946).

Boyanus, S. K. and N. B. Jopson, *Spoken Russian* (London, 1939).

Broch, O., *Slavische Phonetik* (Heidelberg, 1911).

Винокур, Г., *Русское сценическое произношение* (Москва, 1948).
[See my review in *The Slavonic and East European Review*, xxx, 74; London, 1951.]

Всеволодский-Гернгросс, В., *Теория русской речевой интонации* (Петербург, 1922).

Гвоздёв, А. Н., *О фонологических средствах русского языка* (Москва-Ленинград, 1949).

Isačenko, A. V., *Fonetika spisovnej ruštiny* (Bratislava, 1947).
[See my review in *Archivum Linguisticum*, II, 2; Glasgow, 1950.]

Lundell, J. A., *Études sur la prononciation russe* (Stockholm, 1890).

Matthews, W. K., 'The Pronunciation of Medieval Russian' (*The Slavonic and East European Review*, xxx, 74; London, 1951).

Огиенко, И. И., *Русское литературное ударение* (Киев, 1914).

Sweet, H., 'On Russian Pronunciation' (*Transactions of the Philological Society*; London, 1877–9).

Ščerba, L. V., *Court exposé de la prononciation russe* (Leipzig, 1911).

Trofimov, M. V. and D. Jones, *The Pronunciation of Russian* (Cambridge, 1923).

Trofimov, M. V. and J. P. Scott, *Handbook of Russian*, I (London, 1918).

Чернышёв, В. И., *Русское ударение* (СПБ, 1912).

Чернышёв, В. И., *Законы и правила русского произношения*[3] (Петро-град, 1915).

Шаров, В. Г., *Образцовое русское произношение*[3] (Москва, 1915).

Щерба, Л. В., *Русские гласные в качественном и количественном отношении* (СПБ, 1912).

II. Spelling

Бодуэн-де-Куртенэ, И. А., *Об отношении русского письма к рус-скому языку* (СПБ, 1913).

Гвоздёв, А. Н., *Основы русской орфографии*[3] (Москва, 1951).

Грот, Я. К., *Русское правописание*[22] (Петроград, 1916).

[1] The items are listed in the order of their respective alphabets, Cyrillic and Latin.

Ушаков, Д. Н., *Русское правописание*² (Москва, 1917).

Ушаков, Д. Н. и С. Е. Крючков, *Орфографический словарь*⁷ (Москва, 1951).

Ушаков, М. В., *Методика правописания* (Москва, 1930).

Шапиро, А. Б., *Русское правописание* (Москва, 1951).

[See my review in *The Slavonic and East European Review*, XXXI, 77; London, 1953.]

III. DESCRIPTIVE GRAMMAR

Аванесов, Р. И. и В. Н. Сидоров, *Очерк грамматики русского литературного языка* (Москва, 1945).

Бархударов, С. Г. (ред.), *Методические разработки по грамматике* (Москва, 1940).

Berneker, E. und M. Vasmer, *Russische Grammatik*⁴ (Berlin-Leipzig, 1940).⁵

Богородицкий, В. А., *Общий курс русской грамматики*⁵ (Москва-Ленинград, 1935).

Будде, Е. Ф., *Русский язык*² (Казань, 1914).

Будде, Е. Ф., *Основы синтаксиса русского языка* (Казань, 1914).

Булаховский, Л. А., *Курс русского литературного языка*⁴ (Киев, 1949).

Виноградов, В. В., *Великий русский язык* (Москва, 1945).

Виноградов, В. В., *Русский язык. Грамматическое учение о слове* (Москва-Ленинград, 1947).

[See my review in *The Slavonic and East European Review*, XXVII, 69; London, 1949.]

Виноградов, В. В. (ред.), *Современный русский язык. Морфология* (Москва, 1952).

Виноградов, В. В., Е. С. Истрина и С. Г. Бархударов (ред.), *Грамматика русского языка*, I (Москва, 1952).

[See my review in *The Slavonic and East European Review*, XXXII, 78; London, 1953.]

Голанов, И. Г., *Русский язык. Элементы русского языкознания* (Москва, 1930).

Forbes, N., *Russian Grammar*² (Oxford, 1916).

Карцевский, С. И., *Русский язык. I. Грамматика* (Prague, 1925).

Karcevski, S., *Système du verbe russe. Essai de linguistique synchronique* (Prague, 1927).

Кошутић, Р., *Граматика руског језика*, I² (Петроград, 1922), II (Београд, 1914).

Matthews, W. K., *Russian Grammatical Design* (London, 1950).

[Reprinted from *The Slavonic and East European Review*, XXIX, 72; London, 1950.]

Mazon, A., *Morphologie des aspects du verbe russe* (Paris, 1908).

Mazon, A., *Emplois des aspects du verbe russe* (Paris, 1914).

Mazon, A., *Grammaire de la langue russe*³ (Paris, 1949).

Обнорский, С. П., *Именное склонение в современном русском языке*, I–II (Ленинград, 1927–31).

Овсянико-Куликовский, Д. Н., *Синтаксис русского языка*[2] (СПБ, 1911).

Петерсон, М. Н., *Русский язык* (Москва-Ленинград, 1925).

Петерсон, М. Н., *Современный русский язык* (Москва, 1929).

Петерсон, М. Н., *Синтаксис русского языка* (Москва, 1930).

Пешковский, А. М., *Русский синтаксис в научном освещении*[4] (Москва, 1934).

Потебня, А. А., *Из записок по русской грамматике*, I–II[2] (Харьков, 1888); III (Харьков, 1899); IV (Ленинград, 1941).

Trofimov, M. V., *Handbook of Russian*, II (Manchester, 1939).

Trubetzkoy, N., *Das morphonologische System der russischen Sprache* (Prague, 1934).

Unbegaun, B., *Grammaire russe* (Lyon-Paris, 1951).

[See my review in *The Slavonic and East European Review*, XXX, 75; London, 1952.]

Шахматов, А. А., *Синтаксис русского языка*[2] (Ленинград, 1941).

Шахматов, А. А., *Очерк современного русского литературного языка*[4] (Москва, 1941).

IV. DIALECTOLOGY

Аванесов, Р. И., *Очерки русской диалектологии*, I (Москва, 1949).

[See my review in *The Slavonic and East European Review*, XXX, 74; London, 1951.]

Голанов, И. Г., *Русская диалектология* (Москва, 1929).

Дурново, Н. Н., Н. Н. Соколов и Д. Н. Ушаков, *Опыт диалектологической карты русского языка в Европе* (Москва, 1915).

Еремин, С. А. и И. А. Фалёв, *Русская диалектология* (Москва-Ленинград, 1928).

Каринский, Н. М., *Очерки языка русских крестьян. Говор деревни Ванилово* (Москва-Ленинград, 1936).

Карский, Е. Ф., *Русская диалектология* (Ленинград, 1924).

Кузнецов, П. С., *Русская диалектология* (Москва, 1951).

[See my review in *The Slavonic and East European Review*, XXXI, 77; London, 1953.]

Matthews, W. K., 'Modern Russian Dialects' (*Transactions of the Philological Society*, 1950; London, 1951).

Селищев, А. М., *Диалектологический очерк Сибири*, I (Иркутск, 1921).

Соболевский, А. И., *Опыт русской диалектологии*, I[2] (Киев, 1911).

Филин, Ф. П., *Исследование о лексике русских говоров* (Москва-Ленинград, 1936).

Черных, П. Я., *Русский язык в Сибири* (Иркутск, 1936).

V. Historical Grammar

Брант, Р. Ф., *Лекции по исторической грамматике русского языка. I. Фонетика* (Москва, 1892).

Будде, Е. Ф., *Очерк истории современного литературного русского языка. XVII–XIX век.* (Энц. Слав. Фил. XII; СПБ, 1908).

Будде, Е. Ф., *Лекции по истории русского языка²* (Казань, 1914).

Булаховский, Л. А., *Исторический комментарий к литературному русскому языку³* (Киев, 1950).

Буслаев, Ф. И., *Историческая грамматика русского языка, I–II⁵* (Москва, 1881).

Виноградов, В. В., *Очерки по истории русского литературного языка XVII–XIX вв.²* (Москва, 1938).

Винокур, Г., *Русский язык. Исторический очерк* (Москва, 1945).

Горбушина, Л. А. и В, Г. Яковлев, *Русский язык: краткие сведения из истории русского языка и письма* (Москва, 1946).

Григорьев, А. Д., *Русский язык* (Варшава, 1915).

Дементьев, А., *Сборник задач и упражнений по исторической грамматике русского языка* (Москва, 1946).

Дурново, Н. Н., *Очерк истории русского языка* (Москва-Ленинград, 1924).

Дурново, Н. Н., *Введение в историю русского языка. I. Источники* (Brno, 1927).

Entwistle, W. J. and W. A. Morison, *Russian and the Slavonic Languages* (London, 1949).

Истрина, Е. С., *Руководство по истории русского языка³* (Москва-Ленинград, 1923).

Jakobson, R., *Remarques sur l'évolution phonologique du russe comparée à celle des autres langues slaves* (Prague, 1929).

Matthews, W. K., 'The Russian Language before 1700' (*The Slavonic and East European Review*, XXXI, 77; London, 1953).

Meyer, K. H., *Historische Grammatik der russischen Sprache*, I (Bonn, 1923).

Никифоров, С. Д., *История русского литературного языка* (Москва, 1947).

Соболевский, А. И., *Лекции по истории русского языка⁴* (Москва, 1907).

Unbegaun, B., *La langue russe au 16e siècle (1500–1550). I. La flexion des noms* (Paris, 1935).

Филин, Ф. П., *Очерк истории русского языка до XIV столетия* (Ленинград, 1940).

Черных, П. Я., *Историческая грамматика русского языка* (Москва, 1952).

Шахматов, А. А., *Очерк древнейшего периода истории русского языка* (Энц. Слав. Фил. XI, 1; Петроград, 1915).

Шахматов, А. А., *Введение в курс истории русского языка*, I (Петроград, 1916).

Ягич, И. В., *Критические заметки по истории русского языка* (СПБ, 1889).

Яковлев, В. Г., *Русский язык. Краткие сведения из истории русского языка и письма* (Москва, 1946).

Якубинский, Л., *Очерки по истории древнерусского языка* (Москва, 1945).

VI. CYRILLIC ALPHABET AND PALAEOGRAPHY

Беляев, И. С., *Практический курс изучения древней русской скорописи для чтения рукописей XV–XVIII вв.*[2] (Москва, 1911).

Карский, Е. Ф., *Славянская кирилловская палеография* (Ленинград, 1928).

Лавров, П. А., *Палеографическое обозрение кирилловского письма* (Энц. Слав. Фил. IV, 1; Петроград, 1914).

Matthews, W. K., 'The Latinisation of Cyrillic Characters' (*The Slavonic and East European Review*, XXX, 75; London, 1952).

Соболевский, А. И., *Славяно-русская палеография*[2] (СПБ, 1908).

Срезневский, И. И., *Славяно-русская палеография XI–XIV вв.* (СПБ, 1885).

Чаев, Н. С. и Л. В. Черепнин, *Русская палеография* (Москва, 1946).

Щепкин, В. Н., *Учебник русской палеографии* (Москва, 1918).

VII. VOCABULARY AND PHRASEOLOGY

Булич, С. К., *Церковно-славянские элементы в современном литературном и народном русском языке*, I (СПБ, 1893).

Карцевский, С. И., *Язык, война и революция* (Berlin, 1923).

Mazon, A., *Lexique de la guerre et de la révolution en Russie, 1914–18* (Paris, 1920).

Михельсон, М., *Русская мысль и речь*, I–II (СПБ, 1912).

Овсянников, В. З., *Литературная речь. Толковый словарь современной общелитературной фразеологии* (Москва-Ленинград, 1933).

Селищев, А. М., *Язык революционной эпохи*[2] (Москва, 1928).

Смирнов, Н. А., *Западное влияние на русский язык в Петровскую эпоху* (СПБ, 1910).

VIII. DICTIONARIES (DESCRIPTIVE AND HISTORICAL)

Академия Наук (Институт русского языка), *Словарь современного русского литературного языка*, I– (Москва-Ленинград, 1950–). [In progress.]

Даль, В. И., *Толковый словарь живого великорусского языка*, I–IV[4] (СПБ-Москва, 1912–14). [Stereotyped edition.]

(Императорская) Академия Наук (2-ое отделение), *Словарь русского языка*, I (СПБ, 1891–5); II–VIII (СПБ, 1897–1929). [Unfinished.]

Кочин, Г. Е., *Материалы для терминологического словаря древней России* (Москва-Ленинград, 1937).

Лёхин, И. В. и Ф. Н. Петров (ред.), *Словарь иностранных слов*[3] (Москва, 1949).

Ожегов, С. И., *Словарь русского языка*[2] (Москва, 1952).

Преображенский, А., *Этимологический словарь русского языка*, I–III (Москва, 1910–49). [Reprinted in one volume in New York, 1952.] [See my review in *The Slavonic and East European Review*, xxxi, 77; London, 1953.]

Срезневский, И. И., *Материалы для словаря древне-русского языка по письменным памятникам*, I–III (СПБ, 1893–1912).

Ушаков, Д. Н. и Б. М. Волин (ред.), *Толковый словарь русского языка*, I–IV (Москва, 1934–40).

Vasmer, M., *Russisches etymologisches Wörterbuch*, I– (Heidelberg, 1950–). [In progress.]

IX. Prose Style

Винокур, Г., *Культура языка*[2] (Москва, 1929).

Гвоздёв, А. Н., *Очерки по стилистике русского языка* (Москва, 1952).

Рыбникова, М. А., *Введение в стилистику* (Москва, 1937).

Чернышёв, В., *Правильность и чистота русской речи*, I–II[2] (СПБ, 1914–15).

X. Metre

Брюсов, В. Я., *Основы стиховедения* (Москва, 1924).

Жирмунский, В. М., *Введение в метрику. Теория стиха* (Ленинград, 1925).

Тимофеев, Л., *Теория стиха* (Москва, 1939).

Томашевский, Б. В., *Русское стихосложение. Метрика* (Петроград, 1923).

Тынянов, Ю. Н., *Проблемы стихотворного языка* (Ленинград, 1924).

Шенгели, Г., *Техника стиха* (Москва, 1940).

Штокмар, М. П., *Исследования в области русского народного стихосложения* (Москва, 1952).

XI. History of Russian Linguistics

Булич, С. К., *Очерк истории языкознания в России*, I (СПБ, 1904).

Виноградов, В. В., *Русская наука о русском литературном языке* (Уч. зап. Моск. гос. ун. 106, Москва, 1946).

Карский, Е. Ф., *Очерк научной разработки истории русского языка в пределах СССР* (Ленинград, 1926).

Обнорский, С. П., *Итоги научного изучения русского языка* (Уч. зап. Моск. гос. ун. 106, Москва, 1946).

XII. Periodicals

Бюллетень Диалектологического сектора Института русского языка Академии Наук СССР (Москва-Ленинград).

Вопросы языкознания (Москва).

Доклады и сообщения Института русского языка Академии Наук СССР (Москва-Ленинград).

Доклады и сообщения Филологического факультета Московского государственного университета (Москва).

Известия Академии Наук СССР. Отделение литературы и языка (Москва-Ленинград).

Материалы и исследования по истории русского литературного языка (Москва-Ленинград).

Материалы и исследования по русской диалектологии (Москва-Ленинград).

Русский язык в школе (Москва).

Труды Института русского языка Академии Наук СССР (Москва-Ленинград).

Учёные записки Ленинградского государственного педагогического института (Ленинград).

Учёные записки Ленинградского государственного университета (Ленинград).

Учёные записки Московского государственного педагогического института (Москва).

Учёные записки Московского государственного университета (Москва).

XIII. BIBLIOGRAPHY

Unbegaun, B. O. and J. S. G. Simmons, *A Bibliographical Guide to the Russian Language* (Oxford, 1953).

[See my review in *The Slavonic and East European Review*, XXXII, 79; London, 1954.]

ADDENDA (Unclassified)

Борковский, В. И., *Синтаксис древнерусских грамот. Простое предложение* (Львов, 1949).

Булаховский, Л. А., *Русский литературный язык первой половины XIX века*, I–II (Киев, 1941–48).

Виноградов, В. В. (ред.), *Вопросы синтаксиса современного русского языка* (Москва, 1950).

Елизаровский, И. А., *Русский язык XI–XVII вв.* (Архангельск, 1935).

Garbell, A., *Das russische Zeitwort* (Berlin, 1901).

Михайлов, А. В., *Опыт введения в изучение русского литературного языка и письма* (Варшава, 1911).

Никулин, А. С., *Историческая грамматика русского языка. Краткий очерк* (Ленинград, 1941).

Павлов-Шишкин, В. Д. и П. А. Стефановский, *Учебный словарь синонимов русского литературного языка* (Москва, 1930).

Пулькина, И. М., *Краткий справочник по русской грамматике*[3] (Москва, 1951).

Шахматов, А. А., *Курс истории русского языка*, I[2], II[2], III (СПБ, 1910–12).

INDEX

The items in this index refer only to the text of the book and not to the footnotes. A further limitation has been imposed by the exclusion of all reference to illustrative examples.

For EU product safety concerns, contact us at Calle de José Abascal, 56–1°,
28003 Madrid, Spain or eugpsr@cambridge.org.

www.ingramcontent.com/pod-product-compliance
Ingram Content Group UK Ltd.
Pitfield, Milton Keynes, MK11 3LW, UK
UKHW010337140625
459647UK00010B/659